Target
Iran

ALSO BY SCOTT RITTER

Endgame

War on Iraq

Frontier Justice

Iraq Confidential

Waging Peace

Target Iran

THE TRUTH ABOUT THE WHITE HOUSE'S
PLANS FOR REGIME CHANGE

SCOTT RITTER

NATION BOOKS
NEW YORK

TARGET IRAN:
The Truth About the White House's Plans for Regime Change

Copyright © 2006 Scott Ritter

Published by
Nation Books
A Member of the Perseus Books Group
116 East 16th Street, 8th Floor
New York, NY 10003

First published, 2006
First trade paperback edtion, 2007

Nation Books is a copublishing venture of the Nation Institute
and the Perseus Books Group.

Library of Congress Cataloging-in-Publication Data is available.

ISBN-10: 1-56858-356-7
ISBN-13: 978-1-56858-356-3

9 8 7 6 5 4 3 2 1

Printed in the United States of America

Contents

Map   vi

Acknowledgments   ix

Prologue: A Briefing in August   xiii

One: A Crisis Made in Israel   1

Two: The Inspectors   35

Three: The Great Appeasers   73

Four: The Rational Actor   107

Five: The War Party   135

Six: Endgame   169

Conclusion   197

Postscript   215

Afterword   221

Bibliographical Notes   238

Index   241

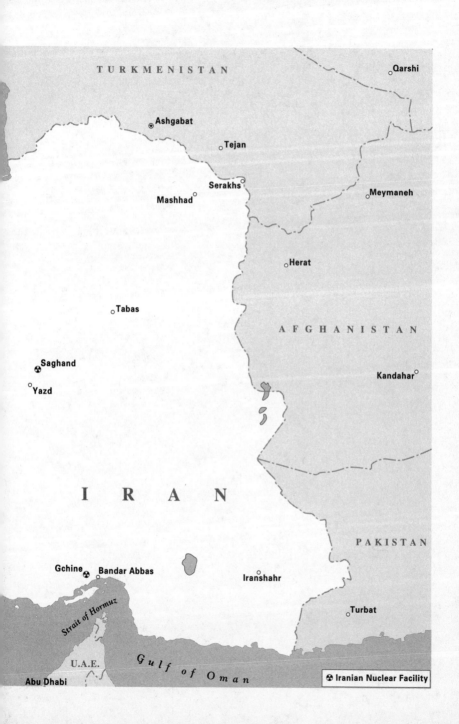

Acknowledgments

WRITING THIS BOOK WAS NOT MY number-one objective for 2006. However, the current affairs of the world have a way of dictating one's actions, and this book emerged as an outgrowth of the writing and speaking I had been doing, and continue to do, about the ongoing debacle that is America's foreign policy in the Middle East, both in regard to Iraq and, increasingly, Iran, both in terms of its nuclear program and its affiliation with Hezbollah in Lebanon and Hamas in Palestine. Nevertheless, this book still would not have been written were it not for the vision and enthusiasm of Hamilton Fish, the energetic and visionary head of the Nation Institute. Ham took a concept developed over beers in a New York City restaurant and helped guide it to fruition. Thank goodness for people like Ham Fish and organizations like the Nation Institute, which are willing to support projects such as this that address critical issues and critical analysis when, almost without exception, all others shy away. I'm forever grateful for this bastion of progressive thinking to have opened its doors to a conservative such as myself.

This project likewise could not have been conducted without the guiding hand of my editor and sounding board, Carl Bromley, who like so many others at the Nation Institute has the ability to grasp ideas and comprehend vision free of outside distractions. Carl also has the innate ability to bring calm to the chaos that emerges from writing a topical book such as this at a time when current events threaten to change everything on a daily basis. His disciplined approach to getting this book done enabled these and other obstacles to be readily overcome. I would also like to thank Ruth Baldwin, Liliana Segura, Taya Kitman and all the others at Nation Books and the Nation Institute for their support and friendship, as well as Anne Sullivan at Avalon, who likewise has made this project and others a joy to be involved with.

Deciding to become a lightning rod for such a controversial topic as Iran and its nuclear program requires the support of friends and colleagues who don't cut and run when the going gets tough. It also requires mentoring and guidance from those who have gone before, and who continue to speak truth to power. I am forever humbled by the brilliance and generosity of America's preeminent investigative journalist, Sy Hersh, who has served as a sounding board for my analysis and prognosis over the years, as well as being one heck of a good friend who can always be counted on for a kind word of support. I am also grateful for the wisdom and advice provided by America's biographer, Gore Vidal, who has been kind enough to make time in his very busy life for a fellow traveler on the road of holding one's beloved nation accountable when it strays off course.

The growing awareness in the United States that something has gone wrong in the way we as a people interface with the rest of the world could not have been accomplished without the courage and dedication of the progressive peace movement, which I have had the honor and pleasure of working with over the years. To Sunny Miller and Charles Jenks and the Traprock Peace Center, Doug Wilson and the Rowe Peace Camp, Jeff Norman at US Tour of Duty, Ray McGovern and the Veteran Intelligence Professionals for Sanity, Medea Benjamin and Code Pink, and the thousands of others who participate as part of nationwide groups such as United for Peace and Justice, American Friends, Veterans for Peace, Peace Action, and all the other community and faith-based outlets for peaceful patriotic expression, I give you my thanks and a promise of continued support.

Writing this book, and participating in social activism, creates demands on time and presence that are draining for friends, colleagues, and above all else, family. My thanks to Bob and Amy Murphy and the rest of the Albany "gang" for their continued support for their "invisible friend", and to my fellow firefighters at the Delmar Fire Department for putting up with my lengthy and sustained absences from my duty station. I would also like to thank my friends and colleagues at the Dutchess County HAZMAT Team, and at the Poughkeepsie Fire Department's Station 2, for their support, inclusive of innovative methodologies that enabled me to train and write at the same time! For my parents, Pat and Bill Ritter, my sisters Shirley, Suzanne and Amy, and their families, and to all my relatives, I apologize for my absence from the family circle during this time, and am thankful for your continued understanding and support. And last but not least, for my loving wife, Marina, her forever patient father, Bidzina, and the most wonderful daughters a father could ever be blessed with, Patricia and Victoria, I dedicate this book in hopes that it contributes to a better world, which we can continue to enjoy together and pass on to our future generations.

Scott Ritter
Delmar, New York
July 2006

Prologue
A Briefing in August

AUGUST 14, 2002, STARTED OFF just like any other muggy summer day in the capital of the world's sole remaining superpower, Washington, D.C. Tensions were running high about the looming crisis with Iraq, with Congressional hearings having just been completed that all but gave a green light to the Bush administration to pursue an aggressive posture vis-à-vis the regime of Saddam Hussein over the issue of weapons of mass destruction.

At the State Department, Deputy Press Spokesman Phillip Reeker approached the podium for the daily press briefing. Iraq was on everyone's mind, and so the briefing started out with questions about the relations between the United States and the Iraqi National Congress, or INC, and the issue of continued funding for the work being done by the Iraqi opposition and its controversial leader, Ahmed Chalabi. Soon the focus shifted from Chalabi to Saddam Hussein and weapons of mass destruction, with a reporter asking about recent intelligence reports indicating that Iraq had restarted a biological weapons program.

Mr. Reeker, ever the professional, handled the question using the standard State Department generic response: "We have been very clear about our concerns about Saddam Hussein's regime and their attempts to have weapons of mass destruction, programs to that effect, and missiles to deliver them, and their support for terrorism. And so I don't think I can add again today anything new or different to our position in terms of our view of Saddam's regime, the threat that that regime poses not only to his own people but to the people of the region, and indeed to peace and security around the world."

The briefing then shifted to the issue of Iran. It was here that things got interesting.

Reporter: The Iranian National Council of Resistance, or National Council of Iranian Resistance, has held a press conference this morning here in Washington. They were classified as a terrorist organization because they're associated with Mujahedin-e Khalq, which is a—

Mr. Reeker: MEK.

Reporter: MEK. So I was just wondering what your position is on terrorist organizations like these, or organizations like these who are affiliated or on the list of terrorism—

Mr. Reeker: It's a terrorist organization. It's listed as such, designated as a Foreign Terrorist Organization under U.S. law. You can read about them in the *Patterns on Global Terrorism Report.*

Reporter: But they're operating openly. They had a press conference here in Washington. I mean, you're not—

Mr. Reeker: For that, you would need to talk to the Justice Department that enforces that law domestically.

Reporter: Well, still on that matter, they actually—the press conference that they had was to disclose information that they had that Iran is in the process of building two new nuclear sites for weapons-grade fuel, and that they said that this information was passed on to the administration. So I guess the question is, do you believe—have you seen this information? Do you believe it to be true? And do you believe that Iran is in the process of building two nuclear sites?

Mr. Reeker: I wouldn't be in a position to discuss intelligence information from whatever source it might be, so I can't help you on that.

I think in terms of Iran, our differences with Iran stem from policies and actions of its government, and we've talked about that for some time, specifically the support for international terrorist groups, the opposition to Arab–Israeli peace process, their pursuit of weapons of mass destruction and the ballistic missile systems with which to deliver such weapons, and their poor human rights record. And these have been the issues and concerns that we have had about the Iranian regime for some time. So that remains our position.

I think the President has been quite clear that the future of Iran will be decided by the people of Iran, and he made a statement on July 12th that I can refer you to in terms of some of the internal debate taking place in Iran and the fact that the United States follows this with interest, but that it's a matter for the people of Iran to decide. And as the President said, an Iran that moves toward freedom and tolerance will have no better friend than the United States.

Reporter: Phil, back on the question of the National Council of Resistance, can you check if it's possible and find out when the last communication was from the State Department to the Justice Department about the—about this group? Because it does seem implausible that it wouldn't raise any eyebrows if a group that's labeled an FTO is giving a press conference in a hotel, you know, at the Willard that's just a stone's throw from the White House. So if it's possible, can you find out when the last time you—it was raised with Justice?

Mr. Reeker: Yes, I mean, Justice enforces the law. We make designations under it and Justice enforces that law. You need to ask them what they may be looking at in terms of—

Reporter: That's what I want to know, if it's possible. Have you guys been kind of saying, look, there's this group out there and they're on the list, and they're still operating.

Mr. Reeker: I'd be happy to check. I'm sure they are equally as aware of the list and the people on it as are we.

Reporter: But if we could stay on the subject, I mean, these people came into the United States. They probably got visas through the State Department. I mean, isn't there some sort of law banning—

Mr. Reeker: I don't know who these people are or whether they were people here in the United States or what their citizenship was, or anything else. I'm afraid I don't have any information on who they are. I did hear that there was a press conference being given today, I believe at 11:00 A.M., by such a group, but I have no further information on them. And as a domestic matter in terms of law enforcement, it would be for the Department of Justice to look into that.

Reporter: If—I mean, this looks very much like the Iraqi resistance movement that was here last week, the leaders from the Iraqi resistance movement. If Iran is developing weapons of mass destruction, nuclear or biological, which this group says they are, with the assistance of Russia, and they're campaigning here in the U.S. The regime in Iran is not exactly free and democratic and open. Will the State Department take some sort of action? Are you in contact with this group to try and do something there like what you're trying to do in Iraq?

Mr. Reeker: Again, I think you're looking at two different situations. I've made quite clear, yet again today, what our concerns are about Iran, what our policy is about Iran. I have invited you to review the President's statement from July 12th. But very much so, our concerns include Iranian government's pursuit of weapons of mass destruction and missile systems. So that remains a concern of ours that we watch very closely.

Reporter: Is it possible that a D.C. representative office of an FTO could be exempted? This is what this group claims—

Mr. Reeker: You'd have to ask the Justice Department because they enforce the law, that is, the Anti-Terror and Effective Death Penalty Act of 1996.

Reporter: So that's not the State Department's—

Mr. Reeker: They would, and we don't have a domestic law enforcement role. You need to ask the Justice Department on that.

Reporter: I'm aware of that. But do you make exceptions—you designate the FTOs.

Mr. Reeker: Right.

Reporter: Do you make exceptions for groups underneath the umbrella name of MEK? It's not about enforcement; it's about designation. If they're not designated an FTO—

Mr. Reeker: This particular group that you're asking about, at least according to the press release or the announcement of their press conference is, we consider, the so-called NCRI, National Council of Resistance of Iran, we consider them to be a Foreign Terrorist Organization, consider them to be under the umbrella of the Mujahedin-e Khalq organization, the MEK.

Reporter: So any of their subsidiaries would be similarly designated?

Mr. Reeker: Right. And if you look in *Patterns of Global Terrorism*, they list a number of them, and there are others I think included in the actual legal documents that designate it. Because obviously people can adopt new names and new acronyms and other things, so that is watched very closely.

As a former U.N. weapons inspector who played an integral role publicly and behind the scenes in formulating and implementing arms control and disarmament policy, the scene that played out at the State Department briefing room on August 14, 2002, was quite remarkable, even to one such as myself who had grown accustomed to the surrealistic atmosphere that often enveloped formal government-sponsored briefings. According to the State Department's own version of events, a spokesperson affiliated with an identified terrorist group was giving a public press conference, with the full knowledge of the U.S. government, in Washington, D.C. This occurred at a time when the U.S. government's condemnation of Saddam Hussein included language accusing the Iraqi leader of his ongoing support of terrorism.

Making this matter even more bizarre was the fact that the terrorist group in question—the National Council of Resistance in Iran—was delivering a presentation on the status of Iran's nuclear program that proved to be more precise and accurate than anything the Iraqi National Congress and its leader, Ahmed Chalabi, ever provided to the United States. I had plenty of personal interaction over the years with Ahmed Chalabi which centered around his possession of so-called "sensitive information" about Iraqi weapons of mass destruction, and had come to accept, cynically, the notion of Middle Eastern expatriate opposition figures using Washington, D.C., as a platform for promoting their own specific cause. It turned out that the "sensitive information" Ahmed Chalabi had been selling America (and the U.N.) was nothing less than snake poison. In a large part due to the lies and distortions peddled by Chalabi concerning the so-called "weapons of mass destruction threat" emanating from Iraq, America finds itself embroiled in an illegitimate war of aggression in Iraq, one that has currently manifested itself as a disastrous occupation of that once sovereign state.

In a large part because of his role in facilitating the war through his fabrications and misrepresentations of fact (although Chalabi likened himself to a "hero in error," as opposed to a simple liar), and also because of some unsavory ties that Chalabi and his INC had developed with the Iranian Intelligence Services (which included passing on to Iran information about U.S. intelligence sources and methods, thus compromising American efforts to combat and contain a growing Iraqi insurgency), Ahmed Chalabi and the INC had lost its "most favored" status, and by the summer of 2002 had its funding, underwritten by the U.S. taxpayer via the U.S. State Department, frozen while his entire operation was being reviewed by the U.S. government. The irony of having a named terrorist group (the NCRI) providing accurate intelligence about potential weapons of mass destruction activity in Iran, a nation identified by the Bush administration as a leading supporter of international terror, while the United States withheld millions of dollars in financial assistance to Chalabi's organization escaped most who were not in the State Department briefing room that day. But I for one did not see irony; I saw the recent past being replayed, with American policy objectives once again being hidden behind a veil of deceit, with regime change disguised as disarmament. Some of the cast of characters had changed, with a Mesopotamian Dictator replaced by Persian Islamist Theocrats, but the stage and the play remained the same.

But the real drama wasn't at Foggy Bottom, but a few blocks away, in the lobby of the Willard Hotel, where a U.S.-educated Iranian citizen, Alireza Jafarzadeh, had delivered a briefing full of dynamite. Mr. Jafarzadeh, the chief Congressional liaison and media spokesperson for the U.S. representative office of Iran's parliament in exile, the National Council of Resistance of Iran, had appeared before a group of reporters and briefed them on some new information about Iraq's nuclear program.

Alireza Jafarzadeh is a man of no small controversy. Born in Mashad, Iran, he left for the United States to attend university prior to the 1979 revolution that ousted Reza Shah Palevi. Jafarzadeh joined the Mujahedin-e Khalq soon after that time, and became a fanatically dedicated member, even going so far as to volunteer to set himself on fire outside the U.N. Headquarters building in New York City to draw attention to the MEK's cause. In 1988 Alireza Jafarzadeh traveled to Iraq, where he received military training at one of the MEK camps then operating under the auspices of Saddam Hussein's Mukhabarat.

The MEK, once part of the Iranian revolution that overthrew the Shah (and, according to some accounts, the force behind the murder of several Americans in Iran prior to 1979), had helped plan and carry out the capture of the U.S. Embassy in Tehran, and the holding of fifty-two American citizens hostage. However, in 1981 the MEK had a falling-out with the theocrats in Tehran, and its members fled to Paris, where they set up headquarters. By 1986 the MEK, with the cooperation of Iraq's President, Saddam Hussein, began setting up military bases in Iraq. From these bases MEK forces would cooperate with Saddam Hussein's regime in its life-or-death struggle with the Islamic Republic of Iran.

In late July 1988, just prior to a cease-fire entering into force between Iran and Iraq (and thus ending a bloody eight-year war), Alireza Jafarzadeh's MEK unit participated in "Operation Forough-e Jaavedaan," or "Eternal Light," a desperate attempt to overthrow the Iranian government. The MEK's forces, which included scores of armored vehicles, drove more than 100 miles into Iran, capturing the town of Islamabad, before being cut off and destroyed by the Iranian military. The MEK suffered thousands of casualties in the process. Jafarzadeh was one of the lucky ones to escape back into Iraq alive.

The MEK consolidated its surviving forces within its main base inside Iraq, known as Camp Ashraf (named for the first wife of the MEK's founder and spiritual leader, Massoud Rajavi). In March 1991, in the aftermath of the defeat of the Iraqi Army during Operation Desert Storm, the MEK was called upon by Saddam Hussein to help suppress the revolt of the Kurds in northern Iraq. The MEK planned and executed Operation Morvarid, or Pearl, in which its forces allegedly killed hundreds of Kurdish civilians, including women and children. This operation, along with the murders of Americans in Iran and the seizure of the U.S. Embassy in 1979, earned the MEK the label of "terrorist organization" by the United States Department of State in 1997, a status that still holds to this date.

As the exchange between the State Department's Deputy Spokesperson and the assembled media on August 14, 2002, illustrated, Mr. Jafarzadeh's status as a spokesperson of the political arm of the MEK, the National Council for Resistance in Iran, or NCRI, remained a matter of no small controversy, as did his participation in military operations (and potential war crimes) against Iran and Iraqi Kurds as a de facto proxy of Saddam Hussein.

When one thinks of the term matchmaker, the President's State of the Union Address doesn't normally trigger an association. However, the first State of the Union Address of the Bush administration, delivered on January 29, 2002, turned out to be a matchmaker of historic proportions. It was in this speech that George W. Bush first publicly coined the phrase Axis of Evil, when referring to Iran, North Korea and, of course, Iraq. "States like these," the President said, "and their terrorist allies, constitute an axis of evil, arming to threaten the peace of the world. By seeking weapons of mass destruction, these regimes pose a grave and growing danger. They could provide these arms to terrorists, giving them the means to match their hatred. They could attack our allies or attempt to blackmail the United States. In any of these cases, the price of indifference would be catastrophic."

The President had reserved most of his rhetoric for Saddam Hussein and Iraq, the number one focus of his administration at the time and a nation for which the United States was busy making preparations for war. North Korea likewise received a great deal of attention in the speech. Surprisingly, Iran only rated a single line of criticism: "Iran aggressively pursues these weapons and exports terror, while an unelected few repress the Iranian people's hope for freedom." But the match had been made, and Iran was now a charter member of George Bush's Axis of Evil. One critical aspect of this match was that Iran and Iraq were now inextricably linked to an overall Bush administration national security strategy which fixated on regional transformation (i.e., regime change) in the Middle East, and embraced preventive unilateral military operations as the prime vehicle for achieving this.

The other match made that night was not so obvious, and took longer to arrange. Alireza Jafarzadeh had been watching the President's speech from his office at the National Press Club in Washington, D.C., and liked what he had heard, considering it a step in the right direction for the Bush administration, bringing America closer to confronting the Iranian regime Jafarzadeh had sworn to remove from power. Up until the State of the Union speech, Jafarzadeh felt that the U.S. government had taken a policy approach toward Iran that was more akin to appeasement than containment.

Jafarzadeh and the others at NCRI (and the MEK) had watched with frustration as Iran and Russia had grown closer over the years, culminating with close economic ties which not only strengthened the theocrats in Tehran economically and politically, but also, because some of these ties were based upon the sale of weapons and technology that could be used to produce weapons, strengthened the mullahs militarily as well. Some of the most worrisome transactions between Russia and Iran involved the transfer of missile-related technologies, and nuclear reactors that the NCRI believed were part of a secret Iranian nuclear weapons program. However, given the pariah status the NCRI enjoyed with American officialdom, these concerns more often than not fell on deaf ears.

But there were other people who shared the same concerns as Mr. Jafarzadeh. In late 2001, in the aftermath of the September 11 terrorist attacks on the United States, a group of like-minded people came together to form a new lobbying entity in Washington, D.C., known as the Committee for a Democratic Iran. At the heart of this grouping were well-known neoconservative ideologues such as

Michael Ledeen (a senior fellow at the American Enterprise Institute), Morris Amitay (the former Executive Director of the American-Israeli Public Affairs Committee, or AIPAC), and James Woolsey (the former Director of the CIA).

The underlying objective of the CDI was to achieve regime change in Tehran. While it was an American-registered lobby, the CDI had an extremely pro-Israel bias, and indeed many of its members were either directly or indirectly associated with powerful pro-Israeli lobbies such as AIPAC or the Jewish Institute for National Security Affairs, or JINSA. The CDI, like AIPAC and JINSA, viewed the MEK, and its political front, NCRI, as worthy of wide-ranging support, in part because the MEK was the only relatively large, well-organized anti-regime force in existence. The fact that the MEK was based in Iraq, and had openly supported the oppressive policies of Saddam Hussein in the past, was apparently of little relevance.

The membership of the CDI had a history of lobbying on behalf of forces hostile to regimes that had been targeted for removal. Ledeen, Amitay, and Woolsey were all active supporters of the Iraqi opposition leader, Ahmed Chalabi. They had spent years working behind the scenes to turn Chalabi into a player on the U.S. scene, and by the end of 2001 Chalabi and his organization, the Iraqi National Congress (INC), had become a major supplier of intelligence information to the Bush administration regarding Iraqi WMD programs. The elimination of Iraq's WMD had become a rallying cry within the Bush administration which served as the heart of its overall policy objective in Iraq of removing Saddam Hussein from power. By the beginning of 2002, it appeared that this was a successful model upon which one could build if regime change in Tehran was to be achieved.

The CDI, in so far as it concentrated together under a single banner so many critical personalities from organizations that have come to be known collectively as the Israeli Lobby, possessed close links with the Israeli government. Despite much speculation about the interplay between the Israeli Lobby and the Israeli government, it is the government of Israel, and not the so-called Israeli Lobby, which formulates the foreign and national security policy of Israel. Of course, there are no absolutes; the 1996 policy paper "A Clean Break" illustrates this point. Written by several American neoconservative ideologues with close links to the Israeli Likud Party, the paper served as a guideline on how the newly elected Prime Minister of Israel, Benjamin Netanyahu, could best leverage Israeli influence within the U.S. national security decision-making hierarchy for the benefit of Israel. This being said, the Israeli Lobby does serve as a useful proxy for promoting the Israeli position, and given the close links between those in the Israeli Lobby and the Israeli government, especially the right-wing Likud, one is able to closely connect the causes that the Israeli Lobby espouses with the official policy line of the Likud Party, whether serving as the government of Israel or the opposition.

Another founding member of CDI, an Iranian-American named Rob Sobhani, is a friend of the former Shah of Iran's son (and ostensible heir to the Iranian throne), Reza Pahlavi. Using the close links the CDI had with the Israeli Lobby, Sobhani and others at CDI, especially Michael Ledeen, were able to forge close contacts between Reza Pahlavi and the Likud government of Prime Minister Ariel Sharon. CDI and other members of the Israeli Lobby, in particular AIPAC, were proponents of building support within the United States government for Reza Pahlavi to be anointed as the logical choice to replace the mullahs in Tehran. A key element of this plan was to elevate Palahvi's status as a legitimate "player" regarding present-day Iran, and not just a bit actor from the past. For help in this, the CDI turned to the Likud government in Israel, taking advantage of a visit to the United States by Sharon in February 2002.

Ariel Sharon, like many others in Israel, was perturbed by the aggressive Iraq-centric focus of the Bush administration. While Israel had long harbored concerns over Saddam Hussein's government, its close links with U.N. weapons inspectors in Iraq during the 1990s provided it with an insight into the true nature of the Iraqi threat, which was found to be minimal and easily contained. Not so, in the mind of the Likud, the case with Iran. While Israel would not shed any tears over the demise of Saddam's regime, there was a widespread belief that if the United States were to engage itself dramatically in the Middle East, to the extent of invading Iraq, then it had better be prepared to stay the course and finish the job, a job which from the Israeli perspective included regime change in Syria and Iran, and nullification of Hezbollah in Lebanon and the PLO/Hamas factions in Palestine.

In early February 2002 a senior Israeli delegation arrived in Washington, D.C., which included both Ariel Sharon and his defense minister, Benjamin Ben-Eliezer. Ben-Eliezer met with Vice President Dick Cheney on February 8, and emphasized that Israel's number one concern was Iran, not Iraq. "The danger as I see it," he told Cheney, "is from a Hezbollah-Iran-Palestinian triangle, with Iran leading this triangle and putting together a coalition of terror." Ben-Eliezer told Cheney that Israel was particularly worried about Iran's nuclear weapons program, and that Israel believed Iran could have nuclear weapons by 2005. Ben-Eliezer shared with Cheney the basis of his concern—Israeli intelligence, already shared with their U.S. counterparts in the CIA, about secret Iranian nuclear weapons facilities operating outside the scope of International Atomic Energy Agency (IAEA) safeguard inspections. The next day, February 9, Prime Minister Sharon repeated these concerns during his meeting with President Bush. The goal of the meeting was to convince Bush that Iran constituted a strategic threat to Israel beyond that posed by Iraq.

But the Bush administration was not to be deterred from its focus on removing Saddam Hussein. When the White House asked the CIA about the Israeli claims, the CIA Director, George Tenet, reportedly replied that this was information the United States was aware of, but didn't give it much credibility. President Bush did raise the issue with Russian President Putin during a summit meeting in May, but focused on the issue of the Russian effort to install a nuclear reactor at Bushehr, as opposed to the Israeli information about secret facilities. The Russians, undeterred, seemed intent to proceed with the deal, U.S. objections notwithstanding. In late July 2002 the Russians surprised everyone by signing an agreement with the Iranians which dramatically increased the scale and scope of Russian–Iranian cooperation well beyond simply the Bushehr deal. In this agreement Russia offered to build five more nuclear power plants in Iran, as well as expand economic cooperation to include oil, gas, and aircraft manufacturing. A senior U.S. delegation visited Russia in early August, protesting the deal, but the Russians pressed ahead. A summit between the Russian and Iranian governments was scheduled for August 20, in which the ambitious ten-year plan of cooperation was to be discussed.

Rebuked by the United States, the Israelis looked for another vehicle to draw attention to the threat they believed Iran posed, and thus spur America to take that threat posed by Iran more seriously. Of critical importance was to get the United States to stop the Russian–Iranian cooperation on nuclear activity. Sobhani and CDI provided an ideal solution, namely that the Israeli government use Reza Pahlavi as the mouthpiece for telling the world about what the Iranians were up to in the field of nuclear weapons, and in exchange Pahlavi would be given immediate credibility and with it front runner status in the race of those trying to rule Iran post-Mullah. Unfortunately for the Israelis and CDI, Reza Pahlavi balked, apparently not wanting to risk his standing inside Iran by having too close of a link with Israeli intelligence.

Undeterred, Ledeen and the CDI turned to the MEK, or more specifically, its political front in Washington, D.C., the NCRI, as the next best option to bring the Israeli intelligence to center stage. CDI reportedly lobbied the NCRI representative, Alireza Jafarzadeh, to serve as the mouthpiece for presenting the Israeli intelligence to the general public. This was not as far a stretch as one might believe; Israeli intelligence had maintained a relationship with the MEK that dated back to the mid-1990s. The stage was now set for Jafarzadeh to deliver his lines.

"What I am going to reveal today," Jafarzadeh said, "is the result of extensive research and investigation by the Committee of Defense and Strategic Studies of the National Council of Resistance of Iran, with the benefit of Command Headquarters Inside Iran of the People's Mojahedin Organization of Iran, which I am going to share with you." This, of course, was not true. According to knowledgeable sources, Jafarzadeh's information came from Israeli intelligence. But this point was irrelevant. For what Jafarzadeh said next literally propelled the world down a path that could change the course of modern history:

Although on the surface, the regime's main nuclear activity revolves around Bushehr's nuclear plant, in reality many secret nuclear programs are at work without any knowledge of International Atomic Energy Agency (IAEA).

One of these top-secret projects is Natanz's nuclear facility. Natanz is about 100 miles north of Isfahan. The other one is Arak's atomic facilities. Arak is a city in central Iran, 150 miles south of Tehran. These two projects have been kept secret until now.

Jafarzadeh went on to provide details about suppliers, manufacturers, bureaucratic entities, and chronological details about the work he claimed was going on at the two facilities. The briefing was attended by reporters from the *Wall Street Journal*, Associated Press, Fox News, the French News Agency, and Aljazeera. Aljazeera had attempted to get the Iranian government to provide a comment on the accusations leveled by Jafarzadeh, but got no reply. The revelations made by Jafarzadeh barely made a blip on the radar screen of mainstream media in the United States or elsewhere, the entire world at that time seemingly solely focused on the issue of Iraq's WMD programs and the increasingly bellicose statements being made by the American government.

At first blush it seemed the Israeli gambit had failed. But in the months and years that followed his briefing, Alireza Jafarzadeh's short presentation on that muggy day in August 2002 would steamroll into a global crisis that, by the summer of 2006, threatened to push the world over the edge of an abyss.

I have decided to tell the story of this journey from Foggy Bottom to the Abyss not because I am a first-hand participant in the events portrayed herein, but rather because I am not. Rather than recounting the events from the perspective of an insider, I offer the perspectives of an informed observer. While I have not participated in any weapons inspections inside Iran, I did participate in numerous U.N.-mandated inspections in Iraq. I have sat in on Security Council discussions about how to deal with the Iraq situation, watched the diplomatic struggles behind the scenes as governments attempt to forge consensus, sat in on meetings at the White House, State Department, Pentagon and CIA as policy was formulated, as well as meetings with the IAEA at its headquarters in Vienna, Austria, and in the field, as these policies were implemented. I have witnessed the frustration of the nation targeted for inspection (in my case Iraq, but it could very well have been Iran), as they wrestled with the inherent contradictions of U.S. policy objectives of regime change being wrapped in layer after layer of disingenuous commitment to arms control and disarmament. I know most of the players of this game, whether they be diplomats in Europe, spies in Israel, or inspectors in the United States. I have spent hours discussing the issue of Iran and its nuclear program with these experts, and have come to the conclusion that, in the issue of Iran, we are seeing history repeat itself. I am struck by the similarity between how the United States, Israel, Europe, Russia, and the United Nations stumbled their collective way toward war in Iraq based upon a false premise (i.e., the existence of WMD in Iraq), and what is transpiring vis-à-vis Iran today, where we seem to be stumbling down that very same path of conflict, driven by ghosts of a nuclear weapons program that has not manifested itself beyond the hyperbole and speculative rhetoric of those whose true agenda lies more in changing the regime in Tehran than it does with genuine non-proliferation and disarmament.

This has been a difficult book to write. The subject matter is complicated on a number of levels, and it is easy to fall into the trap of technical or diplomatic minutia. I have done my best to avoid such traps, and yet lay out the technical and diplomatic framework so that the basics of the story can be understood and followed by the reader. Much of the technical information about Iran's nuclear programs is contained in the reports prepared by the International Atomic Energy Agency about their work in Iran. Where needed, I have consulted specialists in uranium mining and processing for some clarification on certain processes. Sourcing for this book, outside of publicly available materials such as the IAEA reports and media accounts, has been difficult. Given the highly politicized nature of the subject, no one involved in the Iranian issue who did speak with me wanted to be identified in any way, shape or form. As such, I have relied on the information they provided primarily as a guide to help me navigate through the reams of open source reporting on Iran, picking those accounts that best reflect the actual situation as told to me. On occasion I have woven into the narrative data provided directly by a source, always careful to protect the identity of the individual or individuals involved. These include academics from around the world, weapons inspectors involved in the Iranian nuclear issue (both past and present), nuclear experts (both in the field of energy and weapons), intelligence officials in Israel, Europe, and the United States, and diplomatic sources in Europe and the United States.

I made an effort to reach out to the government of Iran, and had been told that I would be granted a visa to visit that country and conduct interviews and visits in support of this book, but literally at the last minute, the Iranian government withdrew its support. I had submitted a list of questions and interviews, and I can only assume that the Iranians were taken aback by the direct nature of some of the questioning. I have tried to remain impartial throughout the telling of this story, but have to admit to being taken aback by the Iranian government's behavior in this regard. However, any prejudice brought on by this encounter is more than offset by my own opinions formed regarding U.S. policy in the Middle East after nearly a decade's worth of involvement in the Iraq issue. So hopefully the two will balance each other out in the telling of the story of the Iranian crisis.

How this crisis came to be, and the story of the individuals and organizations involved, is a tale full of hubris, pathos, integrity, and deception. It is a story of intelligence and indifference, and the fear born of ignorance. Most importantly, it is a story of national overreach, by many parties, and the awful consequences of such. As such, it is a story that is dominated by a sickening sense of déjà vu, as if we have seen this all before, with the accusatory finger being pointed in the direction of Iraq, instead of Iran. Because we have seen this story unfold before, this time we are, in the process of telling the story, able to discern a path that leads away from the abyss of conflict with Iran, and yet at the same time ascertain why, in the end, human foibles might succeed in pushing the world collectively over its edge.

One
A Crisis Made in Israel

TO UNDERSTAND ISRAEL'S PRESENT STANCE on Iran, perhaps the best place to begin is at Yad Vashem, Israel's main Holocaust museum and memorial. It is at Yad Vashem that Israelis reflect on the very reason there is a modern Israeli state, namely because of the genocidal forces that brought so much suffering upon the Jewish people in the past century. Modern Israelis are also reminded here of the political forces that continue to seek the elimination of not only the Jews, but also Israel itself.

Recognizing the powerful influence that the Holocaust plays on the psyche of Israel is not just important in terms of understanding why Israel would never tolerate the existence of forces opposed to its survival, but also how an issue of such emotional depth has the potential to poison an environment, to the point that Israel and its supporters can support policies that can end up being exploited for purposes that are detrimental to the long-term survival and prosperity of the Israeli state.

Anyone who has visited Israel as an official guest, as I have done a number of times, has been provided a tour of that tiny nation, and as such can sense Israel's perceived vulnerability. There is a certain paranoia that dominates the Israeli psyche, one that is not without some merit. The high number of suicide attacks bears witness to the reality that there are in fact organizations and people "out there" who seek to do harm to the state of Israel and the Israeli people.

It should come as no surprise then that senior Israeli politicians chose Yad Vashem as the place from which to make clear the Israeli policy regarding Iran's nuclear ambitions. On this year's Holocaust Remembrance Day two Iranian-born Jews delivered these remarks. "I call on the Western world to not stand silently in the face of the nations that are trying to acquire nuclear weapons and [who] preach the destruction of the State of Israel," Israeli President Moshe Katsav remarked during prepared remarks made at Yad Vashem. On the same day, at the opening of the Center for Iranian Studies at Tel Aviv University, outgoing Defense Minister Shaul Mofaz highlighted Israel's contention that Iran had funded terror groups operating inside the Palestinian territories with close to $10 million in financial assistance since the start of 2006. Mr. Mofaz went on to say that the Israeli policy should be focused on seeking the demise of the current regime in Tehran.

However, there is an element of hypocrisy inherent in the Israeli position. Israel possesses nuclear weapons capabilities that were acquired surreptitiously, and fields a force of modern ballistic missiles capable of firing nuclear warheads into not only Iran, but also every other nation in the region. The irony of Israel, a nation born of the Holocaust and alone among Middle Eastern nations in possessing the holocaust-generating power of nuclear weapons, condemning Iran for its rhetoric while itself espousing the demise of the Iranian government, is lost on few outside of Israel and the United States, and for a large part explains why the legitimacy of the Israeli concerns about Iran to a large extent fall on deaf ears.

The reality of the Holocaust (from an historical perspective) and the concept of the Holocaust (regarding Israel's future) dominate the national security thinking of the Israeli state. It is wrong to characterize the emotions and beliefs of over five million people in the person of a single individual, especially when it comes to the issue of Israel's national security, Iraq and Iran. However, there is one man who has so dominated these issues for over the past decade that it is impossible to speak of these issues without referring to his name over and over again—Amos Gilad.

When meeting Amos Gilad, it is at first hard to imagine such serious matters being rolled up into the personage of such a man. He is medium height, with a thinning shock of white hair, possessing a soft, pudgy frame, and pale skin reflective of a career indoors, rummaging through papers and sitting through briefings; one would be hard pressed equating the physical impression of the man with the near-mythological status he holds as one of Israel's premier spymasters. But when the man speaks, and in doing so exposes his intellect to his audience, the physical no longer matters as the sharp insights and analytical capacity of Amos Gilad becomes clear. Whether one agrees with his assessments or not, there is no escaping the fact that with his soft but firm voice and direct presentation, Amos Gilad projects confidence.

This confidence is born of an adult lifetime spent in the service of the Israel Defense Force, serving as an officer within the Aman, or Military Intelligence. Born in 1954 to a father who immigrated from Czechoslovakia to Israel in 1939, and a mother who was a survivor of the Holocaust, Amos Gilad had the history of the persecution and near-extermination of Europe's Jews seared into his being from youth. The legend of Amos Gilad tells of how he wrote a paper on Auschwitz which involved research so detailed that it enabled the young Amos to correct any errors in stories told by camp survivors. A serious student, he enlisted in the Officer's Candidate Academic Studies Program upon graduating from high school, allowing him to earn a Master's Degree in Political Science from the University of Haifa before going on active duty.

With his advanced degree and sharp intellect, Gilad was a natural for assignment to Military Intelligence. He entered military service in the aftermath of the 1973 Yom Kippur War, and as such joined an intelligence branch stinging from the embarrassment of failed analysis, a process which has taken on the shameful title of "konseptsia," from the Hebrew word for conception, a derogatory reference to the pre-1973 assessment of the head of Israeli Military Intelligence at the time, Eli Za'ira, who "conceived" that Egypt would not launch an attack against Israel, ignoring a huge amount of intelligence the contrary. In the aftermath of Eli Za'ira's konseptsia, the Aman put in place analytical checks and balances throughout the military intelligence system in order to make sure that never again would Israel fall victim to assessments void of fact.

The rigorous training in the art of intelligence paid off. In 1978, as a junior officer, Amos Gilad made a name for himself when he accurately predicted a PLO terror attack along the Israeli seacoast. In 1982, by now a major, he became embroiled in Israel's invasion of Lebanon. Assigned to the Aman's research branch, Gilad was very critical of Israel's close ties with the Lebanese Christian Phalangist militias. Major Gilad predicted that Israel's decision to allow the Phalangist militia into the Palestinian refugee camps of Sabra and Shatila would result in the massacre of the civilian population. On the night of September 16, 1982, Amos Gilad arrived at a forward command post near Beirut, and started immediately to send warnings of an impending slaughter back to his higher headquarters. His warnings were ignored, largely because analysts in the rear headquarters believed that Gilad was responding to a gut feeling, rather than hard fact. The official investigation into the role of the Israel Defense Force (IDF) in Sabra and Shatila revealed that Major Gilad was acting on far more than gut feeling; he had overheard conversations between Israeli officers that indicated that a massacre was underway.

The horrible events at Sabra and Shatila left a mark on Amos Gilad, making him not only more cognizant of the soundness of his analytical thinking, but the absolute requirement to press this analysis home in the face of doubters or bureaucratic inaction. Gilad worked his way through various assignments within the Aman, until fate had him, by this time a Colonel, serving as the head of the Iraq desk on the eve of the escalation of tensions with Iraq over its nuclear program, Saddam's subsequent threat to "burn half of Israel" with a chemical weapon, the Iraqi invasion of Kuwait, and the American build-up in Saudi Arabia in response. As the head of the Iraq desk, Amos Gilad monitored Iraqi military developments continuously, and would brief his findings to the Director of Military Intelligence, and more often than not, to the Defense Minister and Prime Minister.

At the time of Saddam Hussein's invasion of Kuwait, the United States, through the Department of Defense, maintained an intelligence sharing program with the IDF, which operated under the code name Ice Castle. While the history of modern U.S.–Israeli intelligence sharing programs have as their genesis the tumultuous period surrounding the 1973 Yom Kippur War, the specifics of the Ice Castle program were tied to the crisis of Spring 1990, when Israeli intelligence detected a resurgence of activity within Iraq related to nuclear matters, prompting Israeli politicians to publicly speculate about a repeat of the 1982 attack by Israel on the Osirak nuclear reactor outside of Baghdad, an action that many today believe retarded Saddam Hussein's nuclear ambitions by over a decade.

Iraq, for its part, put Israel on notice that any such attack by Israel would result in an Iraqi counterattack, including the use of chemical weapons that would, according to Saddam Hussein, "burn half of Israel." The Ice Castle program revolved around Israel's concerns relating to Iraqi capabilities to launch such an attack, and U.S. intelligence data, specifically satellite photographs of western Iraq, was provided to Israel (via Israeli liaison officers dispatched to Washington, D.C.) to help detect any suspicious Iraqi activity in the deserts of western Iraq. Of specific concern for the Israelis were Iraqi SCUD missiles, armed with chemical warheads, which when operating from locations in western Iraq would be able to range all of Israel. In the period of heightened tensions between Israel and Iraq that followed into the summer of 1990, the Ice Castle cooperation detected a surge of ballistic missile related activity in western Iraq on the part of the Iraqi military, including the establishment of numerous fixed-arm missile launchers oriented toward Israel, and the survey of missile launch sites for Iraq's mobile SCUD launchers.

Theory quickly became reality when, following Iraq's August 1990 invasion of Kuwait, the Iraqi military deployed nearly a dozen chemical warhead-tipped SCUD missiles to the deserts of western Iraq. Even as U.S. forces surged into the Middle East in the months following the Iraqi invasion, Israel pushed the United States for more information on the Iraqi missile threat. However, the U.S. planning priority had shifted away from dealing with an Israeli-centric issue revolving around missile threats in western Iraq, to a larger matter of assembling a large, multi-national coalition comprising many key Arab allies, which would not only defend the eastern oil fields of Saudi Arabia from the threat of expanded Iraqi incursions, but also launch a counterattack designed to liberate Kuwait from Iraqi occupation. Israel's concerns were no longer America's concerns, so much so that Ice Castle imagery was diverted to U.S. military planners (myself included), while Israeli liaison officers sat empty handed in Pentagon briefing rooms.

Israeli military and political leaders grew increasingly irritated by the lack of U.S. sensitivity regarding what they viewed as a serious threat to Israeli security. Many in Israel talked of an Israeli preemptive strike on Iraq, but were pressured by the United States to stand down so as to do nothing that could be detrimental to the Arab-heavy coalition being assembled in Saudi Arabia to confront Iraq. On January 13, 1991, a U.S. delegation led by Assistant Secretary of State Lawrence Eagleburger went so far as to guarantee that after the second day of military action against Iraq, no Iraqi missiles would ever impact on Israeli soil.

This lack of American attention took on considerable political consequence when, in January 1991, Iraq fired SCUD missiles from western Iraq into Israeli cities following the initiation of military action on the part of a U.S.-led coalition designed to liberate Kuwait. In the early morning hours of January 17, the Israeli seaport of Haifa was struck, in rapid succession, by three Iraqi SCUD missiles. Two missiles impacted in the sea off the city proper, exploding on contact with the water. The third missile struck a shopping mall under construction, located near the checkpoint for the northern entrance to Haifa. Fortunately, the shopping mall was empty, most people had left their apartments for bomb shelters, and there were no casualties.

Shortly after the missile attack in Haifa, five more SCUD missiles struck Tel Aviv. The first missile exploded in the air over the suburb of Afeka, spreading debris over the trajectory flight path. The second missile struck a civilian factory structure in Azur, destroying that building. The third missile impacted in the Ezra quarter of Tel Aviv, completely destroying seventy-six housing apartments, and damaging nearly 1,000 more. It was this missile which caused most of the damage and all of the casualties in this first wave of missile attacks, wounding sixty-eight people, several seriously. Two more missiles fell over Tel Aviv that morning, one crashing into an orchard in Rishon Letzion, and the other exploding in the sky above Ganei Tikva.

But the damage had been done. For the first time in its post-1948 history, the heartland of Israel had been struck a heavy blow by the means of a deliberate attack by Arab military forces. Denied through American diplomacy the traditional Israeli defensive tactic of preemptive strike, and now facing the specter of dozens of wounded Israelis being rushed to hospitals amid the debris of their destroyed or damaged homes, all eyes in Israel turned to their military for swift and effective retribution.

Amos Gilad, as the head of the Iraq desk, stood at the center of this controversy. Prior to the war, and blinded by a lack of precise data in the form of U.S. intelligence, he had been under considerable pressure from his leadership to predict the actions of Saddam Hussein. Rejecting the disciplined approach toward analysis that Israeli Military Intelligence had embraced since 1973, Gilad caved in to the pressure and produced his own personal assessment derived more from konseptsia than fact. According to Colonel Gilad, Saddam Hussein was an irrational actor who would shower Israel with ballistic missiles tipped with chemical and biological warheads. As such, Amos Gilad was a vocal proponent of an Israeli preemptive attack.

When the war started in January 1991, Colonel Gilad's assessment was proven to be half-correct: Iraqi SCUD missiles pounded Israel. But the most explosive element of his warnings—that these missiles would be topped with chemical and biological warheads—did not come to pass. However, Gilad's forward-leaning posture in advocating a preemptive strike played well politically in an Israel shaken by scores of missiles impacting its soil, and feeling impotent given its inability to strike back.

Shortly after the news of the Iraqi SCUD attacks on Israel reached Washington, D.C., Israeli Defense Minister Moshe Arens called U.S. Secretary of Defense Dick Cheney. Arens expressed his dismay over the attacks, and sternly pressed for the U.S. to make arrangements for an Israeli counter strike. Secretary Cheney took note of the Israeli request, and quickly placed a telephone call to the National Security Advisor's office in the west wing of the White House, where Brent Scowcroft was sitting with Vice President Dan Quayle, Secretary of State James Baker, Deputy Secretary of State Lawrence Eagleburger, Robert Gates, the Deputy National Security Advisor, and Richard Haass, the National Security Council senior Middle East expert. Cheney outlined his concerns that it would be difficult to stop the Israelis from retaliating, and that Washington should not impede such action if Israel pressed forward.

Following this exchange, Baker immediately placed a phone call to the White House residence, informing President Bush of the Israeli requests. The president urged restraint, and directed Baker to relay this message to the Israelis. Secretary of State Baker finally was able to make contact with Israeli Prime Minister Shamir, passing on the president's message and noting that the U.S. Coalition air forces were even as they spoke were "going full bore," delivering devastating strikes against the Iraqi SCUD forces in western Iraq. Baker acknowledged Israel's right to military retaliation, but stated that such action by Israel at this point in time would only aid Iraq politically, and threaten the coalition of Western and Arab forces that President Bush had assembled for the war. Shamir reiterated his concern over the situation, telling Baker that "Israel has never failed to respond." But for the moment the sword of Zion had been stayed.

Not all in Israel took such a position. There was a large faction within the Israeli government that favored active military retaliation against Iraq. This was prominently displayed at a meeting of the Ministerial Committee on National Security held on January 18, in which Shamir—while forestalling any immediate retaliatory actions—directed the Chief of Staff of the Israel Defense Forces, Dan Shomron, to draw up detailed plans for military action against Iraq should the SCUD attacks continue. Even more foreboding was the fact that the Israeli nuclear-tipped *Jericho* missile force was placed on full alert for only the third time in its history. Shamir called James Baker and informed him that the Israeli cabinet was leaning toward an immediate response to the Iraqi missile attacks against Tel Aviv and Haifa. Baker urged restraint, noting that the fallout of any such Israeli action would be disastrous for both Israel and the coalition.

At the same time as Baker was speaking to Shamir, Secretary Cheney was taking a call from Moshe Arens. Mr. Arens pressed on Cheney his point of how seriously Israel regarded the turn of events. Arens detailed the Israeli plan for destroying and/or disrupting the Iraqi capability to launch its SCUD missiles which had been drawn up by Dan Shamron and General Avi Bin-Nun. (The plan had actually been in place since mid-summer 1990, and was constantly updated by the IDF Chief of Staff to reflect available Israeli assets and the current situation involving coalition forces.) The plan was a modification of a long-standing IDF contingency to conduct pre-emptive and interdiction strikes against Iraqi ground and air forces staged in or moving through western Iraq in time of actual or pending conflict.

Even as Mr. Arens spoke, twelve Israeli aircraft were being sent airborne, assuming what amounted to a large defensive combat air patrol. Based on the types of armament onboard (precision-guided bombs, anti-radiation rockets, etc.), it was obvious, however, that this defensive posture could shift to an offensive one at a moment's notice. Israeli commando forces had already been assembled in the Negev desert, where they were rehearsing their attacks against Iraqi SCUD missiles. The entire operation would take several days, Mr. Arens stated, and was scheduled to begin on January 19 with an initial strike by 100 Israeli warplanes. While he patiently listened to the Israeli counter strike proposal, Cheney in the end remained firm, indicating that the U.S. would do nothing to facilitate any Israeli attack against Iraq, and continued to press home the absolute requirement for Israeli restraint.

Both Baker and Cheney ended their respective phone calls unsure what the Israeli reaction would be. During this moment of uncertainty, the Iraqis struck yet again. Early on the morning of January 19, four more Iraqi missiles slammed into Israel, hitting the Tel Aviv area. One struck the Tikva quarter, near a bomb shelter, where it left a sizeable crater and damaged buildings in the surrounding area. A second impacted at the exhibition gardens, near the Ayalon freeway junction. Again, the explosion left a large crater, but as this was an unpopulated region, the damage was negligible. The third missile impact had the greatest potential for causing a catastrophe, impacting in a residential area at the corner of Allenby and Yehuda Halevi streets. This missile had disintegrated in mid-air, separating the warhead from the missile body. The warhead penetrated into a residential apartment complex, but miraculously failed to explode. Had it done so, the casualties would have been considerable. The fourth and final missile of the morning landed at Rishon Letzion, north of Nahalat Yehuda. The explosion of the warhead set off a fire at a nearby gas station, which burned dramatically in the early morning darkness. In total, some 1,589 apartments were damaged, of which forty-six were considered destroyed. Forty-seven Israelis were wounded in this new round of attacks.

Many within the U.S. administration believed Israel had reached its breaking point. Under instructions from Dick Cheney, the Joint Staff in Washington, D.C., passed on to Central Command the details of the Israeli plan, and initial contingencies were drafted to clear the skies of western Iraq of coalition aircraft if Israel decided to intervene. There was no desire for any armed confrontation with Israel, regardless of the U.S. stance against Israeli intervention. In Israel, Prime Minister Shamir had originally scheduled a meeting of his entire cabinet for Sunday morning, January 20, following the Sabbath. At this meeting the cabinet was to debate the retaliation plans being fine-tuned by the Israeli Defense Force.

However, the continued Iraqi missile attacks on Saturday morning meant that this meeting had to be pushed forward, calling for an extremely rare gathering on the morning of the Sabbath itself. Surprisingly, Prime Minister Shamir, despite the continued Iraqi attacks, formally announced an Israeli policy of non-retaliation, after a lengthy and emotional debate within the Israeli inner cabinet. But it had become obvious to the policy makers in Washington, D.C., that the longer Iraq was able to launch its SCUD missiles toward Israel, the more likely Israel was to enter the conflict, regardless of the consequences. The United States was running out of time.

The continued SCUD attacks against Israel, and the resulting domestic pressure placed upon the Israeli military to retaliate, meant that the threat of Israel becoming actively involved in military operations against Iraq was becoming more real. Before the initiation of hostilities on January 16, the Ice Castle intelligence-sharing program partly mollified Israeli concerns about Iraq, and thus prevented a pre-emptive Israeli attack. Immediately prior to Operation Desert Storm getting under way, when the Israeli concern over the Iraqi SCUD threat became more focused, the Defence Intelligence Agency and the Joint Chiefs of Staff formed a joint crisis response team that was dispatched to Tel Aviv for the purpose of sharing operational information and intelligence derived from and concerning the war effort, as well as to process Israeli concerns into tangible targets for attack by the U.S./Coalition air forces. Once hostilities began, this team sought to alleviate the Israeli fears by keeping the Israelis informed of the progress made by the U.S./Coalition air forces in destroying the Iraqi SCUD threat in western Iraq. This team was reinforced early on in the conflict by a team of imagery and area specialists, who augmented the existing liaison team and provided a direct link with the counter-SCUD cell back at DIA Headquarters.

By January 23, the political leaders of Israel were under significant pressure from their civilian constituency to retaliate, and this pressure was in turn applied to the IDF command. In meetings with the U.S. crisis response team, the IDF highlighted the hair-trigger nature of their retaliatory force, and the fact that they were under considerable criticism for not pulling it. The IDF command pressured the U.S. team to provide information which highlighted the U.S. actions in western Iraq so that they might forestall any rash, politically motivated action by the Israelis. In particular, the IDF requested advance knowledge of targets to be struck in Iraq (especially any suspected chemical munitions storage bunkers), and timely assessments concerning the effectiveness of all attacks. All of this would considerably aid the IDF in placating Israeli political concerns that everything was being done that could be. The U.S. crisis response team agreed to increase the information being provided to Israel, and asked Central Command headquarters in Riyadh to comply.

However, the intensity of the Israeli Defense Force's requests for assistance that was felt by the crisis response team in Tel Aviv was not mirrored by the headquarters of U.S. Central Command in Riyadh. At the same time that the crisis response team was meeting with the IDF in Tel Aviv, battle damage analysts at Central Command were beginning to come to grips with the scope of the failure of the U.S./Coalition air strikes against the Iraqi SCUD missiles. In a blunt assessment the point was made that, despite the considerable amount of effort being placed on locating and destroying the Iraqi SCUD missiles in western Iraq, on the eve of an urgent Israeli request for information and data needed to prevent a spreading of the conflict, the United States had very little of substance to report. In a politically motivated decision, the United States decided to exaggerate its success in hunting down Iraqi SCUDs in an effort to continue holding Israel at bay. All the while, Iraqi missiles continued to rain down on Israeli cities.

The Israelis did not miss the American deception, and as a result the Israeli military began preparing for action. Israelis complained bitterly to the American team in Tel Aviv that the U.S./Coalition strikes had been ineffective. The Israelis believed the U.S. target list used in western Iraq to be totally inadequate. The same vote of confidence was given to the U.S. approach to target prioritization. The Israeli Air Force had developed a comprehensive list of 180 SCUD-related targets which they felt should be attacked. These targets, in their opinion, were being overlooked by the U.S./Coalition mission planners, hence the continued SCUD attacks against Israel.

Despite all of Israel's concerns about how the counter-SCUD campaign was being executed by the U.S./Coalition forces, the time for the implementation of any large-scale Israeli air-ground thrust into western Iraq was past. While the Israeli Air Force continued to make noise concerning the target selection of the allied aircraft, it was by this time quite evident that Israel was in no position to either match the number of sorties being generated over western Iraq, or to complain about the accuracy of the munitions being delivered.

The ongoing attacks on Israel by Iraqi SCUD missiles, which continued unabated up until the end of hostilities in late February 1991, only served to deepen the sense of impotence and betrayal that abounded in Tel Aviv. Israel had bought into the arguments of the United States that American military power would serve to safeguard Israel, and then stood back and did nothing when these American promises turned out to be false. Furthermore, Israel carefully monitored the deceptive nature of American diplomacy regarding the Iraqi missile threat, biting its tongue while the United States delivered poor quality (and often-times deliberately deceptive) intelligence information about the Iraqi threat and the American response.

A clear indicator of this newfound Israeli independence took place in the form of an Israeli aerial reconnaissance mission flown over western Iraq in October 1991. This mission had originally been intended to be flown in late February 1991, at the height of the Iraqi missile assault on Israeli cities. Israeli intelligence personnel had developed information that Iraq had deployed chemical weapons to bunkers in western Iraq (U.N. weapons inspectors later confirmed this to be true). The Israelis were anxious to determine whether or not their repeated requests that these bunkers be bombed were being acted on by the United States. It turned out the Israeli requests were being ignored. In an effort to both assist the U.S. and assuage their own concerns, the Israelis requested up-to-date satellite imagery from the United States so that they could evaluate with their own eyes what the status was concerning the chemical bunkers.

The United States, in an effort to forestall any Israeli attack, provided imagery dating back to November 1990, claiming it was from February 1991. The Israelis were quick to detect the lie (which was explained away by the United States as a genuine mistake). In anger, the head of the Israeli Air Force ordered a pair of Israeli F-15 fighters, equipped with cameras, to fly over western Iraq and take their own pictures. The date of the mission was scheduled to be February 28, the same day the cease-fire was announced. The Israeli reconnaissance flight stood down, but not for long. In October 1991, angered by the refusal of the United States to share U-2 imagery of Iraq taken under the auspices of the United Nations weapons inspection process, Israel launched the two F-15 fighters, flying over western Iraq (and taking pictures of the targets they were interested in) at the same time a large U.N. weapons inspection team was operating on the ground. The message was unmistakable: Israel will trust no one again when it comes to matters concerning its national security interest.

The 1991 Gulf War was a traumatic event for Israel, deeply scarring that nation and branding the Israeli leadership with the reality that, at the end of the day, Israel could only rely upon itself when it came to defending its perceived national security interests. America remained a close ally, but one that had proven it could not be relied upon when left to its own devices. Not only would Israel redouble its efforts to create and maintain truly unilateral defense capabilities, but also in those situations where the use of powerful proxies like the United States was unavoidable, Israel became determined to stack the deck in its own favor, engaging in activities in the United States, directly and through the very powerful and influential pro-Israeli lobby, that can only be described as outright espionage and interference in the domestic politics of a sovereign state. This stance dominated Israeli relations with the United States throughout the 1990s, not only influencing American policy but also, in an odd sort of blowback phenomenon that will be demonstrated, corrupting the very independent character that Israel sought to develop to begin with. And Amos Gilad would be at the center of it all.

When the war ended, Colonel Gilad's political star was on the rise, and he was reassigned as the assistant to the Military Secretary to Prime Minister Yitzhak Shamir. Gilad stayed on in this role when Yitzhak Rabin became Prime Minister in 1993 and named Danny Yatom as his Military Secretary. In this role, Amos Gilad was thrust into the complex world of Israeli–Palestinian relations, traveling to Tunis for secret meetings with Yassar Arafat, and participating in the Washington, D.C.-based negotiations with the Palestinians during the build-up to the Oslo Accords. Politics suited Gilad's post-Desert Storm persona, where "gut feelings" concerning the Palestinian intentions often outweighed cold, professional analysis.

Gilad had become a hard-liner on the issue of Palestinian reliability, and argued vociferously against Israel agreeing to the Oslo Accords. Given the political sensitivity surrounding Israeli–Palestinian relations, the Israeli leadership thought it better to have the hard-liner explaining policy, as opposed to negotiating it, and in June 1994 he was appointed as the Spokesperson for the IDF, a highly public role that was at odds with the acerbic, opinionated Gilad. Amos Gilad did not enjoy his time as the IDF Spokesperson, but his hard-line stance caught the attention of those in higher office, and by 1996 he returned once again to the ranks of the Aman, this time as Chief of the Intelligence Research Division, responsible for the preparation of all national intelligence estimates.

The one-time holder of the Iraq file now found himself responsible for assessing every aspect of Israel's national security. Iraq was still a major issue, but in the years since the 1991 Gulf War much had happened to alter the intelligence picture on that country and the threat it posed to Israel. Under the leadership of Ya'acov Ami Dror, Amos Gilad's predecessor at the Intelligence Research Division, Israel had reached out in unprecedented fashion to its long-time nemesis, the United Nations, and forged close ties with the United Nations Special Commission, the inspection body responsible for overseeing the disarmament of Iraq's weapons of mass destruction. Similar close ties were established between Israel and the International Atomic Energy Agency regarding the Iraqi nuclear program. As a result, Israel was able to improve its intelligence picture regarding Iraq to the point that it possessed as clear an understanding of the threat—or in this case, the lack of threat—posed by Saddam Hussein's Iraq.

A clear example of just how influential the U.N.–Israeli cooperation on Iraq was came in October 1994 when a visit to Israel by U.N. weapons inspectors coincided with a precipitous move by Iraqi forces toward the border with Kuwait, invoking memories of the 1990 invasion. The Israeli government was on high alert, and a decision needed to be made as to whether or not gas masks would be distributed to the general population in anticipation of a replay of the Iraqi missile attacks of 1991. General Uri Saguy, the Director of Military Intelligence, and Ya'acov Ami Dror were called by the office of the Prime Minister for consultation. A decision was needed in short order. While Ya'acov Ami Dror had provided General Saguy with the assessment of his division regarding the Iraqi threat, Saguy decided to take advantage of the presence of the U.N. weapons inspectors to ask about their assessment as to whether or not Iraq possessed a missile threat to Israel. The answer was clear—the Iraqi missile capability had been eliminated, the only issue remaining being a final verifiable accounting of what happened to a few missiles, as opposed to the search for a hidden operational capability. Israel was not under threat. Apparently the assessment of the U.N. inspectors coincided with that of Ya'acov Ami Dror, and the decision was taken not to issue the gas masks.

Under the leadership of Ya'acov Ami Dror, Israeli Military Intelligence was able to assemble a sound assessment of Iraqi capabilities and intentions. Using a post-1973 system known as the Control Office (or as the Israelis refer to it in tongue-in-cheek fashion, the official "doubting Thomas"), all assessments were subjected to a rigorous quality control process by a Colonel who reported directly to the Director of Military Intelligence. No assessments were allowed to go to the desk of the Aman Director until they had been subjected to this screening. The Control Office questioned every conclusion, sought sources for every fact quoted, and in general made sure that the process behind any given assessment remained true to time-tested professional intelligence standards.

Ami Dror also appointed a veteran Israeli intelligence Colonel to take on the role of "becoming Saddam," so that every word or action of the Iraqi dictator could be evaluated not only from the perspective of Israeli security, but also the mind-set and intent of the Iraqi leader. In this manner, Saddam became viewed as a "rational actor" not prone to "suicidal gestures." While the Israelis never bought into the notion of Saddam giving up his dream of possessing weapons of mass destruction, they did view him as a problem that was easily contained. Post-1991 decisions by the Israeli leadership to remove Saddam Hussein from power, which had manifested themselves in the form of

Israeli commando teams trained and equipped to carry out assassinations, were put on hold because of this new approach.

This new Israeli assessment of Saddam dropped him from the number-one threat facing Israel in 1994, to number six by 1998. The Israelis viewed Saddam as the evil they knew, and as such felt that as long as he was contained by U.N. weapons inspections, they would rather live with him in power than confront the great unknown of a post-Saddam Iraq governed by unknown and unpredictable forces.

The security picture confronting Israel when Amos Gilad took over the position of Director for Research and Analysis was far more complicated than simply facing down a Middle East tyrant. The problem of immediate concern was the ongoing quagmire of the Israeli occupation of southern Lebanon, and Israel's complicated relationship with the Palestinians following the signing of the 1993 Oslo Accord, a relationship exacerbated by a string of particularly deadly terrorist bombings inside Israel in early 1996. In April 1996, the Israeli military launched its largest operation in Lebanon since 1993, Operation Grapes of Wrath, designed to punish the pro-Iranian militia, Hezbollah, for firing rockets into northern Israel. The two-week attack proved to be inconclusive from a military standpoint, and a disaster for Israel from an international relations perspective. More than 500,000 Lebanese were displaced from their homes because of the fighting, and harsh Israeli tactics were brought into sharp focus when an artillery barrage fell on the Palestinian refugee camp of Qana, killing more than 100 civilians. Hezbollah, far from being defeated, reinforced its position in Lebanon as the one power willing, and able, to stand up to Israeli aggression.

In May 1996 Israel went to the polls in an election that was widely viewed as a public referendum of the Israeli–Palestinian peace process. The right-wing Likud Party, headed by Benjamin Netanyahu, defeated the Labor government headed by Shimon Peres. Given Peres' role in advocating a more lenient Israeli posture vis-à-vis the Palestinians, the election of Netanyahu was seen as a rejection by Israel of the current status quo concerning the tenuous peace arrangements. In September 1996, while tensions simmered in Lebanon, relations with the Palestinians exploded when the new Netanyahu government opened up the controversial Hasmonean Tunnel, an ongoing archeological excavation some Muslims believed violated the sanctity of sites sacred to Islam.

In the wave of anti-Israeli demonstrations that followed, tensions exploded with Palestinian policemen and Israeli soldiers exchanging heavy fire throughout the West Bank and Gaza Strip, leaving eighty-five Palestinians and sixteen Israelis dead, and more than 1,200 Palestinians and eighty-seven Israelis wounded. Under the Oslo Accord the Palestinian Security Service (PSS) was supposed to be a lightly armed force dedicated to maintaining order among the Palestinian people. The September fighting imprinted in the minds of many Israelis (including Amos Gilad) a quite different perspective—that the PSS was a well-armed fighting force that directly threatened the safety and security of Israel.

Within this troublesome security climate a new threat emerged, this time from Iran. Following the collapse of the Soviet Union in 1991, Israel and the various new republics of the former Soviet Union (especially Russia and Ukraine) worked together to bring to Israel more than 500,000 Russian Jews. This emigration presented yet another point of pressure on Israel, radically changing the demographics of the Jewish state while straining an already burdened economy. However, the opening of relations also provided a bonanza for the Israeli intelligence service, which exploited the chaos and uncertainty that existed within the new republics to recruit networks of agents that dug deep into business and governmental institutions. The Israelis viewed such work as very much being in their national security interest, given the fact that the vast empire that once was the Soviet Military Defense Industrial complex now lay fractured and operating without any central control or guidance.

The Israeli fears, and the wisdom of their decision to put in place these intelligence networks, soon became clear when, in 1995, word started leaking out of Russia about nefarious dealings between former-Soviet missile production facilities and the Islamic Republic of Iran. The Israeli agents were reporting on visits made by Russian scientists to an Iranian missile design center located at Karaj, fifty miles northwest of Tehran, as early as 1994, and a whole slew of similar exchanges that had taken place since then. One aspect of this new cooperation was particularly disturbing—the wholesale transfer by Russian authorities of a missile production line, including airframe and engine, for the SS-4 intermediate-range missile. The former Soviet Union had signed a treaty with the United States in 1987 which eliminated all intermediate-range missiles in their respective arsenals, and in 1995 the Russian government signed the Missile Technology Control Regime (MTCR) agreement, placing a ban on the exportation of specific technologies and material related to missile design and production.

The Israelis, through their networks, were able to assemble a wide variety of damning evidence, including intercepted conversations, technical specifications, shipping documents, and financial invoices, which proved without a doubt that there were ongoing activities between senior Russian personnel associated with the defense industry of the former Soviet Union and the government of Iran. What was hard to discern was whether or not these transactions had the approval of the central Russian authorities. However, the Israelis had been tracking for some time the relationship between Iran and North Korea concerning ballistic missile development, and was very concerned about one program in particular— the Shahib-3 ("Shooting Star").

The Iranian Shahib-3 missile, a derivative of the North Korean No-Dong 1 missile, has a range between 900 and 1,000 miles, making it the only Iranian missile system capable of reaching Israel. The Iranian–North Korean cooperation in ballistic missiles traced back to the Iran–Iraq War of the 1980s, when Iran imported around a hundred North Korean produced SCUD-B missiles, seventy-seven of which were fired at Iraq during the so-called War of the Cities in 1988. The relationship expanded, and Iran soon bought, in the form of missile kits which were later assembled at facilities in Iran, more than 400 longer-range SCUD-C missiles.

However, neither the SCUD-B nor SCUD-C gave Iran the capability of striking Israel. For this, Iran furthered its relationship with North Korea, engaging in an extensive oil-for-missiles arrangement that had the components of some ten No-Dong missiles in Iran by the mid-1990s. In May 1993 an Iranian delegation was on hand in North Korea to watch the initial operational launch of the No-Dong missile. Impressed, Iran reportedly signed a contract for delivery of 150 of the missiles.

The North Korean connection, however, was tenuous, and susceptible to interdiction. What Iran really wanted was the ability to manufacture its own No-Dong missile indigenously. The North

Koreans were not amenable to a complete technology transfer arrangement, however, so the Iranians went shopping, an excursion which brought them to the free-for-all atmosphere of post-Soviet defense industry.

To Amos Gilad, the Russian-Iranian missile deal represented a vital threat to the security of Israel. At first there was some hesitation within the ranks of the Aman to accept the nascent Iranian missile program, backed up with nebulous reporting about shady dealings with Russian businessmen, as representing a threat. Israel was focused on the Palestinian and Hezbollah problems. And another crisis soon emerged—the Mossad was reporting that Syria was preparing to launch an attack on the Golan Heights. The Mossad data was based on reporting by a long-time Mossad agent, Yehuda Gil. Amos Gilad, in evaluating the reporting from Yehuda Gil, took the position that Syria was not, in fact, preparing to attack, and a subsequent investigation showed that Yehuda Gil had fabricated the totality of his reporting. In the light of events to come, this turn of events demonstrates that Amos Gilad, for all of his detractors, was not prone to fabricate intelligence information. But, having ridden out one wave of hostile missile attacks in 1991, Amos Gilad was not about to stand by idly while another threat loomed on the horizon. Despite Israel's focus on troubles closer to home, Amos Gilad took on the task of elevating Iran to the status of the number one threat facing Israel.

Up until a year before the 1979 Islamic revolution that swept the Shah of Iran out of power, Israel had long-standing ties with Iran. The Iranian monarchy was one of the first nations to recognize Israel as a new state in 1948, and from 1948 to 1949, Iran worked closely with Israel to facilitate the relocation to Israel of Iranian Jews who wanted to live in the new Jewish state. In 1958 Israel initiated an intelligence and military exchange program with the Shah of Iran, and that same year, with the cooperation of the Shah, Israel started arming and training Kurds in northern Iraq, using bases inside Iran, in an effort to destabilize the Iraqi government. This cooperation expanded considerably in 1963, to the extent that by 1965 Israeli personnel were on the ground in northern Iraq, training and advising the Iraqi Kurdish rebels. The close nature of this cooperation manifested itself in June 1967 when, at the behest of their Israeli advisers, the Kurds of northern Iraq launched an offensive against the Iraqi Army in an effort to tie down Iraqi forces that might have been offered up in support of Syria, Jordan or Egypt. A similar rebellion by Iraq's Kurds in 1973 was timed to support Israeli military interests.

The focal point in Iraqi Kurdistan concerning Israeli support was Mullah Mustafa Barzani, who secretly visited Israel in 1967 and again in 1973 to cement the relationship. After 1973, the Israeli-Kurdish relationship was expanded to incorporate the CIA, which sent liaison officers to northern Iraq to coordinate the flow of material support coming out of Iran. This tri-cooperation came to a halt in 1975, however, when the United States brokered a peace agreement between Iran and Iraq. Part of the agreement had Iran suspending all aid shipments to the Iraqi Kurds in the north of Iraq, in effect ending the Kurdish revolt.

The 1970s brought a period of difficulty between Iran and Israel, with Iran providing material support to Egypt during the Yom Kippur War, and then in 1975 voting in the United Nations on a resolution equating Zionism with racism. However, both nations were able to navigate these troubled diplomatic waters, and by 1977 Iran was involved in a multi-billion dollar weapons deal with Israel. These deals were abruptly halted in 1979 with the overthrow of the Shah. However, the demise of the Shah left Israel with an outstanding debt of over $5 billion owed Iran. Israel was able to leverage some of this debt off by continuing to ship weapons to Iran in exchange for the emigration of several thousand Iranian Jews anxious to escape the religious fanatics of the new Islamic Republic in Iran. But soon this contact ended, and the matter of the debt remained.

Even after the 1975 peace agreement between Iran and Iraq, the Israeli intelligence service continued to maintain close ties with Iraqi Kurds loyal to Mustafa Barzani, relations which expanded during the time of the Iran–Iraq War. Israeli intelligence was able to create a number of intelligence gathering networks both inside Iraq and Iran that exploited the Kurdish populations of both countries. After the 1991 Gulf War, Israel greatly expanded its presence in northern Iraq, using elite teams of spies drawn from the ranks of Iraqi-borne Kurds living in Israel (Israel has a Kurdish population of around 50,000). By 1995, this Kurdish network was providing the Israeli intelligence services with a huge amount of raw intelligence data, including reporting on Iraq's weapons of mass destruction programs. Likewise, similar Kurdish networks operating in Iran were furnishing Israel with important information about Iran's security posture, including intelligence about Iranian capabilities in the field of chemical, biological, nuclear and ballistic missiles.

However, it was at this time the Kurdish problem in Turkey began to take on an extremely serious character. The recent public nature of Israel's close relations with Turkey are actually reflective of a long-standing relationship dating back to 1958, when Israeli Prime Minister Ben-Gurion signed a secret agreement with Turkish President Menderes calling for Israeli-Turkish cooperation in the face of growing radicalism in the Middle East, as well as countering what the agreement termed as "Soviet influence." The military coup in Ankara of 1960 put a chill on the nascent Israeli-Turkish relationship. However, by 1964 Israeli–Turkish relations were back on track when Prime Minister Eshkol of Israel and Prime Minister Inonu of Turkey met in Paris and revived the dormant 1958 agreement. Inherent in this agreement was the matter of intelligence cooperation. The first public manifestation of this new relationship occurred in 1974, when Israel provided intelligence in support of Turkey's invasion of Cyprus. When the United States cut off the sale of military equipment to Turkey in response, Israel stepped in, and in 1975 signed an agreement with Turkey for the sale of Israeli-manufactured air-to-air missiles, along with other military material.

In order to balance out its strategic relationship with Turkey and its intelligence exploitation of the Kurds, the Israelis reached a compromise where Turkey would turn a blind eye toward Israel's support of Kurds in Iraq and Iran in exchange for Israel's assistance in clamping down on the Kurdish rebellion in Turkey. Specifically, Israel aided and abetted Turkey in its apprehension of the leader of the Turkish Kurdish movement, Abdullah Ocalan, using its considerable communications intercept and tracking capabilities to gather intelligence which was then passed on to Turkish authorities, who subsequently apprehended the Kurdish rebel leader in Kenya in February 1999.

These intelligence tentacles into Iran were extremely important for Israel, especially given the fact that the relations between the two nations had become increasingly violent. Israel's invasion of Lebanon in 1982 opened the door for the dispatch of Iranian Revolutionary Guards to that country to fight back against the Israeli aggression, thus creating a situation that exists to this day. The Iranians became the primary supporters of the radical Lebanese Islamic group Hezbollah, and Lebanon became a nation targeted by Iran for the exportation of Islamic revolution.

The Iranians didn't keep their struggle against Israel limited to the Lebanon front. In July 1994 there occurred the horrific bombing of the Jewish community center in Buenos Aires, Argentina, that left some 100 people dead and 250 wounded. Israeli intelligence was able to link the bombing to an August 1993 meeting of the Iranian Supreme Council for National Security at which the decision to go ahead with the bombing was made. The actual assignment was given to an overseas operational unit belonging to Hezbollah, with Iranian intelligence providing assistance. Israel's Kurdish connection, according to some sources, played an important role in enabling Israel to put together the pieces of the intelligence puzzle leading to Iran.

But these same sources also allowed Israeli intelligence to paint a much more complex picture of Iranian attitudes toward Israel. Through business links established in the 1980s, when Israel facilitated the ill-fated arms for hostages deal that was part of the larger Iran–Contra scandal that plagued the Reagan administration, Israel continued to ship weapons to Iran, first as an effort to help tip the balance in favor of Iran during the Iran–Iraq War, and later to establish and maintain contacts within Iran, governmental and other, which could prove to be useful.

These sources reported on the possibility of a moderation of the Iranian hard-line view against Israel, and that the Iranian focus was increasingly looking inward, toward solving a myriad of domestic problems (the economy being first and foremost). By 1995 Israeli Military Intelligence believed that there might be an opening to scale down the friction between Israel and Iran, especially if the flash point of Lebanon could be brought under control. There was some thought within Israeli Military Intelligence as to whether or not Israel could leverage payment of its nearly $5 billion debt into better relations with Iran.

It is within this complex web of intelligence and shadow diplomacy that Amos Gilad was forced to consider how to assess the intelligence data coming out of Russia concerning Iran's missile program. One of the first assessments Amos Gilad oversaw was the 1996 National Threat Assessment, in which he claimed that Israel was facing two major threats: Palestine and Iran. Amos Gilad held that as long as Yassar Arafat was in charge, the Palestinians could never be seen as true partners in peace, the 1995 Oslo-2 agreement nonwithstanding. Gilad also believed that the nature of the Iranian regime, its fundamentalist Islamic posture, and vehemently anti-Israeli rhetoric which it routinely dispensed meant that there was a fundamental incompatibility between Israel and Iran, and that the best course of action Israel could take would be to seek regime change in Iran. His draft of the 1996 National Assessment reflected these concerns.

Unfortunately for Amos Gilad, the Israeli Military establishment did not share his views. The Control Office (i.e., doubting Thomas), disturbed by what it saw as too much "emotional debate" and not enough hard analysis, insisted that the assessment be re-written to reflect these concerns, and in the end the 1996 National Assessment held that while the Palestinian problem was real, Israel could look toward a negotiated settlement as the path toward peace, even if this meant negotiating with Arafat. The assessment also held that while Iran was a significant threat, it was also a self-moderating threat where the hard-liners in Iran were subjected to considerable pressures from the Iranian population. While Amos Gilad held that Iran would directly threaten the security of Israel by 2005, the 1996 assessment believed that internal political dynamics would result in the demise of the Iranian hard-liners as a political force by that same year.

Undeterred by the weak posture taken in the 1996 National Assessment, Gilad brought the Iranian–Russian missile connection to the United States in late 1996, raising it in the course of a routine intelligence exchange liaison visit. The Americans did not take the bait, so Gilad returned in January 1997, this time with a detailed briefing that incorporated all of the sensitive intelligence Israel had gained from its sources in Russia and Iran. Gilad confronted the Americans with a stunning conclusion: unless something was done to stop these transfers, Iran would in very short time be able to field a missile force composed of these new Shahib-3 missiles, all capable of striking Israel. The U.S. intelligence community viewed the Shahib-3 missile as a product of Iran's relations with North Korea, and perhaps China, but not

Russia. In the U.S. view, Gilad's intelligence reflected nothing more than the rogue activities of some Russian industrialists that, while a nuisance, did not constitute a real national security issue, either for Israel or the United States.

At this point Amos Gilad engaged the services of the pro-Israeli lobby, the American–Israeli Public Affairs Committee, in order to bring the battle to the United States Congress. With AIPAC operatives working behind the scene to apply pressure to the appropriate members, Gilad appeared before the intelligence committees of both the House of Representatives and the United States Senate, and made Israel's case against the Iranian-Russian connection.

With Congress fully behind him, Amos Gilad was able to get an audience with Vice President Gore's National Security Advisor, Leon Fuerth, where Gilad was able to impress Fuerth as to the seriousness of the situation (at least in so far as Gilad perceived it), and the need to press the Russians to stop the cooperation with Iran. Fuerth was able to lobby Vice President Gore sufficiently that the matter was raised during the visit of Russian Prime Minister Viktor Chernomyrdin to the United States in February 1997.

Not surprisingly, Chernomyrdin denied any official Russian involvement in the matter, but promised to look into it. However, there was a catch: the Russians needed specifics. The United States, through Leon Fuerth, shared with Chernomyrdin what it had learned about the Russian–Iranian connection from Amos Gilad. According to Israeli intelligence officials, within months the sources of intelligence Israel had relied upon began drying up as Russian security forces began arresting any and all who might be privy to the data that had been received by the United States.

It is difficult to assess the real, versus perceived, damage to Israeli intelligence because of Fuerth's indiscretion. At the same time that the Israeli–Russian network was generating information about Iran, similar reporting was forthcoming from these same sources about Russian contacts with Iraq. The Israeli information, provided to the United Nations weapons inspectors, proved to be impressively accurate in every regard except context. The Israelis were able to provide the U.N. inspectors (I headed this coordination on behalf of the U.N.) with impressive link analysis, and dead-on specifics about the nature of the transactions underway. The U.N. inspectors were able to intercept a shipment of Russian missile guidance and control material in Jordan before it made its way to Iraq. However, in doing so, the inspectors discovered that far from an official Russian government-Iraqi government scheme, the network tapped into by the Iraqis represented the seamier side of the post-Soviet economy, where state-owned establishments searched for new markets with little or no official guidance or control over how they did it.

Old equipment destined for the scrap heap, or mothballed material long forgotten in the inventory, was now sold by enterprising black marketers. The U.N. weapons inspectors in Iraq uncovered documents concerning Iraqi-Russian connections which mimicked those the Israelis were uncovering about Iran. Much of it was pie in the sky-type activity, with grand schemes set forth on paper backed up by little of substance. The deals with Iran progressed further than those with Iraq, namely because in Iran there were no U.N. weapons inspectors lurking to uncover the deal. But the basics of the overall arrangements with Russia remained the same: shady black market deals with no official standing.

In order to fully understand the Israeli hysteria about the Iranian–Russian missile cooperation, regardless of its unofficial status, one must put it in the perspective of the Israeli concerns over Russia's decision to supply Iran with nuclear power reactors, an activity that Israel deemed unacceptable and providing a mortal danger to the security of Israel. The Russian–Iranian reactor deal dates back to the time of the Shah of Iran, when in the mid-1970s the Iranian monarchy decided to install a network of twenty nuclear reactors which would supply Iran with all of its energy needs. Two such reactors, each capable of operating at 1,300 megawatts, were to be installed at a site in Bushehr.

By the time of the fall of the Shah, the Bushehr site was at 80 percent completion. However, the new Islamic government deemed nuclear power to be "un-Islamic," and construction (being carried out by a German company, Siemens) was halted. Iraqi aircraft bombed the facility in 1981, destroying it. Midway through the Iran–Iraq War, the government in Tehran had a change of mind about nuclear power, and re-approached Germany to take on the project. Germany, however, was pressured by the United States not to provide Iran with nuclear reactors, but rather gas-powered generators. Iran refused the

German offer. Negotiations with a Spanish–Argentinian consortium in 1987 likewise failed to materialize. Following the collapse of the Soviet Union, Iran approached the new cash-starved Russian government of Boris Yeltsin, and in early 1995 signed a $800 million deal for the Russians to provide a single 1,000 megawatt reactor at Bushehr. This arrangement was approved by the Clinton administration.

Almost immediately, the Israeli government balked at the deal. The United States had for some time been playing a cat and mouse game with the Iranians over their professed desire to acquire nuclear technology, ostensibly for a nuclear energy program but which Washington, D.C., and Tel Aviv believed to be part of a larger intent to acquire nuclear weapons. Iran had visited Kazakhstan in 1992–1993, shopping for low-enriched uranium to power a reactor (this prompted a multi-million dollar U.S. program to remove from Kazakhstan its entire stock of enriched uranium).

Iran had approached French and Chinese companies for the acquisition of turn-key factories useful in the production of uranium hexaflouride, the feedstock for enriching uranium via the centrifuge method. The United States again pressured both the French and the Chinese to stop such cooperation. The powerful pro-Israeli AIPAC lobby was cut loose by the Israelis, and soon Congress, in an unprecedented display of just how much influence AIPAC holds over it, pressured the Clinton administration into putting into place stringent economic sanctions against Iran, encompassing not only U.S. investment and trade with Iran, but any foreign companies that did so as well.

Clearly, the Israeli government was overreacting regarding the developments surrounding Iran's nuclear program in 1994–1995. There was absolutely no evidence whatsoever that linked Iran's efforts to acquire nuclear technology to a nuclear weapons program. But the Israeli position, soon mirrored by Washington, D.C., was absolute: Iran had no logical need for a nuclear energy program, and as such any effort in the field of nuclear activity only served as a cover for a secret nuclear weapons program. Significantly, the Israeli "model" concerning an Iranian covert nuclear weapons program was derived from a similar model it had worked out concerning the possible resumption of nuclear weapons activities in Iraq, this despite the fact that U.N. inspectors were active in both countries, and Israeli intelligence was maintaining an active program of liaison with the IAEA in order to monitor the nuclear activities of both Iraq and Iran.

However weak the Israeli case regarding an Iranian nuclear weapons program might have been, the combination of Iran seeking to obtain nuclear technology from Russia with the ongoing developments regarding the secret transfer of missile technology to Iran from Russia created a near hysteria in Israeli military intelligence circles. The Israeli Air Force spent much of 1996 updating its strike options vis-à-vis Iran. In April 1995 the Israelis launched into space a geocentric-orbit photographic reconnaissance satellite known as the OFEK-3. The resolution of this satellite left much to be desired, but was good enough for Israel to locate major facilities for targeting purposes, and to track the air defense systems of both Iraq and Iran. OFEK-3 imagery was used extensively to prepare target folders for possible use against Iran. Even at the height of tensions between the United States and Iraq in the summer of 1996, the primary focus of attention for Israeli intelligence remained Iran and the combined threats posed by its missile and nuclear programs.

Amos Gilad was presented with a quandary. When assessed in isolation, each component of the threat spectrum facing Israel could be moderated on the basis of fact, or in Gilad's opinion, the lack of fact. However, when packaged together, the threats combined into a single package that left no doubt as to the danger Israel faced. Gilad had to assess the entire scope of the threat faced by Israel: the increased militancy of the Palestinian Authority, combined with a dramatic increase in the number of terrorist attacks inside Israel, the increased militancy of the pro-Iranian Lebanese Hezbollah party, and the actions by Iran to acquire nuclear capability and missiles capable of reaching Israel.

In Gilad's mind, these factors combined in a sort of modern konseptsia, where gut feel trumped hard fact. Gilad's tough approach was increasingly welcomed by the hard-line government of Prime Minister Benjamin Netanyahu. In a system which prided itself on a disciplined approach to intelligence analysis, Gilad's konseptsia was heresy. But under Netanyahu, the intelligence process had become quite politicized, and Gilad's konseptsia won out over objections from within the Military Intelligence branch, even when officers senior to Gilad voiced those objections.

By 1997 Amos Gilad was spearheading a bilateral intelligence sharing operation with the United States known as the Leakage Committee, monitoring the Israeli concerns about the transfer of Russian missile-related technology to Iran. In short order, the U.S. intelligence community embraced the Israeli model of thinking, and soon, with the assistance of extensive political lobbying on the part of AIPAC, the U.S. Congress was pushing for the imposition of trade sanctions on Russian companies identified by the Leakage Committee as being involved in illicit trade with Iran.

The work of the Leakage Committee took on even greater urgency after U.S. spy satellites detected an Iranian status test of a liquid-fueled engine ostensibly for use in the Shahib-3 missile. The Israelis were convinced that this test could only have been conducted with the aid and assistance of the Russian experts in Iran. The reality was that the engine tested was procured by Iran from North Korea, and had nothing whatsoever to do with the Russian–Iran missile cooperation. But facts simply no longer mattered. In the konseptsia of Amos Gilad, everything was linked together in one master scheme to bring harm to Israel. By early 1999 the combined impact of the Leakage Committee intelligence cooperation and AIPAC political pressure resulted in the Clinton administration enacting sanctions against Russian companies identified as doing business with Iran.

The Israelis began to seriously look at putting in place the conditions under which the Iranian government might be overthrown. Amos Gilad and his fellow officers knew that this was a task too big for Israel to accomplish on its own. In fact, there was only one nation in the world that was up to this task, that being the United States.

With Amos Gilad as the guiding hand, Israeli intelligence began feeding information to the National Council of Resistance in Iran (NCRI) in Washington, D.C., often using what has come to be known as the "Israeli Lobby" as an intermediary. The National Council of Resistance in Iran was the political face of the Mujahadin-e Khalq, or MEK, which since 1981 had been headquartered in Iraq, serving as a de facto arm of the Iraqi Mukhabarat, or intelligence service. The MEK had been listed by the U.S. government as a terrorist organization, and so de-linking the NCRI and MEK in the minds of the U.S. public and policy makers became a key objective of the Israeli Lobby. *The Middle East Quarterly*, the journal of the pro-AIPAC Middle East

Forum, took the lead in reshaping the public face of the NCRI by publishing a very sympathetic interview with a senior NCRI official in September 1995.

Under pressure from AIPAC, members of Congress began expressing their public support for both NCRI and the removal from power in Tehran of the regime of the Mullahs. The goal of this process was two-fold: to imprint in the psyche of the American body politic the notion of regime change as policy, and to find a deniable outlet for the release of Israeli intelligence into the public eye, where AIPAC could then begin to pressure members of Congress to take action where the Clinton administration would not. In January 1999 NCRI initiated this process when it gave a press conference about Iranian progress in the field of chemical and biological weapons.

The NCRI–MEK link was not the only outlet for regime change being pursued by the Israelis. The contentious and complicated nature of the Israeli–Turkish cooperation concerning the Kurds of the Middle East was borne out again in 1998, when the government of Iran arrested twenty-five members of the Iraqi Kurdish Democratic Party headed by Massud Barzani, the son of Mustafa Barzani, and charged them with spying both for the Israelis and Turks. And, with the assistance of the Turkish government, Israel was able to establish an intelligence presence in Azerbaijan, where by 1996 the Israeli government was beaming propaganda broadcasts into the Azeri-populated north of Iran in support of an anti-regime Azeri nationalist movement, as well as carrying out extensive intelligence collection operations involving both communications interception and cross-border activity by pro-Israeli Azerbaijanis.

Thanks to the unprecedented cooperation between Israel and the U.N. weapons inspectors regarding Iraq, Israel no longer viewed the regime of Saddam Hussein as representing a serious national security threat. The Israeli national assessment of 1998 held that Iraq had been fundamentally disarmed and, as long as U.N. weapons inspectors remained in place, was deterred from reconstituting its past proscribed weapons programs. But in December 1998 the U.N. weapons inspectors in Iraq were ordered out by the United States on the eve of Operation Desert Fox, a forty-eight-hour bombing campaign ostensibly targeting Iraqi WMD sites, but in reality aimed at removing Saddam Hussein from power. When the aerial campaign failed, Iraq refused to allow the U.N. weapons inspectors back in, citing their close ties to the intelligence services of the United States.

Israel, left without the excellent intelligence resources of the U.N. inspectors, was compelled to re-evaluate its position on Iraq. Conservative estimates had held that Iraq could reconstitute important aspects of its WMD programs six to nine months after U.N. inspectors left Iraq, and when the nine-month mark passed, Israeli intelligence assessments began to speculate on what weapons Saddam might have, as opposed to what they actually knew. Amos Gilad was the man responsible for taking this hard-line position on Iraq. He never believed the assessments that held Iraq to be leaning toward compliance with its disarmament obligation. Instead, he held that Saddam always wanted WMD, and would use the absence of inspections as an opportunity to rebuild that which had been lost during the time of the inspections. But even in the environment of post-inspection Iraq, the dual problems of Iran and the Palestinians continued to dominate the thinking of Amos Gilad.

In mid-2001 Amos Gilad was picked by Prime Minister Ariel Sharon to become the IDF Coordinator of Government Activities in the Palestinian Territories. Like Sharon, Amos Gilad distrusted Yassar Arafat, a point of view he reiterated repeatedly and publicly, even after his appointment. Gilad had cemented his reputation for being able to conduct sound assessments of the Israeli–Palestinian relationship, predicting that Benjamin Netanyahu would be able to reach an agreement with Arafat at the Wye River accords in 1999, but that the Palestinians would never abide by them. In 2000, at the Camp David talks, Amos Gilad predicted that Barak would never get an agreement with Arafat. Of course, both assessments take on something akin to a self-fulfilling prophesy when assessed within the poisonous atmosphere of Israeli–Palestinian relations, where deception and distrust are not limited to a single side.

As the coordinator in the territories, Gilad oversaw some of the most tumultuous times in Israeli–Palestinian history, including the efforts by Israel to suppress the Al Aqsa Intifada, which erupted in September 2000, the siege of Yassar Arafat's headquarters in Ramallah, to the intercept of the *Karine A,* a PLO ship carrying a huge arms cache provided by Iran, and the assault on Jenin in April 2002. During this time, Amos Gilad's influence on Israeli policy grew to the point that he was considered one of the four most influential men surrounding Ariel Sharon, part of the so-called Quartet, which advised the Israeli Prime Minister on Israeli security policy, to the exclusion of even the traditional intelligence channels normally available to the Israeli leadership.

Through his membership in the Quartet, Amos Gilad was able to pursue his fixation on his konseptsia linking Iran and the Palestinians. However much he tried to pass on this konseptsia to his counterparts in the United States, he kept running into one major problem: Iraq. Iraq was dominating the policy formulations of the Bush administration, to the extent that when the Israelis passed on information garnered from their satellite surveillance of Iran to the NCRI, which went public with the information in August 2002, there was barely a reaction in Washington, D.C. All eyes were on Baghdad, not Tehran.

Quick to catch on, Sharon assigned Gilad the additional duty of liaison officer to the Pentagon's Office of Special Plans, where he passed on for American use Israeli intelligence estimates on Iraqi WMD activity. The actual impact of this information on U.S. policy formulation is unknown; the U.S. decision to invade Iraq had been cemented by the summer of 2002. But one thing is for certain: Amos Gilad pressed home to his U.S. counterparts the notion that the upcoming U.S. invasion of Iraq must serve as a springboard for a larger transformation within the Middle East, one that swept away not only Saddam Hussein, but also anti-Israeli elements in Syria, Palestine, and, of course, Iran.

To cement his role as the Israeli orchestrator-in-chief when it came to the U.S. invasion of Iraq, in December 2002 Sharon appointed Gilad to the unprecedented position of National Commentator on the crisis with Iraq. His role was ostensibly to explain the position of the Israeli government vis-à-vis Iraq to the people of Israel and the rest of the world. But in every way, Gilad became not only an apologist for the U.S.-led invasion of Iraq, but also a cheerleader for his own konseptsia, this time linking Iraq's looming demise with that of his archnemesis in Damascus, Ramallah, and Tehran.

In February 2003, on the eve of war with Iraq, Gilad went on Israeli television, where he delivered the following public assessment: "Our estimate was then, and still is, that if [Saddam] is pushed with his back against the wall, he might take desperate measures that will ensure his place in history, including the use of non-conventional capabilities. . . . In general terms I will only say that we are preparing for three main scenarios: one scenario is that Saddam Hussein will try to attack Israel with conventional or non-conventional missiles; another scenario is that he will try to attack with a manned or unmanned aircraft; and the third scenario involves terrorist activity, mainly non-conventional, that can be carried out in Israel or overseas."

A few days later Amos Gilad told reporters that Saddam "kept astounding quantities of chemical weapons aimed at half the world. He apparently also has biological weapons and is engaged in building nuclear weapons," a stunning statement backed up by no serious assessment from within the Israeli military intelligence system. And, invoking the memory of 1991, Gilad warned Israelis that the upcoming war with Iraq might be even worse than the Gulf War, "because this time, unlike during the Gulf War, Saddam is fighting for his life." This statement directly contradicted the more modest assessments put out by the IDF Chief of Staff, Moshe Ayalon, who noted that he was not losing any sleep from the threat posed by Saddam Hussein.

Such statements are less likely to soothe the nerves of the citizens of Israel than they would justify the hostile intent of America. Amos Gilad, like the rest of the Israeli intelligence establishment, knew all too well that Iraq posed a direct threat to no one, least of all Israel. Iraq had no ties to Al Qaeda or Iran, as well. Indeed, outside of Saddam's disbursing payments to the families of Palestinian suicide bombers (an emotional issue in terror-stricken Israel, but on the strategic scale of threats, not a large one), Iraq represented the sort of secular foundation that a nation like Israel would normally expect to counter the forces of Islamic fundamentalism, especially that coming from Iran.

But the die was cast, and the secular regime of Saddam Hussein was to be no more. Amos Gilad called the American invasion of Iraq a "miracle for Israel." Another member of Ariel Sharon's Quartet, the former head of the Mossad, Efraim Halevy, predicted that the U.S. toppling of Saddam "would create dramatic change in the Middle East because Saddam is a leading symbol to tyrants like Arafat and others."

Halevy painted a utopian picture of a post-Saddam Middle East which had a post-Yasser Arafat Palestinian leadership negotiating in good faith with Israel, a progressive and prosperous Iraq rejoining the family of nations, and Syria, no longer feeling a need to compete with Iraq, loosening its ties with Iran. Iran would, in turn, be driven from Lebanon, accompanied by a withdrawal of Syrian forces, and Hezbollah would disarm, leading to a lasting peace between Israel and Lebanon. And, of course, the growing isolation of the regime of the Mullahs in Tehran would lead to the rise of a popular movement among the moderate majority within Iran, who would sweep the Islamic fundamentalist government from power, foreswear nuclear weapons and all other weapons of mass destruction, and peacefully co-exist with Israel.

The only voice of caution came from the veteran intelligence officer Ya'acov Ami Dror. The American plans to transform the Middle East through its invasion of Iraq were too optimistic. The glowing American predictions in the aftermath of the fall of Saddam, like those of Amos Gilad and his fellow travelers in Israel, were unlikely to come to fruition, Ami Dror warned, and as a result the failure of the American adventure in Iraq would only exacerbate tensions between the United States and the Muslim world, including Iran. And, by extension, there goes the fate of Israel.

The Holocaust remains a yin-yang influence on Israel, simultaneously pushing and pulling the Israeli state in directions that may ultimately result in its demise. The Iranian situation represents such a case, where fears of the repetition of the Holocaust may very well result in Israel unleashing forces, either directly or through proxy, that may end with a Holocaust-type event being revisited on Israel and the Jews who have populated its sacred soil (not to mention the millions of non-Jews who would be caught up in such a maelstrom). Of course, while Israel employs many proxies in the service of its security interests, the proxy of choice, and by far the most powerful and capable of these proxies, is the United States. While much has been made of the hand-in-glove relationship enjoyed between Israel and the United States, and in particular between Israel and the current Bush administration in power in America today, the reality is much more complex and nuanced.

The vision of the Holocaust and sympathy with Israel may in fact drive many Americans, Jew and non-Jew alike, to act in support of what they believe to be a mutually beneficial relationship born of common goals and interests. But ultimately, it's memory of the Holocaust, and the sense of betrayal contained within that memory, that means at the end of the day Israel truly can have a deep-seated common interest with no one, even a compliant superpower such as the United States. While many in the United States feel compelled to support Israel out of a sense of moral duty and obligation, Israel in the end does not share the same moral bond in terms of supporting the United States. America, in the eyes of those who formulate Israeli security policy, is but a tool to be wielded in support of the larger Israeli interest.

So it was with Iraq, and so it shall be with Iran. And while Israel may desperately want to separate the Iranian issue from the ongoing debacle that is Iraq, from the mindset of the Americans who are now calling the shots in the Middle East, the two nations are inextricably linked. By engaging the services of the NCRI in August 2002 to expose the existence of secret Iranian nuclear activities, Israel helped define the international focus of attention on Iran in purely nuclear terms. The other issues of concern, namely Iran's support of Hezbollah and radical elements within Hamas and the PLO, Iran's rabid anti-Israeli rhetoric, and Iran's ongoing support of international terror, were now secondary to the nuclear issue.

Israel had unwittingly thrust its national security into the arms of an organization that Israel had shunned for many years—the International Atomic Energy Agency, or IAEA. Israel's own undeclared nuclear weapons program, and ongoing refusal to sign on to the provisions of the non-proliferation treaty (NPT), put it naturally at odds with the IAEA. And so it was with no small amount of irony that Israel, a nation struggling to maintain independence in the field of national security, found its very survival (if the reports of an Iranian nuclear weapons program were in fact true) in the hands of IAEA weapons inspectors, or to be more specific, the head of the IAEA, an Egyptian named Mohammed El-Baradei.

Two
The Inspectors

OVER THE COURSE OF TWO cloud-filled days in Paris, during February 1896, the French physicist Henri Becquerel helped change the world, whether for better or for worse only history will tell. Carrying out experiments related to the emission of X-rays (the discovery of which had occurred only a few months back, on November 8, 1895, by a German physicist named Wilhelm Roentgen), Becquerel had coated a series of photographic plates with a phosphorescent mixture of potassium uranyl sulfate, which he then exposed to sunlight and wrapped in black paper. When developed, the photographic plates revealed an image of the uranium crystals contained in the substance Becquerel had used to coat the plates. Becquerel interpreted his initial findings as evidence of the sun's energy being absorbed by the uranium, which then emitted X-rays.

However, the follow-up experiments Becquerel planned were thwarted by the cloudy skies of Paris, and he returned his seemingly underexposed photographic plates to a drawer. A few days later, when the plates were developed, Becquerel was stunned to discover that the images of the uranium crystals were clear—the uranium had emitted the radiation without an external source of energy such as the sun. Radioactivity, or the spontaneous emission of radiation by a material, in this case uranium, had been discovered. Becquerel went on to show that the spontaneous release of radiation from uranium was not caused by X-rays, but rather through the release of charged particles. However, it took another

German physicist to develop a theory that would transform Becquerel's discovery into a force as powerful as the sun.

In 1905 the German physicist Albert Einstein wrote a letter to a friend, in which he exclaimed, "The relativity principle . . . demands that the mass is a direct measure for the energy contained in bodies; light transfers mass . . . This thought is amusing and infectious, but I cannot possibly know whether the good Lord does not laugh at it and has led me up the garden path." Einstein then proceeded to develop his special theory of relativity, which held that the deep connection between energy and mass could be expressed in the equation $E=mc^2$, where E represents energy, m represents mass, and c^2 the square of the speed of light.

In 1933 Einstein's theory was captured on film by the French physicist couple Irene and Francis Joliot-Curie, in an image that showed a quantum of light, accelerated, changing into mass, two particles which rapidly moved away from one another. A year earlier, in Cambridge, England, the British physicists John Cockcroft and E. T. S. Walton bombarded lithium with high energy protons, transmuting the lithium into helium and other chemical elements. The resulting fragments had slightly less mass in total than did the original atom, but they flew apart with great energy. This was the first occasion on which an atomic nucleus of one element had been successfully changed to a different nucleus by artificial means, an accomplishment which became known as "splitting the atom," and which continues to enthrall and terrify the world today.

The study of the atom, and more specifically the release of energy caused by nuclear transformations such as that achieved by Cockcroft and Watson, led to the discovery of nuclear fission, where a nucleus splits into several smaller fragments, or fission products, which are equal to about half of the original mass. Two or three neutrons are also emitted. The sum of the masses of the fission products is less than the original mass, the "lost" mass having been converted into energy. When neutrons released through fission produce additional fission in at least one additional nucleus, which in turn produces neutrons which produce fission in other nuclei, and so on and so forth, a fission chain reaction occurs. This process can produce the controlled release of energy, used in nuclear energy, or uncontrolled release of energy, such as is found in nuclear weapons.

Becquerel's discovery of uranium as a self-emitting source of radioactivity led to further investigations into its usefulness as a source of fission. A particular uranium isotope, uranium-235, was found to be a particularly effective material for sustaining a nuclear chain reaction. However, uranium-235 is rarely found in its pure form. Instead, it exists in small quanities (around .07%) in natural uranium (the remaining 99.3% is in the form of uranium-238). Uranium-235 and uranium-238 are chemically identical, but differ in their physical properties, particularly their mass. The nucleus of the U-235 atom contains 92 protons and 143 neutrons, giving an atomic mass of 235 units. The U-238 nucleus also has 92 protons but has 146 neutrons, resulting in a mass of 238 units.

The difference in mass between U-235 and U-238 allows the isotopes to be separated and makes it possible to increase, or enrich, the percentage of U-235 by making use of this small mass difference. Over the years several methodologies have been developed to accomplish this enrichment of U-235. These methods involve a tremendous amount of technological skill, and equally as important, energy consumption to achieve a useful level of enrichment, which for nuclear energy generation purposes involves U-235 enriched to between 3.5 percent and 5 percent (low enriched uranium, or LEU), and for nuclear weapons, U-235 enriched to over 90 percent (although high enriched uranium, or HEU, is defined by the IAEA as being U-235 enriched to levels greater than 20 percent).

Naturally occurring uranium is not, in and of itself, able to be enriched. It must first be converted into a form that facilitates enrichment, either as a metal (for enrichment through the use of lasers), or gas (for enrichment using magnetic separation, gaseous diffusion, or enrichment through the use of centrifuges). Uranium usually leaves a mine as the concentrate of a stable oxide known as uranium trioxide (U_3O_8), at which point it is further refined, through a reaction with hydrogen in a kiln known as hot pressing, into uranium dioxide (UO_2). The uranium dioxide is then reacted in another kiln with hydrogen fluoride (HF) to form uranium tetrafluoride (UF_4). The tetrafluoride is reacted with gaseous fluorine to produce uranium hexafluoride, or UF_6. Since naturally occurring uranium contains many impurities (such as molybdenum), additional chemical processes are required at each step of conversion to remove these impurities.

Removal of impurities takes place at each step (an alternative "wet process" involves making the UF_4 from UO_2 by a wet process, using aqueous HF).

Of all the enrichment processes available, two (gaseous diffusion and centrifuge) have been found to be viable for large-scale enrichment of uranium. Diffusion plants are considered simpler to operate, but are very large operations requiring a tremendous amount of resources. Centrifuge processes are more economical, and can be developed at smaller stages than can gaseous diffusion plants (around 150 stages versus 1,400). Like gaseous diffusion, centrifuge enrichment uses uranium hexafluoride gas as its feedstock, and makes use of the slight difference in mass between U-235 and U-238. The gas is fed into a series of vacuum tubes, each containing a rotor one to two meters long and 15–20 centimeters in diameter. When the rotors are spun rapidly, up to 70,000 revolutions per minute (rpm), the heavier U-238 molecules concentrate toward the cylinder's outer edge. There is a corresponding increase in concentration of the U-235 molecules at the center of the cylinder. This, of course, sounds much easier than it is in reality. The rotors must spin with perfect balance, operate in a vacuum, and function as part of a complex series of similarly flawlessly functioning rotors in order to work as designed.

This enriched gas then forms part of the feed for the next centrifuge processing stage, while the depleted uranium hexafluoride gas is removed and introduced back to the previous stage. This process is repeated until the uranium-235 is produced at the desired percentage level. The same enrichment process can be used to produce uranium-235 useful for energy applications (i.e., 3.7 percent) and weapons use (i.e., more then 90 percent). Due to the high separation factor of a modern gas centrifuge system, only a small number of stages are required to enrich uranium to significant uranium-235 levels. The hold-up time of the material in each stage reportedly is in the order of 10–20 seconds and, as a consequence, the total mass of uranium (in the form of uranium hexafluoride gas) present in the cascade is extremely low, typically between several hundred grams and one kilogram. As such, it does not require a large inventory of feedstock material to obtain a noticeable rise in the level of enrichment. Accordingly, one could achieve significant enrichment (say from .07 percent to 1.2 percent) within an hour.

Around 1970 many nations started to realize that the old methods of enriching uranium (diffusion) were not practical for economically sound nuclear energy programs. This was especially true in places such as Europe, where in 1970 the governments of Germany, Belgium, and the Netherlands formed a joint corporation for the purpose of enriching uranium using the centrifuge method known as URENCO. URENCO's goals were peaceful, yet the technology it was perfecting, if it fell into the hands of the wrong person or nation, was perfect for producing highly enriched uranium for use in nuclear weapons.

This overlap between the peaceful use of nuclear technology for energy purposes, and the utility of nuclear technology for weapons development, has always represented an Achilles heel of sorts. President Dwight D. Eisenhower referred to the quandary in the course of his famous "Atoms for Peace" speech before the General Assembly of the United Nations on December 8, 1953, where he spoke of not just "the mere reduction or elimination of atomic materials for military purposes. It is not enough to take this weapon out of the hands of the soldiers. It must be put into the hands of those who will know how to strip its military casing and adapt it to the arts of peace." To do this, President Eisenhower talked of devising "methods whereby this fissionable material would be allocated to serve the peaceful pursuits of mankind. Experts would be mobilized to apply atomic energy to the needs of agriculture, medicine and other peaceful activities. A special purpose would be to provide abundant electrical energy in the power-starved areas of the world."

From this dream was born the International Atomic Energy Agency (IAEA), operating under the auspices of the United Nations. The IAEA was established in 1957. In keeping with Eisenhower's call for safeguarding nuclear weapons and weapons-grade fissionable materials, the IAEA was charged with, among other tasks, the responsibility of establishing and administering "safeguards designed to ensure that special fissionable and other materials, services, equipment, facilities, and information made available by the Agency or at its request or under its supervision or control are not used in such a way as to further any military purpose; and to apply safeguards, at the request of the parties, to any bilateral or multilateral arrangement, or at the request of a state, to any of that state's activities in the field of atomic energy."

But the safeguards system was not good enough, at least in the minds of the five superpowers which emerged from the ashes of the Second World War, all of whom had developed in the decades following the end of that conflict into nations possessing nuclear weapons. The sudden jump in the number of nations desiring to gain access to nuclear technology brought with it an increase in the potential of nations using the technology to develop their own nuclear weapons capability. The result of this vexing problem was the Non-Proliferation Treaty (NPT), which was signed July 1, 1968, and entered into force March 5, 1970.

The NPT divides "parties" into two classifications: those that tested nuclear weapons before 1968, and those that did not. The former states—known as nuclear-weapon states—are China, France, Russia (then the Soviet Union), the United Kingdom, and the United States. These states were allowed to maintain their nuclear status, although under the terms of the NPT they would seek to disarm gradually over time. The latter countries joined the NPT as non-nuclear-weapon states. In return for committing never to develop or receive nuclear weapons, these non-nuclear-weapons states were promised access to the peaceful benefits of nuclear technology.

All non-weapon-state parties to the NPT were required to comply with IAEA Safeguards, under Article III of the NPT, "for the exclusive purpose of verification of the fulfillment of its obligations assumed under this Treaty with a view to preventing diversion of nuclear energy from peaceful uses to nuclear weapons or other nuclear explosive devices." However, Article IV of the NPT provided a loophole of sorts, when it stated that "Nothing in this Treaty shall be interpreted as affecting the inalienable right of all the Parties to the Treaty to develop research, production and use of nuclear energy for peaceful purposes without discrimination and in conformity with Articles I and II of this Treaty . . . all the Parties to the Treaty undertake to facilitate, and have the right to participate in, the fullest possible exchange of equipment, materials and scientific and technological information for the peaceful uses of nuclear energy."

Article IV has been seen by many advanced Western nations, especially those already possessing access to nuclear enrichment technology (i.e., the nuclear fuel cycle) as a dangerous loophole. While export control laws are not directly stipulated by the NPT, Article III does oblige states not to transfer fission materials or technologies to non-nuclear-weapons states that are not covered by safeguards. Soon after the NPT came into force in 1970, two groups of states formed to voluntarily restrict the export of dual-use materials. The Zanger Committee and the Nuclear Supply Group (NSG) both drew up guidelines on the kind of sensitive materials and technologies that could be transferred across borders. Many nations, especially those with developing economies, viewed the work of the Zanger Committee and the NSG as violating not only the spirit, but also the letter, of the NPT when it came to Article IV, and moreover that the work of these groups are discriminatory in nature and harm their respective economies.

Waiting in the wings were individuals like A. Q. Khan, and nations like Pakistan, who had no obligation to abide by the NPT (Pakistan, like India, had refused to sign the treaty). Throughout the 1970s, and into the 1980s, Pakistan used the energetic brilliance of A. Q. Khan to acquire uranium enrichment technologies such as centrifuge cascades from places such as URENCO, and to assemble these centrifuges into giant uranium enrichment facilities such as the one built in Pakistan by Khan at Kahota. The world suspected that something was going on in Pakistan, but was powerless to do anything to stop it. In 1998 Pakistan, responding to earlier underground nuclear tests carried out by India, conducted its own series of tests, officially propelling it into the status of a nuclear weapon state.

The Pakistan debacle notwithstanding, classic safeguard inspections were carried out by the IAEA in accordance with the NPT for nearly two decades without major incident. For the most part, these were gentleman-type arrangements, with the IAEA playing polite guest to the inspected party. Then, in 1991, in the aftermath of the first Gulf War, the international community came face to face with the fact that Saddam Hussein's Iraq had carried out a clandestine nuclear weapons program right under the noses of the IAEA safeguard inspectors. While the Iraq case was handled through inspections mandated by Security Council resolutions, for the rest of the world it was now apparent that the traditional IAEA safeguards were not sufficient. As a result of the Iraq experience, the IAEA in 1993 sought to revise the classic safeguards, and in its place created what was known as Program

93+2, which sought to broaden the safeguards system to incorporate inspections of undeclared sites, and increased inspection capabilities designed to detect clandestine activities. These new capabilities included the taking of random air and swipe samples from a wide range of locations, and analyzing these samples for any abnormalities that could detect undeclared activity.

Program 93+2 was the basis for what became known as The Model Protocol, which was approved by the Agency's Board of Governors in 1997. The new safeguard measures became effective through a process in which member states would sign an Additional Protocol beyond their existing safeguards arrangement with the IAEA.

The Model Protocol requires states to report a range of information to the Agency about their nuclear and nuclear-related activities and about the planned developments in their nuclear fuel cycles. This includes expanded information about their holdings of uranium ores and ore concentrates, of other plutonium and uranium materials not currently subject to IAEA safeguards, general information about their manufacturing of equipment for enriching uranium or producing plutonium, general information about their nuclear fuel cycle-related research and development activities not involving nuclear material, and their import and export of nuclear material and equipment. Not all nations having safeguards agreements with the IAEA have signed the Additional Protocol, including Israel and Iran, two nations headed on a collision course over their respective nuclear programs.

Caught in the middle of the ongoing crisis over Iran's nuclear program is the IAEA itself, in particular the Director General of the IAEA who is responsible for overseeing and implementing the NPT. The man currently reaping the whirlwind of both Becquerel's discovery of radiation, and Einstein's theory of relativity is a quiet Egyptian diplomat named Mohamed El-Baradei. According to his official biography, Mohammed El-Baradei was born in Cairo, Egypt, in 1942, the son of a distinguished Egyptian lawyer. El-Baradei earned a Bachelor's degree in Law in 1962 at the University of Cairo, and a Doctorate in International Law at the New York University School of Law in 1974.

Dr. El-Baradei began his career in the Egyptian Diplomatic Service in 1964, serving twice in the Permanent Missions of Egypt to the

United Nations in New York and Geneva, responsible for political, legal, and arms control issues. From 1974 to 1978 he was appointed the special assistant to the Foreign Minister of Egypt. In 1980 he left the Egyptian Diplomatic Service to join the United Nations and became a senior fellow in charge of the International Law Program at the United Nations Institute for Training and Research. Since 1984, Dr. El-Baradei has been a senior staff member of the IAEA Secretariat, holding a number of high-level policy positions, including Agency's Legal Adviser and subsequently Assistant Director General for External Relations. He was appointed to his post of IAEA Director General on December 1, 1997.

Mohammed El-Baradei took over the reigns of the IAEA during a time of great turmoil. The situation with Iraq was very much unresolved. While the IAEA inspectors had succeeded in eliminating the Iraqi nuclear program, political agendas beyond simple disarmament were at play, with the United States seeking to overthrow Saddam Hussein, and using disarmament (or at least the excuse of disarmament) as a vehicle to achieve this objective. Similarly, the IAEA was caught up in a power play between the United States and North Korea that had nearly brought those two nations to war in 1994. Since then the IAEA had been trying to carry out a series of inspection and verification tasks, but again found its work hampered by the political maneuvering of both the United States and North Korea.

Complicating even this complicated situation were the events of September 11, 2001, and the aggressive stance taken by the United States, and more pointedly, the administration of President George W. Bush, in responding to the terrorist attacks against New York City and Washington, D.C. The issue of weapons of mass destruction, and more pointedly, nuclear proliferation, had become a cause célèbre for the U.S. government, and the work of the IAEA was coming under close scrutiny in so far as it performed to a level demanded by the United States in a post-9/11 world.

President Bush's evocation of the Axis of Evil in the form of Iraq, North Korea, and Iran had been followed by a never-ending stream of allegations emanating from these three countries about their suspected nuclear weapons programs. Top on the list was, of course, Iraq. The Bush administration had been beating the war drums for some time, and by August 2002 the push for confrontation with Iraq from within the highest levels of government in the United States was in full gear.

The United States Senate, on July 31, 2002, convened a hearing in front of the Senate Foreign Relations Committee, where testimony about Iraq's weapons of mass destruction programs was taken from a number of witnesses. Typical of the rhetoric was the testimony of Dr. Khidir Hamza, the self-proclaimed "Saddam's Bombmaker," who had defected from Iraq in 1994, and had since that time been peddling stories about Iraq's nuclear ambitions. Citing German intelligence sources, Hamza testified that Iraq retained more than ten tons of uranium and one ton of enriched uranium, giving Iraq enough weapons-grade uranium to build three nuclear weapons by 2005.

Hamza's performance was immediately followed up by Vice President Dick Cheney, who in a presentation to the Veterans of Foreign Wars on August 26, took America by surprise when he said, "We know that Saddam has resumed his efforts to acquire nuclear weapons . . . many of us are convinced that Saddam will acquire nuclear weapons fairly soon." Left unnoticed was the fact that Cheney cited as proof for his conclusions the testimony of Saddam's son-in-law, Hussein Kamal, who had defected from Iraq in August 1995. The Vice President stated that the United States had gotten its information from Hussein Kamal, when in fact what Hussein Kamal had actually told his CIA debriefers (and U.N. weapons inspectors) was that Iraq had abandoned its nuclear programs back in 1991. El-Baradei knew that Hussein Kamal had also fingered Khidir Hamza as a liar and a fraud, something also known to the senators who called Hamza before their committee to testify in open session.

But facts did not seem to matter much in this high-stakes game of winning over public opinion. The IAEA knew that it had dismantled Iraq's nuclear weapons program by 1994, and that by 1997 it could state with a high degree of certainty that there was no ongoing nuclear-related activity in Iraq of any consequence. U.N. inspectors had not operated in Iraq since their expulsion in December 1998 (under orders to leave not from Saddam Hussein, but rather the United States, who wanted the inspectors out before starting a seventy-two hour bombing campaign designed to target Saddam Hussein under the guise of going after weapons facilities). Even so, the IAEA kept a close look at Iraq through analysis of satellite imagery, and noted nothing that would indicate that Iraq had reconstituted any aspect of its past nuclear weapons program. However, without inspectors on the ground, the IAEA was in no position to offer any judgment on Iraq's compliance, something El-Baradei had noted in his report to the Security Council in April 2002.

Despite the fact IAEA inspections mandated by Security Council resolutions had been halted, the IAEA was still able to conduct its normal safeguards inspection program as part of the NPT, and as such was able to keep tabs on Iraq's stocks of uranium. In fact, while President Bush was issuing his State of the Union speech, the IAEA had a team of inspectors in Iraq, where they carried out a verification inspection as to the stocks of uranium stored there. These inspections found no discrepancies, and El-Baradei had no reason to believe the information being put forward by Khidir Hamza and the others had any veracity. But the political pressure brought to bear when the Vice President of the United States openly declared Iraq to be reconstituting nuclear weapons was a completely different matter. For El-Baradei and the IAEA, returning inspectors to Iraq was a top priority.

Any hope for movement on that matter was soon dashed as the Iraqis reacted to being labeled part of the Axis of Evil by President Bush and, in February 2002, rejected any return to Iraq by inspectors it referred to as being nothing more than spies. However, by early May there appeared to be some hope of a breakthrough concerning Iraq, when El-Baradei, together with U.N. Secretary General Kofi Annan and Hans Blix, his counterpart with the United Nations Monitoring and Verification Commission (UNMOVIC, charged with carrying out chemical, biological, and ballistic missile inspections inside Iraq), met in New York with Iraqi officials to discuss technical issues relating to the work of weapons inspectors in Iraq. While inconclusive, these talks served as the foundation for follow-up discussions held at the U.N. offices in Vienna, Austria, in early July.

By August the Iraqi government was inviting Hans Blix and Mohammed El-Baradei to Baghdad to hold technical talks about the return of inspectors. But the Iraqis were linking any return of inspectors with the lifting of economic sanctions that had been in place since Iraq's invasion of Kuwait in August 1990, and since April 1991 linked to Iraqi compliance with its disarmament obligation. Statements by successive U.S. presidential administrations had made it clear that the

U.S. policy was for economic sanctions to be continued until Iraq's president, Saddam Hussein, was removed from power.

This position, of course, put the U.N. weapons inspectors, including the IAEA, in a very difficult situation. There could be no discussions between the inspectors and Iraq that linked the return of inspectors with the lifting of sanctions, as this was a matter for the Security Council. And, given America's veto on the Council, there was no chance of sanctions being lifted in order to facilitate the return of inspections. This stalemate, coupled with Dick Cheney's disturbing pronouncements regarding Iraq's nuclear programs, caused El-Baradei no small amount of consternation.

But Iraq was not the only issue the IAEA was wrestling with. El-Baradei was also concerned about developments with North Korea, which had long been problematic in terms of its compliance with the NPT. The IAEA had engaged in a fitful program of enhanced safeguards inspections in North Korea since 1994, when the Clinton administration concluded the so-called Agreed Framework signed in November of that year. North Korea joined the NPT in 1985, and by 1992 had agreed to submit to NPT safeguards inspections. Within months of starting its work in North Korea, however, the IAEA detected serious discrepancies in the initial North Korean declaration concerning plutonium production, and the results of IAEA analysis based upon inspection samples.

The IAEA requested access to two undeclared sites in North Korea that, according to intelligence information made available to the IAEA from the United States, seemed related to the storage of nuclear waste. The IAEA wanted access to these sites, believing that an analysis of the waste material stored there might resolve the inconsistencies. North Korea refused, and in response the Director General of the IAEA, Hans Blix, invoked in February 1993 procedures for special inspections that had been provided for in the Safeguards Agreement. North Korea again refused the IAEA access, and in April 1993 the IAEA Board of Governors declared North Korea to be in non-compliance with its Safeguard Agreement, and referred the North Korean case to the U.N. Security Council. Soon thereafter, North Korea threatened to withdraw from the NPT.

Throughout the remainder of 1993, and into 1994, North Korea permitted IAEA inspectors to conduct limited-scope safeguard inspections, focused on maintenance, containment, and surveillance activities. But such limited inspections were not enough to permit the IAEA to certify North Korea's peaceful use of nuclear technology and in March 1994 the Security Council called upon North Korea to fully cooperate with the IAEA inspectors. The crisis between North Korea and the IAEA came to a head in May 1994, when North Korea hastily removed the fuel from a nuclear reactor covered by the safeguards agreement. The IAEA wanted to inspect the fuel to ensure that it was the original load, as claimed by North Korea, and not a new fuel core, thereby signaling that North Korea could have extracted plutonium from the irradiated uranium fuel rods.

The IAEA called upon North Korea to cease its activities at the nuclear reactor, and to start fully cooperating with the inspectors. In response, in mid-June 1994, North Korea withdrew as a member of the IAEA, and claimed that it was no longer bound by the Safeguards Agreement, and as such would permit no further IAEA inspections. Speculation ran high in the United States about North Korea's nuclear capabilities, and with American military forces being rushed into the region, war looked imminent. The intervention of former President Jimmy Carter in June 1994 lowered tensions, and subsequent negotiations between the U.S. and North Korea led to the coming into being of the Agreed Framework, in November 1994.

The Agreed Framework called for increased North Korean cooperation with the IAEA in order to resolve the outstanding technical issues pertaining to its nuclear program, in exchange for U.S.-brokered economic assistance, including the shipment to North Korea of light-water nuclear reactors (which could not be used to support or sustain a nuclear weapons program) and bunker oil for fuel. However, the North Koreans linked the U.S. making good on its commitments with its cooperation with the IAEA. By December 2001 there had been seventeen technical meetings between North Korea and the IAEA, with no agreement on how to go forward with inspections.

This did not mean that there were no inspections taking place in North Korea. The IAEA Safeguards Division A maintained a North Korea unit that carried out basic monitoring inspections in North Korea. Using a North Korean guesthouse as their base, a team of two IAEA inspectors, operating on a two-week tour of duty, would travel to the sites in North Korea that were under IAEA seal and camera surveillance, checking on the integrity of these operations. The usual rate of activity was one inspection per day, with the North Koreans being informed of the site to be inspected the night before. Ostensibly these inspectors could also carry out surprise inspections, where a site would be declared and the inspectors on their way within an hour of declaration, but this type of inspection had not taken place since the implementation of the Agreed Framework.

Starting in early 2002 Mohammed El-Baradei and the IAEA had been receiving disturbing reports about undeclared uranium enrichment activities ongoing inside North Korea. The U.S. Under-Secretary of State for Arms Control, John Bolton, in January 2002, had publicly stated that North Korea had an undeclared nuclear weapons program, and was in violation of the NPT. This was followed up in February 2002 with members of Congress pressuring President Bush to withhold delivery of materials scheduled to be shipped to North Korea under the Agreed Framework, citing an undeclared program carried out by North Korea to enrich uranium. El-Baradei and the IAEA knew nothing of such programs, and every effort to reach out to the North Koreans to engage in discussions was rebuked. Starting in June 2002 there were whispers within diplomatic circles at the IAEA headquarters in Vienna about a bombshell U.S. intelligence report which proved the existence of a North Korean uranium enrichment program, but again nothing was forthcoming on an official basis to El-Baradei and the IAEA.

With the two issues of Iraq and North Korea boiling over, it came as no surprise to most observers at the IAEA that the news of two suspect nuclear sites in Iran, put out by a relatively unknown Iranian opposition group, NCRI, which had been linked in the past to terrorist activity, was greeted with little more than a shrug by the embattled IAEA Director General. The allegations put forward by NCRI were not unknown to the IAEA. For years, Israeli intelligence had maintained a shadowy relationship with the IAEA, passing on intelligence information concerning nuclear non-proliferation activities through the Israeli Mission in Vienna (although not a signatory to the NPT, Israel has been a member of the IAEA since 1957, and permitted IAEA safeguard inspections of Israeli nuclear research reactors in Israel, although the Dimona nuclear weapons facility and related nuclear reactor remained off limits). This relationship was dramatically expanded in the mid-1990s, when Israel provided an unprecedented level of support to the IAEA Action Team regarding inspections in Iraq.

Israeli intelligence teams would often travel to Vienna, and rendezvous with IAEA personnel in hotel rooms used as impromptu safe houses. On the issue of Iraq, the Israelis had established a similar level of cooperation with the IAEA's Iraq Action Team (re-named the Iraq Nuclear Verification Office, or INVO, in 1999). The relationship involved not only the provision by Israel to the IAEA of intelligence information, but also placing at the disposal of the IAEA the extensive resources of Israel's intelligence analytical community, where the IAEA could pose questions to selected technical experts, or have the results of inspections or other intelligence data reviewed by the Israelis. This relationship, controversial as it was, proved to be very fruitful for the IAEA, and operated with the expressed permission of the Director General (up until December 1, 1997, Hans Blix, and after that time, Mohammed El-Baradei).

The Israelis, according to some sources, maintain a similar relationship with the leadership of Operations Division B (responsible for Iran, among other nations) within the Safeguards Inspection Department, and through that office, with the Deputy Director General of Safeguards. In 2002 the Chief of Operations Division B was the newly appointed Finnish nuclear expert named Olli Heinonen (prior to this appointment Heinonen had served as Chief of Operations Division A, responsible for Asia, including North Korea). His boss, Pierre Goldschmidt, had served as the Deputy Director General for Safeguards since 1999. Both men were familiar with the intelligence data Israel was shopping around concerning undeclared nuclear enrichment facilities operating at Natanz and Arak. However, without any formal mechanism for using the Israeli information, there was really nothing that could be done except to file the information away for later use. The NCRI briefing changed all of this. However, in the context of the Iraq and North Korea situations, the Iranian problem was not seen as representing the most pressing issue for the IAEA.

By September 2002 the Iraq issue was heating up considerably. As usual, the fuel that fed the flame was political rhetoric, this time coming from not only Dick Cheney, but also the National Security Advisor, Condoleezza Rice. On September 8, both Cheney and Rice took to the airwaves to promote the concept of Iraq as a nuclear threat. Appearing on NBC's *Meet the Press*, Cheney stated that Saddam:

> ". . . has been seeking to acquire . . . the kinds of tubes that are necessary to build a centrifuge. And the centrifuge is required to take low-grade uranium and enhance it into highly enriched uranium, which is what you have to have in order to build a bomb. This is a technology he was working on back, say, before the Gulf War . . . we do know he's had four years without any inspections at all in Iraq to develop that capability . . . we do know, with absolute certainty, that he is using his procurement system to acquire the equipment he needs in order to enrich uranium to build a nuclear weapon."

But the ultimate fear factor was raised by Condoleezza Rice, in an interview with CNN's Wolf Blitzer. Rice not only repeated Cheney's mantra about Iraqi efforts to procure aluminum tubes, but went on to say, "We know that he has the infrastructure, nuclear scientists to make a nuclear weapon. And we know that when the inspectors assessed this after the Gulf War, he was far, far closer to a crude nuclear device than anybody thought, maybe six months from a crude nuclear device. The problem here is that there will always be some uncertainty about how quickly he can acquire nuclear weapons. But we don't want the smoking gun to be a mushroom cloud."

Across the Atlantic, in London, another headache was emerging for El-Baradei. The British government, headed by Prime Minister Tony Blair, had released its so-called dossier of intelligence concerning Iraq's ongoing weapons of mass destruction programs. Included in this dossier was information concerning Iraq's attempts to acquire "significant quantities of uranium" from an unnamed African country, "despite having no active civil nuclear power program that could require it."

The British paper was released at the same time senior CIA officials, including the Director, George Tenet, were briefing select members of Congress on Iraq's alleged efforts to acquire aluminum tubes useful only in centrifuge enrichment programs, as well as the uranium "yellowcake" referred to by the British. Many senators and representatives who attended this briefing later said it was this information that swayed them to vote in favor of using military force to disarm Saddam Hussein. El-Baradei needed to get to the bottom of both of these allegations, but without inspectors on the ground in Iraq, this was virtually impossible.

On September 16, 2002, the Iraqi government agreed to allow U.N. weapons inspectors, including those from the IAEA, to return to Iraq without pre-conditions in order to resume inspection activity. Mohammed El-Baradei, together with Hans Blix, met with a senior Iraqi delegation in Vienna, Austria, at the end of September to discuss the technical details surrounding the return of inspectors to Iraq. However, the return of the inspectors was delayed by the insistence on the part of the United States and Great Britain that a new framework for the conduct of the inspections, in the form of a U.N. Security Council resolution, be developed before the inspectors were allowed to return. This new resolution was required, it was argued, because Iraq had repeatedly violated the arrangements for inspections set forth in past resolutions. Iraq, the United States said, was to be given one last chance to come clean on its weapons.

However, many in the Security Council, including veto-wielding Russia, France and China, viewed the U.S.–U.K. bid for a new resolution as nothing more than a blank check for using military force against Iraq. For over a month, throughout October and on into November, the members of the Security Council haggled over the precise wording of the proposed resolution, while the weapons inspectors in Vienna and New York cooled their heels.

Given the evolving situation regarding Iraq, El-Baradei took this time to turn his attention to the NCRI allegations concerning Iran. When the IAEA Board of Governors met in September 2002, the Iranian vice president, Gholamreza Aghazadeh, who is also president of the Atomic Energy Organization of Iran (AEOI), visited it. Aghazadeh told the IAEA that Iran was planning to develop a 6,000-megawatt nuclear power program over the next twenty years, and that the program would include "all out planning, well in advance, in various field of nuclear technology such as fuel cycle, safety and waste management."

During the General Conference, El-Baradei met with Aghazadeh, and asked that Iran confirm whether it was building a large underground nuclear related facility at Natanz and a heavy water production plant at Arak, as reported by the NCRI in August. Aghazadeh was able to provide some information on Iran's intentions to develop further its nuclear fuel cycle, including work at Natanz, and agreed that the IAEA Director General, accompanied by safeguards experts, could visit Natanz in October 2002 (heavy water production facilities, such as the one at Arak, are not nuclear facilities under comprehensive NPT safeguards agreements, and are not required to be declared to the IAEA, nor are they subject to safeguard inspections). The Iranian vice president promised that Iran would, during the planned meetings, provide the IAEA with an update on Iran's plans regarding nuclear energy. In some respects, the NCRI gambit was working: Iran's nuclear program was being flushed out.

Unfortunately for Mohammed El-Baradei, it was Iraq, not Iran, which dominated the first half of the month of October. While the Security Council continued to wrestle with the precise wording of a resolution concerning the return of inspectors, the IAEA was trying to reassemble a team of experts not only to go back to Iraq, but also to track down and verify the source of the information concerning the shipment of aluminum tubes and uranium yellowcake to Iraq. However, both El-Baradei and the head of the INVO, a Frenchman named Jacques Baute, were having no luck in prying loose any details.

Then, on October 16, El-Baradei received a new bombshell: the Bush administration, on the same day that the U.S. Congress voted to authorize the use of military force against Iraq, revealed that earlier that month, during the visit to North Korea by Assistant Secretary of State James Kelly on October 3–5, the United States had confronted the North Koreans about intelligence information, dating back to 1998, which showed the North Koreans were seeking to enrich uranium using centrifuges imported from Pakistan. According to the United States, the North Koreans admitted that this was, indeed, the case.

The North Koreans had a different version of events. They said that they told Kelly that the charges concerning a uranium enrichment program were fabrications, but that North Korea had every right to possess nuclear weapons if the United States violated the Agreed Framework. The Agreed Framework required the United States to provide the North Koreans with formal assurances that the

United States would not threaten North Korea with a nuclear attack. According to the North Koreans, the United States had flagrantly violated this condition. Not only had President Bush cited North Korea as being part of an Axis of Evil in his January 2002 State of the Union Address, but the Bush administration's classified Nuclear Posture Review, a version of which was leaked to the press in January 2002, listed North Korea as a country the United States should be prepared to use nuclear weapons against.

This flagrant violation of the Agreed Framework commitment not to threaten North Korea with nuclear attack was exacerbated in September 2002 when the Bush administration released a report, the National Security Strategy of the United States, which emphasized the new U.S. doctrine of pre-emptively attacking countries that were developing weapons of mass destruction. This report explicitly mentioned North Korea. The combination of these reports, together with the aggressive posture the Bush administration was taking concerning regime change in Iraq, pushed the North Koreans close to the brink.

Suddenly, there was no time for a visit to Iran. With the situation in Iraq threatening to devolve into war and the situation in North Korea suddenly in free-fall, Mohammed El-Baradei and the IAEA had their hands full. While the IAEA struggled to get more precise information about what was going on in North Korea, the United States unilaterally declared the 1994 Agreed Framework to be null and void. As October turned into November, the rhetoric between Pyongyang and Washington, D.C., became harsher. At the end of November, the IAEA Board of Governors called upon North Korea to accept without delay IAEA inspections of its uranium enrichment facilities. Three days later, North Korea rejected the IAEA demand. On December 12, North Korea informed the IAEA that it was restarting its nuclear reactor, and on December 14 told the IAEA that the nuclear matter was between the United States and North Korea, and that the IAEA had no role to play.

On December 21, North Korea began cutting IAEA seals off of surveillance cameras at Yongbyon, and redirecting the cameras so that they either pointed toward walls, or else were covered by cloth. The Yongbyon facility was used for extracting plutonium from spent uranium fuel rods. On December 26 the North Koreans began removing spent fuel rods from their storage facilities at Yongbyang. All IAEA inspectors were expelled from North Korea the next day. On January 10, 2003, North Korea announced that it was withdrawing from the NPT, noting that, in response to a requirement in the NPT that compels a member state withdrawing from the treaty to explain the extraordinary circumstances compelling it to take such action, it was "most seriously threatened by the United States."

The situation with Iraq wasn't going much better for the IAEA. On November 8, 2002, the Security Council finally agreed upon the language for a new resolution, 1441, mandating inspections inside Iraq. Almost immediately arguments broke out between Washington, D.C., and London on one side, and Paris, Beijing, and Moscow on the other, as to whether or not the resolution in and of itself provided authorization for the use of military force should Iraq fail to comply, or whether a second resolution would be required. The Americans and British held that all the authorization they needed was contained in the new resolution (although behind the scenes officials inside Tony Blair's government seemed less sure).

The French, Russians, and Chinese accused the United States and Britain of negotiating in poor faith, and insisted that a second resolution would in fact be required before any military action could be authorized. The fact that the Security Council was debating the authorization of military force, before Iraq had even responded to its initial requirement to provide new information to the U.N. weapons inspectors, did not bode well for the process. For many, war with Iraq seemed like a foregone conclusion.

Even as the Bush administration pushed forward aggressively for war with Iraq, its case for war, at least as far as the IAEA was concerned, was rapidly falling apart. In September and October 2002 the U.S. intelligence services had published a list of some twenty-five sites in Iraq which it claimed were known to be currently used by Iraq for purposes related to weapons of mass destruction. One site in particular, the Al Furat gas centrifuge manufacturing facility, had been singled out by the White House in early October 2002, when it released overhead imagery showing that the Iraqis had repaired some key buildings in the Al Furat facility between 1998 and 2002, leaving open the possibility that Iraq was, in concert with the intelligence information concerning aluminum tubes and yellowcake shipments, reconstituting its nuclear weapons program. Condoleezza Rice's warning about a "smoking gun" coming in the form of a "mushroom cloud" had become a mantra within the Bush administration.

Unfortunately for the United States, the intelligence-based case it was making against Iraq was falling apart, largely because of the work being done by Jaques Baute and the IAEA inspectors from INVO. The Al Furat site was but one of eight nuclear-related sites highlighted by the United States as being of particular concern. All eight sites were inspected, and nothing related to nuclear activity was noted. The Iraqis submitted a detailed declaration of their nuclear program, in accordance with the requirements of resolution 1441. While the declaration did not answer some minor technical questions the IAEA had about past programs, it did remain consistent with the IAEA's overall conclusion that Iraq's nuclear weapons program had been dismantled, that Iraq did not have an ongoing program, and that Iraq was largely in compliance regarding its obligation to disarm.

In the midst of trying to juggle the North Korea and Iraq issues, Mohammed El-Baradei was suddenly once again compelled to take on the issue of Iran. The NCRI briefing from August just wouldn't go away. The IAEA and Iran had agreed to reschedule the visit to Natanz, originally scheduled for October 2002, for sometime in December 2002. Given the ongoing crises with North Korea and Iraq, it was hard to pin down a precise date.

Then, in early December, the IAEA received word that a private American nuclear watchdog organization, the Institute for Science and International Security (ISIS), headed by David Albright, a physicist who had enjoyed a brief stint as an IAEA inspector (he served on a single inspection mission to Iraq, in June 1996), was going to go public with commercially available satellite imagery of both the Natanz and Arak facilities. Albright and a colleague had purchased the imagery on their own, and were prepared to provide pictures to back up the August claims of the NCRI.

Albright was working in cooperation with CNN to get the widest possible attention for his work when El-Baradei ordered his staff to intervene. The IAEA tried to dissuade Albright from going public with the pictures, saying it might make the Iranians less likely to cooperate with the IAEA. In all actuality, El-Baradei believed that the timing was wrong; Iran had already agreed to a site visit to be conducted in December. The attention that would be brought to bear on the Iran issue brought on by the publication of the photographs of Natanz and Arak would only be a distraction, and perhaps undermine the IAEA's efforts to get into Iran.

Albright thought otherwise, and on December 12 aired the photographs and accompanying analysis on CNN. The Iranians were aware of the CNN–ISIS program in advance, and had notified the IAEA that, given the irresponsible actions of the press, the visit to Natanz would not be on for December, and suggested that instead the trip be rescheduled for late February 2003, thus bringing El-Baradei's fears to fruition.

Compounding this situation, the U.S. government immediately went public with a response to the CNN–ISIS report. A State Department spokesman, Richard Boucher, said during a December 13 State Department briefing that the United States has "reached the conclusion that Iran is actively working to develop nuclear-weapons capability." Boucher discussed both the construction of the heavy water facility at Arak and the possible uranium-enrichment facility in Natanz.

The CNN–ISIS broadcast, and the U.S. State Department's responses, presented the Iranian nuclear program in an irresponsibly hyped-up manner, something the IAEA was well aware of. While in 1992 the IAEA Board of Governors had asked all states to provide information about the design of new nuclear facilities as soon as the decision to construct or to authorize construction was taken, this decision was not binding, and while every other member state had agreed to this new provision, Iran had not. Therefore, Iran, by keeping the construction of the Natanz site secret, was not in violation of any aspect of its current safeguard inspection agreement with the IAEA, nor was it in violation of the NPT, as long as it had not introduced any nuclear material into the site. One of the verification tasks the IAEA had set for a visit to Natanz was to confirm whether or not this was the case. The CNN–ISIS broadcast, and U.S. State Department statement, prejudged Iran as already having done so.

Likewise, Iran had not signed an Additional Protocol (the so-called 93+2 enhanced comprehensive safeguards inspections) with the IAEA. El-Baradei had hoped to work with the Iranians, away from the spotlight, to convince them to accept both the 1992 Board of Governors declaration requirements, and to sign an Additional Protocol.

Now that the matter was being aired publicly, El-Baradei had no choice but to publicly call upon Iran, on December 16, to sign an Additional Protocol with the IAEA so as to remove any ambiguity that might exist about Iran's nuclear programs.

Almost immediately Iran expressed its dismay at the comments by the U.S. State Department. The Iranian vice president and head of the AEOI, Mr. Aghazadeh, replied on December 17, 2002 that Iran rejected U.S. accusations that it was attempting to acquire weapons. Aghazadeh went on to say that this was a matter for the IAEA, not the United States. The next day, December 18, Iran's president, Mohammad Khatami, likewise rejected U.S. allegations that Iran was developing a nuclear-weapons capability. Khatami reiterated Iran's peaceful intent, noting that "Iran is working under the supervision of the International Atomic Energy Agency, and Iran is a signatory to the [Nuclear] Nonproliferation Treaty and does not seek nuclear arms."

January 2003 brought no respite for the embattled IAEA Director General. North Korea's decision to withdraw from the NPT and to move aggressively toward the manufacture of nuclear weapons took the world by storm. The American rush to war with Iraq was likewise dominating the international scene, with the IAEA at the center of the storm. On January 26, El-Baradei and his UNMOVIC colleague, Hans Blix, reported to the Security Council that the inspection process in Iraq, although not perfect, was yielding results, and that the inspectors needed more time to finish their tasks. The next day, January 27, El-Baradei appeared before the U.S. Senate, where he discussed the issues of North Korea and Iraq, and informed the senators that he was planning to travel to Iran in February to discuss the issue of the two nuclear facilities that the NCRI had brought to the world's attention the past August.

Sources close to the IAEA claim that the Israeli–IAEA interaction had increased considerably in the period between August 2002 and February 2003. Both the Deputy Director General for Safeguards, Pierre Goldschmidt, and the Chief of Operations Division B (responsible for the Iranian file in the IAEA), Olli Heinonen, had been meeting, with the permission of Mohammed El-Baradei, Israeli intelligence personnel. In these meetings a great deal of information was shared by the Israelis concerning the specifics of both the Natanz and Arak operations. The Israelis pressed the IAEA personnel on the importance of this information, and the fact that, from the Israeli perspective, the Iranian actions could be explained only as part of a nuclear weapons program.

The Israelis also shared additional intelligence files with the IAEA inspectors, files which discussed Iran's efforts to mine uranium, and assemble and test centrifuges used in the enrichment of uranium. The IAEA was aware of the mining activity (Iran had declared its mining activities to the IAEA as far back as 1992). However, the information about the assembly and testing of centrifuges was new. While the Iranians could make a case that their failure to declare the Natanz site was not a violation of the NPT, if what the Israelis were saying about centrifuge testing was true, and the Iranians had introduced nuclear material into a centrifuge, then the Iranians had in fact violated the NPT, a fact which changed dramatically any interpretation about their ultimate intent regarding the overall Iranian nuclear program.

The Israelis shared precise information about a centrifuge test facility located in Tehran called Ab-Ali, operating under the cover of a watch-manufacturing company known as the Kala Electric Company. The main problem facing the IAEA was how to make use of this information without compromising its sources. The Israelis told the IAEA not to worry, that they would make sure that the information was put into the public domain prior to the IAEA visit to Iran in February.

The IAEA was, on the issue of Iran, being squeezed between those who portrayed Iran as an irresponsible state seeking to acquire nuclear weapons in violation of its obligations under the NPT, and the Iranians themselves, who held that all they wanted was a peaceful nuclear energy program. On February 9, a little less than three weeks before the scheduled IAEA visit to Iran, Iran's president, Mohammad Khatami, made a speech in which he said the Islamic Republic of Iran had decided to utilize advanced technology, including those related to nuclear industry, for peaceful purposes.

Khatami said that the Iranian government had adopted plans to exploit its indigenous uranium mines in the Saghand region. He stated that a facility to produce uranium oxide—or yellowcake—is under construction near Saghand. He added that a uranium conversion facility, which converts uranium oxide to uranium hexa-fluoride (the feedstock for centrifuges used to enrich uranium), had neared completion and was located close to Isfahan (this was not a new revelation—in 2000, the Iranian government informed the IAEA Secretariat that a plant for uranium conversion was being constructed at Isfahan). Khatami also said that a uranium-enrichment facility, used to turn uranium hexafluouride into reactor-grade fuel, is under construction near Kashan (also known as Natanz), and that a fuel fab-rication plant was being built.

"Iran has discovered reserves and extracted uranium," Khatami said. "We are determined to use nuclear technology for civilian pur-poses . . . we assure the world that the Islamic Republic of Iran is making use of all domestic facilities to acquire peaceful nuclear technology and considers this its right to do." Khatami went on to say, "If we need to produce electricity from our nuclear power plants, we need to complete the circle from discovering uranium to managing remaining spent fuel. The government is determined to complete that circle."

Khatami's pronouncements sent shockwaves through Washington, D.C. Richard Boucher, the State Department's spokesperson, denounced the Iranian announcement, stating on February 10 that Iran's "plans for a complete fuel cycle clearly indicate Iran's intention to build the infrastructure for a nuclear weapons capability." Iran's stated intent to control the nuclear fuel cycle reinforced concerns in the U.S. government (and Israel) that Iran might reprocess spent fuel it obtains from a nuclear reactor, thus enabling Iran to extract pluto-nium. This is what had happened in the case of North Korea. The United States was determined to make sure it didn't happen with Iran.

Boucher noted that an Iranian decision to reprocess spent fuel "directly contradicted" an agreement between Iran and Russia concerning how nuclear fuel for the Bushehr nuclear reactor under construction would be handled. Under that agreement, Moscow would supply the fuel for the reactor, but Iran had to return the spent fuel to Russia. Iran and Russia had in fact agreed to the terms of the Bushehr fuel deal, but the agreement had not yet been signed as of February 9.

Boucher's claims were exaggerated and largely unfounded. Khatami had not made any reference to reprocessing spent fuel, and

Iran's intent to possess the complete nuclear fuel cycle did not contradict its commitments with Russia concerning Bushehr, but rather reinforced Iran's earlier statements that it intended to build even more nuclear energy reactors in the years to come. But politics often trumps reality, and the State Department was busy trying to impress upon the United States and world opinion its perceptions of the Iranian nuclear program.

On the eve of the visit to Iran by an IAEA delegation, consisting of Mohammed El-Baradei, Pierre Goldschmidt, and Olli Heinonen, the Israelis made good on their promise to release the additional information on Iraq in a manner usable by the IAEA. In a replay of the August 14 press conference, the NCRI again trotted out Alireza Jafarzadeh, accompanied by Soona Samsami, the U.S. representative of the NCRI, in a press conference in Washington, D.C.

Jafarzadeh started the presentation with a statement drafted in Tel Aviv: "For many years, the Iranian regime has tried to procure nuclear weapons . . . the secret nuclear project began several years ago in Natanz, Arak and Saghand. The Tehran regime was seeking to acquire a nuclear arsenal by the year 2004 or 2005. This project, he went on to say, "has three main parts. Uranium is extracted in Saghand. Uranium is enriched in Natanz. Heavy water is produced in Arak."

Jafarzadeh went on to provide details about Natanz, Saghand, Arak and a centrifuge assembly facility in Isfahan. In the process, he released the following information: "Testing for centrifuge systems is taking place at a location called Ab-Ali. The site is under the cover of a company called Kala Electric. It has been registered as a watchmaking factory. But there are two research workshops next to it. The Ab-Ali site has two large warehouses, 450 meters long each, which are used as workshops. It has also several administrative buildings. The address in Tehran is: Kilometer 2.5, Ab-Ali highway, next to Kemi Daroo Company. Kala Electric is located in the alley." In retrospect, neither Jafarzadeh nor the Israelis could have predicted the impact this tiny piece of information would have on world events.

El-Baradei, accompanied by Goldschmidt and Heinonen, arrived in Tehran on February 21, where they were immediately greeted by senior members of the Iranian government, including President Khatami, Majlis (Parliament) Speaker Mehdi Karroubi, and the

Chairman of the Expediency Council, Akbar Hashemi Rafsanjani. The Iranians briefed the IAEA team on its plans for achieving the complete nuclear fuel cycle, and stressed that Iran's nuclear program was for civil purposes only, and as such insisted that Iran had the right under the NPT to develop them. The Iranians looked to the IAEA for assistance in developing these capabilities, and hoped that the Iranian transparency would result in concrete rewards.

Furthermore, the Iranians, in keeping with their new spirit of increasing transparency, agreed that they would, in the future, abide by the 1992 IAEA Board of Governors request for nations to provide the IAEA with early design information regarding any new nuclear facilities. During these meetings, El-Baradei called on the Iranians to also conclude an Additional Protocol (the so-called 93+2 protocol) to its existing Safeguards Agreement, an act which would result in more rigorous inspections, including those of undeclared facilities. The Iranians indicated that they were not opposed to signing the Additional Protocol, but that it would be discussed and signed in the course of future negotiations.

The IAEA team had to tread lightly. Their presence in Iran was dictated by the provisions of the NPT, and more specifically, by the conditions set forth in the comprehensive safeguards inspection agreement that was currently in place between Iran and the IAEA. Ever the diplomats, El-Baradei and his colleagues had to proceed carefully, cognizant of their limitations. Following the initial discussions between the IAEA and the senior Iranian officials, the Iranians officially declared to El-Baradei the existence of two facilities in Natanz as being part of a uranium enrichment program. These facilities were a Pilot Fuel Enrichment Plant (PFEP), which was nearing the end of its construction, and a commercial-scale Fuel Enrichment Plant (FEP), which was still under construction. The Iranians also confirmed that they were constructing a heavy water manufacturing plant at Arak, but that this plant was not covered either by the NPT or the safeguards agreement. El-Baradei then requested that the Iranians allow him and his delegation to visit the Natanz facilities.

Before departing to Natanz, El-Baradei asked the Iranians for clarification concerning certain nuclear materials of interest. Unbeknownst to the Iranians, the IAEA had prevailed upon China to provide a full declaration of all nuclear material it had exported to

Iran. Armed with this information, El-Baradei now sought clarification in the face of Iran's newly stated intent to be totally transparent.

Iran acknowledged that it indeed had received in 1991 several shipments of natural uranium, which had not been reported previously to the IAEA. This uranium came in the form of uranium hexafluoride (1,000 kilograms), uranium tetrafluoride (400 kilograms), and uranium oxide (yellowcake, 400 kilograms). The Iranians stated that this material was being stored at a previously undeclared facility, the Jabr Ibn Hayan Multipurpose Laboratory (JHL), located at the Tehran Nuclear Research Center (TNRC). The Iranians also declared that most of the uranium tetrafluoride had been converted into uranium metal back in 2000, at the JHL facility.

El-Baradei and his IAEA delegation then asked to be taken to Natanz, an ancient city better known in Iran for its famous pear trees than uranium enrichment plants. Located at the foot of Vulture Mountain, where Darius III met his fate at the hands of the soldiers of Alexander the Great, Natanz was a place where the past met the present, and given the stakes at play, it was hard to say which took on a greater significance.

Once at Natanz, the IAEA delegation was taken to the PFEP, where 164 centrifuge casings had already been installed. The IAEA officials were stunned at the advanced state of affairs they were witnessing. They were also shocked to see that the centrifuges being used by Iran appeared to be of European design, looking suspiciously like centrifuges produced by URENCO in the 1970s. The Iranians refused to discuss the origins of the centrifuges, except to note that they were of Iranian manufacture.

The PFEP also contained components for an additional 1,000 centrifuges, which were scheduled to be installed by the end of 2003. The large-scale commercial FEP was still under construction. The Iranians told the IAEA that this facility was expected to hold over 50,000 centrifuges. The FEP was not scheduled to begin receiving centrifuges until early 2005, once the centrifuge design had been confirmed by the planned tests scheduled to take place in the PFEP. The Iranians informed El-Baradei that the PFEP was scheduled to begin operations in June 2003, initially with a test of a single centrifuge, and then on a small pilot scale level using a 10-centrifuge cascade. The IAEA officials were stunned to hear the Iranians declare that the design and research and development work, which began in 1997, was based on extensive modeling and simulation, including rotor tests with and without inert gas, and that these tests were carried out on the premises of the Amer Khabir University in Tehran, and at the AEOI facility in Tehran, and that none of these tests involved the use of nuclear material.

At this juncture, the IAEA Director General was summoned back to Vienna, where he was needed to deal with the rapidly disintegrating situation regarding Iraq. However, El-Baradei left behind both Pierre Goldschmidt and Olli Heinonen to continue on with the program of work.

Goldschmidt and Heinonen were taken to the JHL facility, where the Iranians provided a briefing on the disposition of the uranium material they had received from China. The IAEA officials were shown one large (1,000 kilogram) and two small (400 kilograms each) uranium flouride (UF) containers, which the Iranians claimed contained the totality of the imported uranium hexafluoride. The Iranians then described how they converted uranium tetrafluoride into uranium metal. The Iranians stated that this process was complete, and that the equipment involved had been dismantled and placed into containers for storage (both IAEA representatives were shown the container in question). The Iranians told the IAEA representatives that they were refurbishing that part of the JHL facility for use as a uranium metal processing laboratory. The Iranians promised to make all uranium metal, and all associated waste material, available to the IAEA.

The Iranians also informed the IAEA representatives that some of the imported uranium oxide had been used by Iran in tests related to the purification and conversion processes associated with the uranium conversion facility. The Iranians provided the IAEA with a technical description of how this was done, and what happened to the materials used in these tests. The Iranians also informed the IAEA inspectors about small amounts of uranium oxide expended in process tests at the Molybdenum, Iodine, Xenon Radioisotope Production facility (MIX).

Expanding on this new-found spirit of transparency, Peter Goldschmidt then brought up the issue of the Kala Electric Company, which he had been made aware of through the IAEA's Israeli intelligence connections, and which was now part of the public record thanks to the NCRI briefing of February 20. The Iranians corrected the record, stating that the proper name of the facility was the Kalaye Electric Company, and admitted that the workshop had been used for the production of centrifuge components. However, the Iranians noted, at no time did the Iranians introduce nuclear material into a centrifuge, either at Kalaye or anywhere else in Iran. All testing had been carried out using simulation studies.

Goldschmidt acknowledged that, under the existing safeguards agreement between the IAEA and Iran under the NPT, the Kalaye centrifuge component production facility was not a nuclear facility subject to being declared by Iran, but, in the interest of transparency, the IAEA would like to visit the site and take environmental samples in an effort to verify the Iranian declaration and confirm that there was no undeclared nuclear material, and thus nuclear activity, taking place at the site. The Iranians turned Goldschmidt down; noting that this represented an activity that would be covered by an Additional Protocol, and as such would be handled in the context of the IAEA–Iranian discussion pertaining to that issue.

Before leaving Iran on February 26, Pierre Goldschmidt handed over to the Iranians a paper he had prepared together with Olli Heinonen in which the IAEA laid out a number of questions regarding Iran's centrifuge program. The IAEA officials were particularly interested in Iran providing a detailed chronology of all research and development activities undertaken which related to bringing the Iranian centrifuge into operation, especially in light of the Iranian declarations that it had achieved this impressive accomplishment without introducing uranium hexafluoride gas into the centrifuge cylinder. The IAEA officials asked for similar clarifications from the Iranians about the processes used by Iran at its declared large-scale uranium conversion facility, which was stated to be used for the manufacture of uranium oxide, uranium tetrafluoride, and uranium hexafluoride, all without testing, even on a small scale, any nuclear material.

The Goldschmidt–Heinonen letter also raised questions about Iran's laser enrichment programs and its heavy water programs. According to one account, Goldschmidt had taken advantage of the Iranian spirit of transparency to press them on some of the intelligence he had received from Israel concerning laser enrichment activities (without disclosing the source). While the Iranians acknowledged the existence of a substantial program on lasers, they categorically denied that any enrichment-related laser activities had taken place. The Iranians promised a response on both matters in the near future.

Overall, the trip had been a success. The IAEA had been able to gain unprecedented access to critical nuclear related sites inside Iran, and bring these sites, and their related activities, under safeguard control. While the Iranians had not been required to declare the activities at Natanz, they were required to have declared the importation of the nuclear materials (defined by the IAEA as "material of a composition and purity suitable for fuel fabrication or for being isotopically enriched, and any nuclear material produced at a later stage in the nuclear fuel cycle") they had received from China in 1991, as well as any activity which resulted in a change in the overall inventory of this material. On the surface, this discrepancy was a very minor one, as the total effective nuclear weight (i.e., the amount of fissile material that could be produced using the material in question, once it was processed and enriched) of the material involved was well under one kilogram (anywhere from 12 to 20 kilograms of highly enriched uranium are required to manufacture a nuclear weapon).

Iran tried to explain away this discrepancy by noting that its safeguards agreement precluded declaring any nuclear material with an effective nuclear weight of less than a kilogram. But the IAEA pointed out, rightly, that all material was subject to declaration. The Iranians, in a letter handed to Goldschmidt and Heinonen before they departed Tehran on February 26, promised to make good on their commitments in this regard. In their letter, the Iranians also agreed to the modifications to the Subsidiary Arrangements proposed by the IAEA, which now required Iran to inform the IAEA of all new nuclear facilities and any modifications to existing facilities by providing preliminary design information as soon as the "decision to construct, authorize construction, or modify has been taken."

Upon his return to Vienna, Mohammed El-Baradei discovered that the United States was moving forward aggressively toward armed conflict with Iraq, regardless of what the facts regarding Iraqi WMD were. This was especially true in the case of Iraq's nuclear weapons program, and the statements being made by the Bush administration.

The IAEA had investigated the issue of aluminum tubes imported by Iraq, and found not only were they related solely to the production of artillery rockets, not nuclear-related centrifuges, but were totally incompatible for use in centrifuge-enrichment applications.

Even worse for the Americans, Jacques Baute had finally gotten his hands on a copy of the documents linking Iraq to the procurement of yellowcake in Niger. Within hours these documents had been exposed as forgeries. The entire case made by the Bush administration concerning Iraq's nuclear weapons program had collapsed, but it didn't matter. Even a bold presentation by Mohammed El-Baradei before the Security Council on March 7, 2003, in which he refuted point by point every allegation put forward by the United States regarding an Iraqi reconstituted nuclear weapons program, proved futile. The IAEA was compelled by the United States to withdraw its inspectors from Iraq on March 14. On March 16, the U.S.-led invasion of Iraq began.

As disturbing as the news about the U.S. invasion of Iraq was, the IAEA's Director-General still had work to do. On March 17 he delivered an initial report to the IAEA Board of Governors concerning the February 21–26 visit to Iran by the IAEA. El-Baradei had, by this time, been able to assimilate the information that had been collected during that initial visit, as well as a follow-up inspection in early March. During that inspection, the IAEA representatives presented the Iranian authorities with a safeguards approach to inspections, which included a visit to the Natanz PFEP, where the inspectors took a series of environmental samples.

Under safeguard inspections, samples are collected to detect what are known as nuclear fingerprints, which forensically reveal indicators of past and present activities in locations handling nuclear materials. This process is particularly effective when dealing with facilities involved in uranium conversion, fabrication, and enrichment. The environmental "dust" collected by this sampling is expected to match the declared activities at a given site, or uncover any clandestine production or handling of nuclear materials.

The IAEA maintains a high-tech Safeguards Analytical Laboratory at its Seibersdorf Lab near its headquarters in Vienna, Austria (as well as other laboratories located around the world), which is capable of obtaining a vast amount of information from even the smallest amount of material contained in a sample. Working inside a highly secure and contamination-free Clean Lab, IAEA scientists use a number of screening techniques, such as X-Ray fluorescence and gamma spectrometry, to evaluate samples where any plutonium or uranium can be detected down to a picogram, or a trillionth of a gram.

Using special swipe kits, IAEA inspectors use cotton swabs to collect dust samples from walls, floors, ducts, or pieces of equipment at inspected sites. Surfaces are wiped using 10 x 10 centimeter squares of a specially clean cotton cloth. The Seibersdorf Lab prepares certified clean sampling kits that contain six cotton swabs, special gloves, plastic bags (for storing the swab once the sample is taken), data forms, and a pen. One kit is used per environmental sample at a given inspection location, so that the sample can be sent to different analytical laboratories for analysis. Similar results obtained from parallel sampling increases the confidence in the findings that are obtained from this process.

Armed with these sampling kits, the IAEA inspectors continued with their mission, taking numerous samples at the Natanz PFEP. Heinonen and his team also visited the JHL facility, where they carried out environmental sampling and were given access to the uranium hexafluoride canisters at the JHL facility. When the canisters were weighed, the inspectors detected that a total of 1.9 kilograms of uranium hexafluoride was missing from both of the smaller (400 kilogram) canisters. The Iranians declared that this was due to leaking valves on these canisters.

However, this development again highlighted the probability, in the minds of the IAEA inspectors, that the Iranians had in fact carried out a test of a centrifuge using actual uranium hexafluoride, as opposed to the inert gas they had declared back in February. The inspectors then visited the Kalaye facility, but were granted only limited access to the site. Indeed, when the inspectors tried to gain access to one of the large warehouse buildings the Israelis had identified as being a workshop, only to find the building locked, the Iranians claimed that they had no keys to the facility. The IAEA team requested permission to take environmental samples at the Kalaye facility, but again was turned down by the Iranians, who claimed this was an activity that could only take place in the context of an Additional Protocol.

Back in Vienna, the Deputy Director for Safeguards, Pierre Gold-schmidt was receiving additional indications that the Iranians were up to no good at Kalaye. In the rough-and-tumble world of global non-proliferation, replete with covert weapons programs, illicit man-ufacturing, and black-market supply networks, the Austrian capital, home to the IAEA headquarters, had always had a certain spy-versus-spy atmosphere. The embassies of the United States, Great Britain, Russia, and France were constantly receiving teams of diplomats who roamed the corridors and halls of the IAEA building, conducting hushed meetings with various staff members about nuclear activity being conducted around the world. Embassy functions became ideal events for the unofficial exchange of information, not just between an interested party and the IAEA, but between the various intelli-gence services themselves, so that the cocktail circuit of Vienna began to resemble those of times past in Moscow, where during the height of the Cold War spies and diplomats from around the world rubbed elbows in an effort to pry a snippet of information from whatever source they could.

Given the extreme sensitivity of the work being conducted by the IAEA, not just in Iran, but also around the world, there could be no hint of impropriety on the part of any of its staff when it came to protecting confidential information garnered as part of its global activities. IAEA officials were expected to attend embassy functions, and to socialize with diplomats, real or other, in an effort to expand contacts and improve relations. But at no time were they permitted to cross the boundary between what was proper, and what might be seen as compromising their impartiality.

But a case like Iran, as had been the case with Iraq, created a quandary of sorts for the IAEA. When a nation like Iraq or Iran chooses not to fully cooperate with the IAEA, then there is a premium placed by the inspectors on gaining access to information that can facilitate their investigation. While the inspection tools available to the inspec-tors inside a country to be inspected are quite impressive, they require the identification of a facility as being of interest, and then the guar-antee of access to a facility so that the appropriate investigations can be conducted. Since Iran had, by March 2003, yet to enter into the Advanced Protocol, the IAEA lacked the authority to demand access to Kalaye and carry out intrusive environmental sampling operations.

While the IAEA inspection team was in Iran in early March, the CIA was tasking U.S. satellites to take imagery of Kalaye (and other locations) to see if any Iranian reaction to the IAEA inspection activity could be detected. Sure enough, shortly after IAEA inspectors departed Kalaye (and after they had been denied access to one of the warehouse buildings believed to be used as a workshop), the satellite images showed an increase in activity around the building in question. This activity was assessed by the CIA as showing the Iranians removing items from the building. Pierre Goldschmidt was made aware of this information, as was Olli Heinonen. Both men were convinced that the Iranians were up to no good in Kalaye. But the inherent weakness of the IAEA safeguards regime was made painfully obvious to both. Void of an Iranian decision to permit inspector access to Kalaye, there was nothing the inspectors could do except to continue to request access.

Kalaye wasn't the only area of concern for the IAEA inspectors. During the IAEA inspections in March, the Iranians followed up on their earlier declaration that most of the uranium tetrafluoride that had been imported from China had been converted into uranium metal by describing to the IAEA inspectors some 113 experiments conducted between 1995 and 2000, none of which had been declared to the IAEA, even though under the terms of the NPT, such experiments represented a declarable activity.

The IAEA safeguards inspectors were kept busy in the weeks between early April and early June 2003. A total of three inspections were carried out at the Natanz PFEP, where environmental samples were taken and design drawings of the facility evaluated (the Iranians provided the IAEA with a full set of drawings of the PFEP facility in early May). In May the IAEA inspectors were again granted access to the Kalaye facility and were able to gain entry into the previously locked warehouse. The inspectors noted that the building was large enough to house a pilot-scale cascade of a few hundred centrifuges, and noted with suspicion that part of the building was walled off by a pile of boxes.

The Iranians again refused the IAEA's request to conduct environmental sampling at the Kalaye facility. However, the Iranians did tell the IAEA that they might be receptive to sampling at the Kalaye facility in June, when the IAEA was dispatching a team of centrifuge enrichment specialists to follow up on technical questions pertaining to how Iran proceeded in the field of centrifuge enrichment without using any nuclear material in tests.

Also in May, the Iranians informed the IAEA of their intent to construct a 40-kilowatt heavy water nuclear reactor at Arak, and a fuel manufacturing plant at Isfahan. Both sites would be under IAEA safeguard inspections.

The events regarding the Iranian nuclear program were progressing along three primary avenues. The first, or Iranian, avenue held that significant progress was being made, especially in light of the fact that the IAEA–Iranian cooperation had only just begun in June. The Iranians appeared receptive to new inspection modalities, but were insistent that they had the right under the NPT to carry out their work in nuclear enrichment.

The second avenue, that of the IAEA, was previewed during the March 17 briefing by El-Baradei to the IAEA Board of Governors. At that time El-Baradei had dealt with the Iranian issue in broad terms, but already information had leaked out about the Kalaye plant and the stockpiles of undeclared nuclear material of Chinese origin. The IAEA knew that it was treading on sensitive turf. Any finding that Iran had breached its obligations under the NPT would warrant referral of the Iran case to the U.N. Security Council. El-Baradei knew better than most what such a transfer could mean; the United States invaded Iraq on March 16, having used its position on the Security Council to twist the rule of law and manipulate facts. El-Baradei needed to be careful not to give the U.S. any opening that could be used to carry out the same sort of manipulation that had occurred with Iraq.

The U.S. wanted action taken against Iran. According to the information coming from Iran, the U.S. believed that Iran already could be found to be in breach of its obligations under the NPT. U.S. Ambassador Brill requested that El-Baradei make a full presentation to the IAEA Board of Governors in June 2003 that would spell out exactly what had been found in Iran by the IAEA, and how this related to Iran's compliance with the NPT. The U.S. was looking for a referral to the Security Council, thereby opening the door for economic sanctions to be imposed on Iran, or even the authorization of military force to be brought to bear should Iran not comply with a growing consensus that it cease and desist with its nuclear program as a whole, especially those aspects related to obtaining the entire nuclear fuel cycle.

A preview of the diplomatic struggles that the IAEA could expect during its June meeting of the Board of Governors was played out at the Second Preparatory Committee (PrepCom) for the 2005 Review Conference of the NPT Parties, which was held from April 28 to May 9, 2003, in Geneva, Switzerland. Somewhat surprisingly, North Korea's dramatic withdrawal from the NPT took a back seat to the growing concern that existed in many Western nations about the scope and sophistication of Iran's nuclear program. The American delegation in particular adopted a very aggressive stance, accusing the Iranians of carrying out a program that could only be explained in the context of a nuclear weapons program.

The United States took the lead in arguing that Iran, as a leading producer of oil, had no justifiable economic explanation for its nuclear program, further reinforcing the conclusion by Washington, D.C., that the program was a cover for nuclear weapons acquisition. The United States joined the other nations at the PrepCom to call upon Iran to sign an Additional Protocol with the IAEA, opening Iran up to more intrusive inspections.

Iran rejected the suggestions that it was pursuing nuclear weapons, declaring that nuclear weapons had no place in its defense doctrine. The Iranian delegation also objected to having its nuclear program prejudged prior to the June IAEA meeting, noting that it wanted the merits of its nuclear program to be judged free of the "political burden of U.S.–Iranian bilateral relations."

The PrepCom confrontation provided the first clear indication to many observers that the issue of Iran's nuclear program was in danger of being hijacked by U.S.–Iranian animosity. El-Baradei in particular desired that the Iranian nuclear program be addressed in the framework of an international issue, not simply an extension of U.S. foreign policy objectives.

During the PrepCom the issue of Iran's signing an Additional Protocol with the IAEA was also raised. Iran had committed to signing such a protocol, but did not want to do so until it had received assurances that existing restrictions on the supply of nuclear-related technologies and materials imposed on Iran by the United States, the

United Kingdom, and other members of the Nuclear Suppliers Group (NSG) would be lifted.

There was a certain element of inconsistency on the part of the position being taken by the United States and the United Kingdom regarding Iran, the Additional Protocol, and the NSG sanctions. The United States had made the point of raising at the PrepCom the conditions that signing onto the Additional Protocol was a precondition for receiving nuclear exports. The United States also insisted that Iran not only sign such a protocol void of any assurances that such exports would be forthcoming, but also in the face of American objections to Iran obtaining such technology until all questions about its nuclear program were answered.

Given the recent history of the U.S.-led invasion of Iraq, which used U.N. Security Council resolutions as a cover and pretext for action, and in light of the increasingly harsh rhetoric coming from Washington, D.C., concerning the desirability of regime change in Tehran, there was wide recognition within the IAEA membership that the IAEA needed to maintain control over this matter, but in a manner which maintained the integrity and viability of the NPT and IAEA.

This was to be for El-Baradei, and the IAEA inspectors he led, the greatest challenge.

Three
The Great Appeasers

THE CITIZENS OF THE SMALL French village of Chatellerault could not have known that a dentist-turned-scientific advisor, working on behalf of their one-time mayor, would be responsible for bringing down the European Commissioner and his entire twenty-person commission. The repeated visits to Chatellerault by Rene Bertholot, a close friend of Edith Cresson, a European Commissioner responsible for Research, Training, Education and Youth, were cited by a special investigatory body appointed by the European Parliament to look into charges of corruption made against the former French Prime Minister. Bertholot had been appointed to a position for which he seemed to lack any professional qualifications, and had made scores of "business trips" to Chatellerault which apparently had nothing whatsoever to do with his mandate. The Cresson case led to the resignation on March 16, 1999, of the European Commission President, Jacques Santer, and the entire twenty-person commission he headed, and thereby thrust the European Commission, and as such the European Council which it served.

The resignation of Jacques Santer threw Europe into turmoil, not so much as it was indicative of corruption at the highest levels of government, but rather because the charges of corruption were but the manifestation of a larger power struggle taking place within Europe concerning the broader issues of political and economic power sharing between the European Union on the one hand, and established Euro-

pean nation states on the other. The Cresson-Santer affair exploded
on January 21, 1999, just two weeks after arguably one of the European Union's greatest accomplishments, that being the establishment
of a unified currency, the euro, throughout most of Europe. The
issue at hand stemmed from a growing clash of wills between Santer's
European Commission and the European Parliament over the ratification of the commission's budget. While the European Parliament
enjoys the perks and privileges accorded to national members of parliament, it has none of the power. Budget ratification is normally
meant to be a rubber-stamp process, but on this occasion several
members of the European Parliament were concerned about
seeming irregularities in the 160 billion Deutch Mark (the budget in
question was pre-euro) spending package presented by the Commission. When the European Commission arrogantly rejected any criticism of its budget, and refused to turn over any documents
concerning the budget to the E.U. Parliament, the scene was set for
a confrontation. Control over the management of public finances of
the European Commission is one of the few tasks for which the parliament has responsibility.

It appeared to be no accident that the escalation of the conflict
between the European Parliament and the European Commission
coincided with the introduction of the euro. The concentration of
economic power away from traditional national control mechanisms
into a singular trans-European entity was seen as a threat by certain
interested parties, especially in Germany. The forty-year-old
European Commission existed as a bloated bureaucracy, with over
20,000 employees, ostensibly subordinated to the European Council
of Ministers, comprised of senior officials from individual European
nation states. For the decade prior to the March 1999 crisis, the
primary role of the European Commission was to dispense some 120
billion Deutch Marks' worth of agricultural and economic subsidies
to struggling economies within Europe, helping the targeted recipi-
ents meet the prerequisites for a single European market. With the
establishment of the euro, many in Europe, especially in Germany,
felt that the level of economic integration represented by the euro
could no longer be adequately represented by the antiquated
European Commission as it was currently configured. The challenge
to Jacques Santer, manifested through the Cresson scandal, was less

about bringing down the European Commission than it was about establishing the principle of the need for change, especially on the eve of Germany taking the helm of the European Presidency. The Germans wanted to establish a new framework for leadership within the Union, one that increased the political influence of the European Union by removing a unanimity requirement for voting within the European Parliament, thereby freeing up the Parliament and Commission to be able to take action on wide-ranging issues involving both economic and political matters. Far from being a simple scandal, the Santer–Cresson affair represented nothing less than a struggle for the very future of Europe.

Into the midst of this crisis was thrust a mild-mannered former Italian University professor named Romano Prodi. A former Prime Minister of Italy, Prodi had surprised many when he succeeded in getting Italy accepted as a member of the single European currency, an impressive feat given Italy's many serious economic difficulties. Now, in the midst of the greatest crisis in the history of the European Commission, Prodi was once again called upon to do the impossible, tasked with bringing the European Commission back on its feet, and marching Europe back on track toward not just a common economic policy, but foreign and defense policy as well. At first glance, the mild-mannered, bespectacled man whose lack of popular charisma earned him the nickname *Le Mortadella*, or bland sausage, seemed an odd choice for such a daunting task. But Prodi proved himself to be a careful manager who governed with a combination of careful over-sight and strict fiscal discipline, two things that were lacking in the European Commission at the time of his appointment.

Prodi's success in getting Italy economically qualified for inclusion in the single European currency was matched with his skill in getting eleven more European nations to adopt the euro by 2002. Moreover, under his leadership, the European Union looked toward expansion, with some thirteen nations submitting applications to join the Union by mid-2002. Things were going well for Prodi and Europe. In December 2002 he felt confident enough to address the need for a single European foreign policy during an address in Brussels. "If we are to keep pace with this changing world and shoulder our growing global responsibilities," Prodi said, "we, as the Union, have to take the necessary measures. If we want to satisfy the rising expectations and hopes of countries abroad and the peoples of Europe, we have to become a real global player. We are only beginning to act as one. The Balkans, Afghanistan and the Middle East are only three examples of the challenges facing the world community. The E.U. has to play its part in dealing with them. The E.U.'s foreign policy must be brought up to speed. It must be expressed with one voice and vested with the necessary instruments. There is no other way to guarantee our security in the long term."

The reality of the tenuous nature of any notion of European unity on matters relating to defense and foreign policy came crashing down in the face of America's unbridled rush toward war with Iraq in 2002. The ease with which the Bush administration was able to exploit the fractures existent in European diplomatic circles surprised many in Europe, especially Romano Prodi. The unpleasant dualities of the European Union and NATO were exposed as the United States outmaneuvered Europe repeatedly by trumping the E.U.'s ability to pressure European unity through the promise of E.U. expansion with America's own ability to facilitate membership into NATO.

The Americans made a mockery of European unity, exploiting the political strategy of divide and conquer. When, in January 2003, Germany and France appeared united in their opposition to the American march toward war with Iraq, the U.S. Secretary of Defense, Donald Rumsfeld, dismissed their stance as representative of outdated things. "Germany has been a problem and France has been a problem," Rumsfeld said. "But you look at vast numbers of other countries in Europe, they're not with France and Germany . . . they're with the U.S. You're thinking of Europe as Germany and France. I don't," he said. "I think that's old Europe."

Rumsfeld went on to note that the planned eastward expansion of NATO as far as the three Baltic republics made France and Germany, the traditional stalwarts of European economic and political power, increasingly irrelevant. "If you look at the entire NATO Europe today, the center of gravity is shifting to the east," Rumsfeld said, referring to the 1999 decision to admit Hungary, Poland, and the Czech Republic into NATO. These three nations had also been approved for membership into the E.U. NATO was also aggressively moving toward the admittance of the former Soviet Republics of Estonia, Latvia, and

Lithuania, three nations that were also vying for E.U. membership. Clearly, the U.S. strategy was to use NATO expansion as a tool to counter any leverage anti-war nations, such as Germany and France, in the European Union might have on other E.U. countries, as well as those nations aspiring toward E.U. membership.

In this political maneuvering the Bush administration had a close ally in Great Britain and its pro-American Prime Minister, Tony Blair. The question of E.U. expansion and consolidation of economic and political power had interwoven itself into British domestic politics over the course of many years. Ever since assuming office, Tony Blair had adhered closely to the traditional British view of the European Union more as representing a cooperative venture among European countries rather than the precursor to a United States of Europe. But Blair did envision an E.U. role that went beyond purely economic matters, noting in a speech delivered in January 1998 that "If you look at the way the world is developing, countries that have interests in common are moving closer together, and not just in an economic but in a political sense as well." But any notion of Europe coming together in a "political sense" over Iraq was shot down early on in the lead up to war, when Tony Blair proclaimed that Britain was willing to pay a "blood price" to maintain the special relationship it enjoyed with the United States. Blair then became a co-conspirator with George W. Bush in "fixing intelligence around policy," actively participating in the hyping up and falsification of intelligence to sustain the notion that Iraq maintained WMD stockpiles and programs in violation of Security Council resolutions.

It was Tony Blair and Britain that initiated the process of driving a wedge between old Europe and new Europe, orchestrating an open letter of support for the Bush administration's stance on Iraq in January 2003. This letter, signed by Britain, Spain, Portugal, Italy, Denmark, Poland, Hungary, and the Czech Republic, sent shockwaves through much of Europe, especially among the ranks of those who were posturing for a unified European position on Iraq. The British intervention was seen by many in the European Union, especially France and Germany, as undermining Europe's potential collective power in influencing America's aggressive Iraq policy. An emergency summit was called for mid-February 2003 to discuss Iraq, with the goal

of defining a single European policy position on Iraq. At this summit
a unified E.U. statement was crafted which, through its language, only
proved Europe could not take a strong stance on the issue of Iraq.

"We are committed to the United Nations remaining at the center
of the international order. We recognize that the primary responsibility for dealing with Iraqi disarmament lies with the (U.N.) Security
Council," the statement read.

> We pledge our full support to the Council in discharging its
> responsibilities. The Union's objective for Iraq remains full
> and effective disarmament in accordance with the relevant
> United Nations Security Council resolutions, in particular
> Resolution 1441.

> We want to achieve this peacefully. It is clear that this is what
> the people of Europe want.

> War is not inevitable. Force should be used only as a last resort.
> It is for the Iraqi regime to end this crisis by complying with the
> demands of the Security Council.

> We reiterate our full support for the ongoing work of U.N.
> inspectors. They must be given the time and resources that the
> U.N. Security Council believes they need.

> However, inspections cannot continue indefinitely in the
> absence of full Iraqi cooperation.

> This must include the provision of all the additional and
> specific information on the issues that have been raised in the
> inspectors' reports.

> Baghdad should have no illusions: it must disarm and coop-
> erate immediately and fully. Iraq has a final opportunity to
> resolve the crisis peacefully.

The E.U. statement on the surface exhibited a sense of European
unity and harmony. It was a compromise that synthesized the more

hawkish position on Iraq taken by Britain, Spain, and Italy, and the comparatively dovish position taken by France and Germany. But the fact that the European Union had excluded from the summit any participation by the so-called candidate countries, such as Romania and Bulgaria, angered some, including Tony Blair, who took the opportunity provided to have the ten excluded candidate countries sign a letter of support for the American stance on Iraq similar to the one Britain and others signed in January 2003. This new letter, which directly challenged the image of European unity that was being fostered by the summit's joint statement, caused an explosion. France, which together with Germany had taken the lead in opposing the U.S. position, was withering in its criticism of the new letter, and those who signed it. French President Jacques Chirac chastised the signatories, noting, "These countries have been not very well behaved and rather reckless of the danger of aligning themselves too rapidly with the American position. It is not really responsible behavior. It is not well brought-up behavior. They missed," Chirac said, "a good opportunity to keep quiet. I felt they acted frivolously because entry into the European Union implies a minimum of understanding for the others." The French outburst prompted immediate retorts from the governments of the signatory countries, and altogether created an impression of a Europe that was fractured and weak.

This, of course, was not the image that Romano Prodi wanted to foster. Prodi warned that the "total lack of a European common foreign policy" was a disaster in the making.

"If Europe fails to pull together, all our nation states will disappear from the world scene," Prodi told the European parliament in Strasbourg. "Unless Europe speaks with a single voice, it will be impossible to continue working closely with the U.S. on a longstanding basis while retaining our dignity."

Prodi was saddened by the decision of the candidate countries to sign the new letter because their pro-Americanism signaled they had failed to understand that the European Union was more than a mere economic union. "I would be lying if I said I was happy," Prodi said. "I have been very, very sad, but I am also patient by nature, so I hope they will understand that sharing the future means sharing the future."

Prodi's vision of a European disaster became reality when the United States, together with Britain, invaded Iraq in March 2003 absent of any authorization on the part of the Security Council of the United Nations. Prodi's vision of a unified Europe was under attack, a reality he underscored in a statement he made on March 20, 2003 regarding the U.S.-led invasion of Iraq.

> This is a sad and somber day for all nations around the world. The onslaught of war has paid to the international community's efforts to find a peaceful solution to the Iraq crisis within the United Nations.

> Whatever the outcome of the war, there can be no denying this is a bad time for the Common Foreign and Security Policy, for the European Union as a whole, for the authority of the U.N., for NATO, and for transatlantic relations. In war there are no winners, just losers.

> Today the leaders of the E.U.'s nations will meet in Brussels to discuss the situation. The Commission urges all Member States to strive to build on what we share in our approach to the conflict now commencing.

> The Commission has worked hard with the Presidency of the Union to seek a common position and it will continue to do so.

> These difficult circumstances also show it is time to draw the lessons from this crisis. Europe can make an effective contribution to peace in the world only if its nations pull together within the European Union. We all agree that we owe our wealth and prosperity to the Union. It is not in our interest to continue relying on others when it comes to defending our values militarily.

As March turned into April, and April into May, Romano Prodi and the rest of the European Union watched as American military might made quick work of Saddam's battered military, capturing Baghdad and driving the Iraqi dictator into hiding. President Bush made his triumphant landing aboard the *USS Abraham Lincoln*, and proclaimed "mission accomplished" in Iraq. Those in Europe who had supported the U.S. position suddenly found their political stock to be sky-high, while those who had opposed the war were wallowing in a political purgatory. For Romano Prodi, a leader striving for European unity, purgatory was not the ideal place to be. So when, in June 2003, Europe once again found itself on a collision course with the United States, this time over the issue of Iran, Prodi chose to take a new approach toward European diplomacy vis-à-vis the American super-power, modifying the old adage, If you can't beat them, join them.

In fact, Prodi was not a proponent of total capitulation to the American position on Iran. He was heartened by the May 15, 2003 statement by U.S. Secretary of State Colin Powell that the United States was not planning to take military action to stop Iran's nuclear programs. Secretary Powell had said, "We are concerned about what Iran is doing (with its nuclear program). . . . We will work with the international community to persuade Iran they should not move in this direction. . . . But it's not a matter for the armed forces of the United States at the moment." The phrase "at the moment" was key. If Europe was to have any viability on the world stage as a political force, it would need to find a way to make sure that "at the moment" became "never." The best route to "never" lay in walking a diplomatic tightrope between confrontation and conciliation. Given Europe's weakened position in the aftermath of Iraq, this was not an easy route to choose.

Romano Prodi did have considerably more leverage when it came to Iran than had been the case regarding Iraq. First and foremost, Iran did not have comprehensive economic sanctions imposed on it by the United Nations, and as a result Iran had been engaged in a lengthy process of trade negotiations with the European Union that had compelled even the fractured E.U. to develop a common approach to dealing with Iran. The E.U.–Iran relationship took on an even more important light in the aftermath of the election of Mr. Khatami as Iran's president in May 1997. Seen by Europe to be a moderate reformer, Khatami provided an opportunity to improve Euro–Iranian relations, and in 1998 the European Union entered into what was called a comprehensive dialogue with Iran, in the form of semi-annual meetings. This dialogue manifested itself in dis-cussions on regional issues, including the Middle East peace process, non-proliferation of weapons of mass destruction, human rights and the fight against terrorism. The European Union also explored possibilities for cooperation with Iran in the areas of energy, trade and investment, refugees, and drugs control. After the Iranian parliamentary elections in February 2000, a decision was taken to develop closer relations with Iran, and in November 2000 the European Union and Iran met for the first time to discuss economic cooperation.

By early 2001 the European Commission was well on the path toward developing closer relations with Iran, and was beginning to frame what was known as a Trade and Cooperation Agreement, or TCA. The mandate for such an agreement was adopted by the European Council in July 2002. Building on the movement toward a TCA, the European Union initiated discussions with Iran toward what was known as a Political Dialogue Agreement, and later, a Human Rights Dialogue.

Of course, Europe being Europe, something as controversial as an E.U.–Iran dialogue could not proceed without controversy. Human rights was a critical issue for many in Europe, and the developing E.U.–Iran rapprochement was being disrupted by the case of a Tehran university student named Amir Abbas Fakhravar, who had been arrested in 2002 for the crime of criticizing the leader of the Islamic Republic, Ayatollah Ali Khamenei. In November 2002 Fakhravar was sentenced to eight years in prison for this "crime," a decision many in Europe were outraged over. The European Union decided to link improved human rights in Iran with progress in other areas of discussion taking place as part of the Comprehensive Dialogue meetings, including the ongoing negotiations over the TCA.

By the spring of 2003 the issue of human rights in Iran had eroded some of the confidence within the European Union as to the viability of proceeding full-speed with the Comprehensive Dialogue, especially in the context of the TCA. The war in Iraq influenced every aspect of E.U.–U.S. relations, especially in terms of Europe's failure to present a unified position concerning the U.S. decision to invade Iraq. As such, when the United States confronted Europe over Iran at the IAEA PrepCom held in Geneva in May 2003, the Europeans found themselves in a weakened position when it came to standing up to the United States. The best policy posture, it was decided, was to create a European buffer between Iran and the United States, leveraging Europe's ongoing trade negotiations with Iran as a means of compelling Iran to change direction vis-à-vis its nuclear policy.

On June 16, 2003, Mohammed El-Baradei issued his report to the Board of Governors concerning the ongoing investigations in Iran. Based on this report, the IAEA Board of Governors issued its own statement on June 19, which found that Iran had "failed to meet its obligations under its Safeguards Agreement with respect to the reporting of nuclear material, the subsequent processing and use of that material and the declaration of facilities where the material was stored and processed." In this the Board was referring to the nuclear material Iran had received from China, subsequently declared to the IAEA, and presented for inspection. The Board went on: "Although the quantities of nuclear material involved have not been large, and the material would need further processing before being suitable for use as the fissile material component of a nuclear explosive device, the number of failures by Iran to report the material, facilities and activities in question in a timely manner as it is obliged to do pursuant to its Safeguards Agreement is a matter of concern. While these failures are in the process of being rectified by Iran, the process of verifying the correctness and completeness of the Iranian declarations is still ongoing."

Given the acknowledgment by the IAEA that Iran had violated its safeguards agreement, the United States pushed hard to have IAEA declare Iran in violation of the Nuclear Nonproliferation Treaty. The matter could then be sent to the U.N. Security Council for possible action. "Can the IAEA or anyone else be confident under these circumstances that there are no other clandestine facilities that have yet to be revealed?" U.S. Ambassador Kenneth Brill asked the Board during the meeting.

The level of polarization that was taking place between the Iranians and the United States was reflected in the Iranian statement to the Board, in which the Iranian Ambassador, Ali Salehi, admitted the negligence on the part of Iraq in delaying its declaration of a "small amount of nuclear material" which, according to the Iranians, fell far below the inspection threshold set by the IAEA (the Iranian material amounted to 0.13 effective kilograms of uranium-235; the IAEA inspection threshold for uranium-235 was twenty kilograms). The Iranians made note of fifteen other member states that likewise failed to meet the quantity component of the IAEA inspection goal (i.e., failed to declare amounts of material required by the IAEA, and in particular questioned why the "transfer of nuclear shielded ammunition in hundreds of kilograms" had not been reported to the Agency, referring to the use of depleted uranium ammunition by the United States during the invasion of Iraq.

A few days prior to the IAEA Board meeting, U.S. Secretary of Defense Donald Rumsfeld upped the rhetorical ante by publicly declaring the Iranian nuclear program to be affiliated with manufacturing weapons. "The intelligence community in the United States and around the world currently assess that Iran does not have nuclear weapons," Mr. Rumsfeld said during a visit to Germany. "The assessment is that they do have a very active program and are likely to have nuclear weapons in a relatively short period of time."

Rumsfeld went on to add a new dimension to the U.S.–Iranian dynamic, that of Iraq, by accusing Tehran of seeking to infiltrate agents into Iraq for the purpose of undermining the U.S. occupation.

"We're going to actively oppose any Iranian influence in that country that attempts to make Iraq an Iran-type model and we'll do it with words to start with and we'll do it energetically," Rumsfeld said, in a not too veiled threat.

The IAEA Board of Governors was not about to get into a debate between the United States and Iran. It continued to press Iran on the need to sign an Additional Protocol, and welcomed Iran's "reaffirmed commitment to full transparency and expected Iran to grant the Agency all access deemed necessary by the Agency in order to create the necessary confidence in the international community." The Board, noting that the Natanz enrichment plant was now under IAEA safeguards, encouraged Iran, pending the resolution of related outstanding issues, "not to introduce nuclear material" at the pilot enrichment plant, as a "confidence-building measure." The Board also pressed Iran to permit the IAEA access to the Kalaye facility, so that environmental samples could be taken.

Romano Prodi recognized the reality that the European Union was Iran's main trading partner, and that the two had been talking for months about boosting trade and political ties. The E.U.–Iran initiative was still viable, and as such not only distanced the European Union from the United States, which a year ago listed Iran as part of the so-called Axis of Evil, but also created an opening for constructive diplomacy.

The United States and the E.U. leaders held a summit near the end of June, in Washington, D.C., where the United States pressured the European Union to keep Iran from developing nuclear weapons. Underscoring the total lack of dialogue between the United States and Iran on the issue, Romano Prodi reminded President Bush that the European Union was in daily contact with Iran on the issue.

The Bush administration lobbied hard for a strong European Union stance, but in the end had to settle for a more conciliatory joint statement which declared:

> Proliferation of weapons of mass destruction and their delivery systems constitutes a major threat to international peace and security. The threat is compounded by the interest of terrorists in acquiring WMD. This would undermine the foundations of international order. We pledge to use all means available to avert WMD proliferation and the calamities that would follow.

> We express our continuing serious concern at Iran's nuclear program in particular as regards the pursuit of a full nuclear fuel cycle, as announced by President Khatami. We are troubled by the information in the IAEA's report detailing Iran's failures to meet its safeguards obligations and we fully support ongoing investigation by the IAEA to answer the unresolved questions and concerns identified in that report. Iran must cooperate fully with the IAEA, remedy all failures and answer all questions. It must also sign and implement an Additional Protocol, without delay or conditions, as a significant first step toward addressing those concerns.

On June 25, in an act that not only ignored the IAEA's request that all enrichment operations be halted until the full extent of the Iranian nuclear program was understood by the IAEA, but undermined the diplomatic stance taken by the European Union, Iran announced that it had introduced uranium hexafluoride gas into a single centrifuge at the Natanz facility as a test of the operability of the centrifuge. The gas was from the Chinese stockpile purchased in 1991, and now under IAEA safeguards. There was nothing illegal about the Iranian action, since it had been declared to the IAEA and subsequently monitored. However, it sent a strong signal that Iran was not going to back away from its right to develop the full fuel cycle associated with nuclear energy. The move also reinforced in the minds of those who were distrustful of Iran that the Iranian program was nothing more than a weapons program in disguise, and that the Iranians were using diplomacy as a means of buying time while they proceeded with a crash weapons program.

As tensions heightened and rhetoric became more biting, especially in American circles, British Foreign Secretary Jack Straw paid Tehran a visit, his fourth in less than two years. Britain had proven itself to be a staunch ally of the United States on the issue of Iraq, and on matters pertaining to non-proliferation in general. The diplomatic exchange with his Iranian counterparts was sometimes harsh. Straw, during a joint press conference, called on the Iranian government to sign the NPT Additional Protocol "unconditionally" and warned that Iranian–English relations may suffer if it does not. Iranian Foreign Minister Kamal Kharazi bluntly replied in the same press conference that Iran would not make any concessions on the Additional Protocol until the international community made some concessions toward Iran. Despite this, the British Foreign Secretary made it clear that the United Kingdom was not aligning itself with the Axis of Evil doctrine being espoused by the Bush administration. "No one should ever compare Iran with Iraq in terms of their political systems or their danger," he stated. When asked by a reporter, "Do I take it from that that there are no circumstances in which we would agree to an attack on Iran?" Jack Straw replied: "Yes, and I can conceive of no such circumstances."

While Washington, D.C., spoke in terms of veiled threats, it appeared as if the United Kingdom was aligning itself with the European Union on how best to deal with Iran, choosing diplomatic engagement as the tool of first choice. But diplomacy was proving to be a frustrating path. Even Russia, a longtime ally of Iran, was having trouble forcing any concessions from Iran, especially on the issue of an Additional Protocol. In Moscow the Russian Foreign Ministry, following meetings between Foreign Minister Igor Ivanov and the head of the Iranian Atomic Energy Organization, Gholamreza Aghazadeh, noted, "There are plans to sign this protocol in the near future. This has been agreed with Iran." Aghazadeh, however, replied that Iran "is ready to sign the Additional Protocol . . . but only in an atmosphere of transparency and trust regarding the participants of this document."

Clearly, getting Iranian acquiescence on this major issue was not going to be easy.

Events have a way of driving themselves, and the standoff with Iran over its nuclear program was no different. Stymied on the issue of the Additional Protocol, the IAEA continued to press Iran on the issue of gaining access to the Kalaye site for the purpose of conducting environmental sampling. On July 23, 2003, the IAEA received from Iran a letter proposing a timetable for actions to be taken by August 15, 2003, in relation to "urgent outstanding issues," including the matter of Kalaye. The IAEA agreed to send a team of technical experts to Iran in August, and from August 9–12 the team was finally granted access to Kalaye for the purpose of taking environmental samples. The inspectors were disturbed to find that the site had undergone significant alterations since the last visit in May, with floors changed, walls painted, and equipment removed. The IAEA nevertheless took the samples, noting however that the Iranian actions could make moot the ability of the samples to verify their declarations about what had transpired at the facility.

However, the Iranians weren't trying to assist in verification at Kalaye; their task was to eliminate any evidence whatsoever of what had actually transpired there. The stalling tactics they had engaged in since March had bought them enough time, they believed, to sanitize the facility to the point that the IAEA sampling would fail to detect anything suspicious. But by early September, thanks to the work done at the IAEA's Seibersdorf Lab, it became clear that the game was up. Contrary to the Iranian claim that no nuclear material had been handled at Kalaye, the IAEA sampling detected numerous traces of uranium, enriched both at a low level (LEU), and more disturbing, at a high level (HEU).

And it wasn't just Kalaye which was coming up positive for HEU: the PFEP at Natanz, which had been subjected to a series of sampling campaigns between March and June 2003, well before any nuclear material was said by the Iranians to have been introduced, also tested positive, as samples taken from chemical traps during this time period revealed the presence of HEU particles. Additional environmental sampling revealed the presence in Iran of at least two other types of highly enriched uranium, as well as low enriched uranium and natural uranium. Clearly, the Iranian story was no longer holding water. Making matters even more urgent, the Iranians announced on August 19 that they were introducing uranium hexafluoride gas into a small 10-centrifuge cascade as a continuation of their test program leading to a full-scale test of a 164-centrifuge cascade.

When confronted by their inconsistencies, however, the Iranians were quick to try and make amends. Iran maintained that while it had never produced HEU, its story about the origins of its centrifuge program had been incorrect, and that it would seek to set the record straight. Iran also admitted uranium conversion experiments it had conducted during the 1990s, and which should have been declared to the IAEA but had not been. Iran, again, promised to set the record straight on this matter as well. Clearly, Iran was seeking to hide aspects of its program from the IAEA. The question that needed answering revolved around whether the Iranians were shielding information pertaining to the suppliers of the material it was using in its program, aspects of the actual program (such as the enrichment of uranium), or both?

On August 26 Mohammed El-Baradei submitted his report to the IAEA Board of Governors. The IAEA Director General was convinced that the Iranians were on the path toward coming clean, and so did his best to downplay the more spectacular elements of his agency's findings. While pointing out Iran's various shortcomings, El-Baradei concluded:

> Since the last report was issued, Iran has demonstrated an increased degree of cooperation in relation to the amount and detail of information provided to the Agency and in allowing access requested by the Agency to additional locations and the taking of associated environmental samples. The decision by Iran to start the negotiations with the Agency for the conclusion of an Additional Protocol is also a positive step. However, it should be noted that information and access were at times

slow in coming and incremental, and that, as noted above, some of the information was in contrast to that previously provided by Iran. In addition, as also noted above, there remain a number of important outstanding issues, particularly with regard to Iran's enrichment program, that require urgent resolution. Continued and accelerated cooperation and full transparency on the part of Iran are essential for the Agency to be in a position to provide at an early date the assurances required by Member States.

El-Baradei's report frustrated the United States, which believed that the discovery of HEU and LEU samples proved its contention that Iran was pursuing a secret nuclear weapons program. The United States wanted the Iranian case referred to the United Nations Security Council, where Iran could be subjected to crippling economic sanctions or, worse, military action. But El-Baradei's report was void of the kind of inflammatory language that would be required to pursue such a recommendation.

The United States was running out of patience, something that Ambassador Kenneth Brill, in a statement to the IAEA Board of Governors on September 8, 2003, made loud and clear:

"Some have claimed the United States is seeking to 'politicize' the IAEA process," Brill said. "Nothing could be further from the truth."

What we seek to ensure is that the IAEA meets its responsibilities. Finding peaceful resolutions to critical nonproliferation issues means, among other things, that relevant institutions must serve their intended functions. Is it politicization to support the NPT, or to expect NPT signatories to meet their safeguards obligations, as the U.S. is doing? Is it politicization to imply that "cracks" in treaties and unexpected reactions could result from the IAEA pressing for answers to outstanding questions? It is no secret . . . that the United States believes the facts already established would fully justify an immediate finding of non-compliance by Iran with its safeguards violations. We have taken note, however, of the desire of other member states to give Iran a last chance to stop its evasions, and have agreed today to join in the call on Iran to take "essential and urgent" actions to demonstrate that it has done so. Passing a resolution on this issue that firmly backs the IAEA's efforts is the least the Board could credibly do to meet its responsibilities.

On September 12, 2003, the IAEA Board of Governors issued its resolution on Iran. The Board made note of El-Baradei's report, both in terms of where Iran had failed to perform, and where Iran was cooperating, and decided that "it is essential and urgent in order to ensure IAEA verification of non-diversion of nuclear material that Iran remedy all failures identified by the Agency and cooperate fully with the Agency to ensure verification of compliance with Iran's safeguards agreement by taking all necessary actions by the end of October 2003." Iran now had a deadline of October 31 to comply.

The Board also requested that Iran ". . . work with the Secretariat to promptly and unconditionally sign, ratify and fully implement the additional protocol, and, as a confidence-building measure, henceforth to act in accordance with the additional protocol." El-Baradei was instructed to continue his work, and to report back to the Board in November regarding the implementation of this resolution.

As soon as the IAEA Board of Governors adopted the resolution on Iran, the Iranian representatives walked out of the meeting. At a press conference in Vienna, shortly after he stormed out of the IAEA Board's meeting, Iran's Ambassador Salehi iterated the position of his country:

"You can't impose deadlines on a sovereign country," Salehi said. "We will have no choice but to have a deep review of our existing level and extent of engagement with the Agency vis-à-vis this resolution . . . The Western Group in the Board of Governors, in line with their political goals, have made illegitimate, illegal and impractical requests of Iran . . . Even if all the claims on Iran's program's shortcomings are true, they cannot be resolved within the 45 days given to Iran . . . We are dealing with extremist countries not wishing to resolve the issue technically and legally. . . . It is no secret that the current U.S. administration, or at least its influential circle, entertains the idea of invasion of yet another territory, as they aim to re-engineer and reshape the entire Middle East."

In Tehran, hard-line clerics publicly demanded that Iran should ignore the IAEA's resolution and pull out of the NPT. While it seemed unlikely that Iran would take such a harsh measure, the IAEA was again faced with the prospect of a repetition of the North Korea debacle. Pressure needed to be turned up on Iran in order to bring it in line with the requirements set forth by the IAEA.

On September 29, following intense discussions among many E.U. officials, the European Council publicly warned Iran that lucrative trade ties could be jeopardized if Iran failed to submit to IAEA oversight of its nuclear program. The E.U. foreign ministers insisted that Iran accept tough inspections of its facilities as set forth by the Additional Protocol, and refrain altogether from fuel enrichment, which could be used to produce fissile material for nuclear weapons. The European Union had adopted a very hard-line stance, one that was difficult to distinguish from that of the United States, especially in that it sought to ban Iran from doing that which it was permitted under the terms of the NPT, namely the enrichment of uranium for use as a fuel for nuclear energy.

By October 3 the Iranians seemed to come to grips with the reality that they were facing a crisis of confidence when it came to how the world viewed the Iranian nuclear program. In order to deal with this pressing matter, Iran appointed a five-member committee to shape Iran's policy regarding the IAEA's deadline. The members selected were Foreign Minister Kamal Kharrazi, Minister of Information Ali Yunessi, Defense Minister Ali Shamkhani, Secretary of the High National Security Council Hassan Rowhani, and the supreme religious leader's (the Ayatollah Khomeini) adviser for international affairs, Ali Velayati.

Soon the committee was put to the test. Acting on yet another NCRI press conference (this one delivered by Alireza Jafarzadeh back on July 8, 2003), an IAEA inspection team requested to carry out a short-notice inspection on October 5 of the Kolahdouz military base in Iran. According to Jafarzadeh, the Kolahdouz facility represented the military side of Iran's nuclear program. As per the usual methodology when it came to information of this sort, according to sources familiar with the information, the Israeli intelligence services had provided the IAEA inspectors with detailed information about the site. The hope had been that the IAEA would have inspected this facility back in July, shortly after the NCRI went public with the data.

However, the Kalaye facility standoff had dominated the IAEA's agenda, and following that, the September Board of Governor's meeting. The IAEA was confident that given its advanced technological capabilities to detect radiation, now field tested at Natanz and Kalaye, if the Iranians had indeed carried out any nuclear-related activity at Kolahdouz, it would be detected. The Kolahdouz facility turned out to be very sensitive indeed, related to the manufacture and maintenance of military equipment for the Iranian armed forces. But no traces of uranium enrichment or other nuclear activity were found by the IAEA.

The inspection of the Kolahdouz facility provoked a cry of outrage on the part of Iran's Secretary of the Supreme National Security Council, Hassan Rowhani, a member of the committee overseeing Iran's policy formulation regarding cooperation with the IAEA. On October 7 Rowhani protested what he labeled the United States' abuse of the IAEA and biased actions toward Iran. "This is the worst kind of interference in international law and order when a specialized United Nations agency and its legal authority are exploited for political objective of the United States," Rowhani said, speaking to religious leaders from across the country.

But Rowhani's anger couldn't stop the irrepressible NCRI which, back in Washington, D.C., held yet another press conference that very same day. The subject this time was an alleged secret centrifuge test facility located outside the Iranian city of Isfahan. While again the NCRI representative, Jafarzadeh, provided very specific information about the location, personnel and activity of the suspect site (again, courtesy of Tel Aviv), this time the rhetoric associated with the release of the data likewise seemed to have been dictated by forces either in Washington, D.C., Tel Aviv, or both. "This information," Jafarzadeh said, "again reveals an extensive and clandestine program pursued by the clerical regime to acquire nuclear weapons as a strategic weapons need for the survival of the regime and its regional domination in the sensitive Persian Gulf region." He continued:

> The Iranian regime is sparing no effort to procrastinate and buy time to go beyond the point of no return in its drive to acquire the capability to produce nuclear weapons.

At present, the regime is engaged in a delay tactic in response to IAEA's October 31 deadline. Khatami said a few days ago that even if the government were to accept to sign onto the Additional Protocol, the Majlis and the Guardian Council must also approve that decision. This means that while Tehran is unwilling to abide by its international obligations, it has engaged in these maneuvers to reduce international pressure.

The clerics view nuclear weapons as strategic guarantee for their survival. They believe that once they acquire the bomb, they would have freer rein to export terrorism and Islamic Revolution as nobody would be in a position to challenge them.

The fact is that the Iranian regime has acknowledged bits and pieces of its nuclear program only after revelations by the Iranian Resistance. It is continuing to conceal its nuclear program, which clearly contradicts the claims that its nuclear program is peaceful.

The only way to prevent the world from having to deal with the nightmare of a nuclear-equipped fundamentalist regime is for the U.N. Security Council to dismiss the regime's ploys and impose binding and comprehensive sanctions against this medieval regime.

The NCRI information only served to heighten the growing tension surrounding Iran and its nuclear program. Despite Iran's willingness to allow snap inspections of sensitive military facilities, the IAEA was still flustered by the lack of information being made available by the Iranians concerning the overall uranium enrichment effort. There were still considerable gaps and inconsistencies in the Iranian story that the IAEA needed to fill in and/or investigate. The lack of any comprehensive disclosure by Iran frustrated Mohammed El-Baradei to the extent that he finally spoke out publicly on October 9, stating that Iran ". . . has promised information will be forthcoming but it has not yet been provided. The central question is whether Iran has any enrichment activities that we have not been informed about. On that question I haven't got satisfactory information."

With the October 31 deadline rapidly approaching, the Iranian committee on dealing with the IAEA wrestled with the reality that they had not been completely forthcoming about the history of Iran's nuclear program. On the critical issue Iran had been very consistent: the Iranian nuclear program was for peaceful purposes only, relating to the strategic need of Iran to develop nuclear energy as an alternative to diminishing oil production capacity anticipated over the course of the next few decades. However, the effects of U.S. sanctions, combined with an overall hostile atmosphere when it came to international trade (especially on such sensitive issues as the acquisition of nuclear technology) had driven Iran into the black market in order to acquire what it needed to move forward on the full scope of its nuclear energy ambitions, which were inclusive of the complete nuclear fuel cycle. This flirtation with the black market had resulted in Iran circumventing its obligations under the NPT on many levels, something it would now have to admit if Iran was to be able to comply with the demands of the IAEA's September resolution.

On October 13 a new round of IAEA inspections, led by Pierre Goldschmidt and Olli Heinonen, got under way. Once again the Iranians had to grit their teeth as the IAEA sought to act on the briefings provided by the NCRI, in this case an inspection of the Isfahan facility, and other locations around Tehran. The IAEA team also continued its safeguard inspections of Natanz and Kalaye, including follow-up activities related to the issue of the HEU and LEU traces that had been detected at thee locations.

On October 16, the Iranians decided to come clean. The IAEA committee determined that it could no longer hide the reality of its past activities, and invited Mohammed El-Baradei to come to Tehran and receive their confession. El-Baradei met with the Secretary of the Supreme National Security Council, Hassan Rowhani. What Rowhani had to tell El-Baradei confirmed that which the IAEA had suspected all along: that Iran had used nuclear material, uranium hexafluoride, to test its centrifuges at the Kalaye facility as a precursor step to installing a cascade system at Natanz. Rowhani promised that Iran would provide the IAEA with a full disclosure of Iran's past and present nuclear activities, as well as conclude an Additional Protocol with the IAEA. Rowhani stated that Iran would, pending the entry into force of the Additional Protocol, act in accordance with the protocol and in keeping with the new policy of full transparency.

The Iranians followed up on the October 16 meeting by providing the IAEA a letter, dated October 21, from the head of the Atomic Energy Organization of Iran, Gholamreza Aghazadeh, which acknowledged that Iran had, between 1998 and 2002, carried out testing of centrifuges at Kalaye using uranium hexafluoride imported from China in 1991. These tests accounted for the 1.9 kilograms of uranium hexafluoride that was missing from the Chinese stocks, which the Iranians had earlier claimed had leaked out due to faulty valves. The Iranian tests at Kalaye resulted in the production of small quantities of uranium enriched to 1.2 percent levels. However, this admission did not explain the presence of HEU and LEU traces detected at Natanz and Kalaye which differed from the 1.2 percent LEU the Iranians now acknowledged making.

To counter the IAEA suspicions, Iran claimed that the HEU and LEU contamination had come into the country via imported centrifuges and related enrichment equipment. Despite their policy of complete transparency, the Iranians claimed not to know the original source of the centrifuges. The IAEA requested from Iran a list of all imported and domestically produced centrifuge components, material and equipment, together with an indication as to which batches of equipment Iran claimed to be the source of the contamination.

Armed with this information, the IAEA carried out a detailed environmental sampling campaign at the end of October, at which time all major imported and domestically produced components, as well as various pieces of manufacturing equipment, were sampled. The IAEA was able to test the actual centrifuges used by Iran during the enrichment tests, despite the fact that Iran had originally declared that these centrifuges had been scrapped. It turned out that the Iranians had stored the centrifuges elsewhere in Tehran, and then transported them to Natanz.

Once again the Iranians found themselves on the receiving end of intelligence information provided to the IAEA by Israel, and made public by the NCRI. Back in May 2003, the NCRI had provided a press conference in which it described undeclared "nuclear sites at a large agricultural location" near the village of Lashkar Ab'ad. The IAEA, briefed in full about the Lashkar Ab'ad site by Israeli intelligence, requested Iran to permit environmental sampling at Lashkar Ab'ad back in August 2003. Finally, in early October, the IAEA inspectors were granted access. Inspectors were also shown warehouses in the Karaj Agricultural and Medical Center of the AEOI.

Lashkar Ab'ad turned out to be the location of a pilot plant for the enrichment of uranium using lasers, and had been established since 2000. Uranium enrichment experiments using lasers had been conducted at Lashkar Ab'ad between October 2002 and May 2003 using uranium metal. The experiments made use of 50 kilograms of natural uranium metal, which was imported by Iran in 1993. The equipment was able to enrich uranium up to the contracted level of 3 percent U-235, and even slightly beyond, in the course of the experiments. The pilot plant, together with the uranium metal, was disassembled and taken to the storage facilities located at Karaj. The activities related to the enrichment of uranium using lasers should have been declared to the IAEA under the safeguards agreement, and had not been. Iran promised to provide the IAEA will all information and access required to clarify this aspect of the Iranian nuclear program.

In the atmosphere of these dramatic revelations, the tension between Iran and Israel was ratcheted up considerably when, on October 11, the Israeli government leaked information to the press, through its intelligence service, the Mossad, about plans being drawn up for a pre-emptive attack by Israel on Iran's alleged nuclear weapons programs.

The Iranian government responded to these reports by noting, through a spokesperson, that Iran was ". . . used to such foolish rhetoric from Israel and consider it not even worth replying, but still Israel knows not to mess around with us."

Israel had picked an odd time to interject in such a dramatic and disruptive manner. Things were going well between the IAEA and Iran, perhaps too well for the Israelis' liking. Israel had hoped that the United States would have been able to manage the Iranian issue in a manner which resulted in the total eradication of the Iranian nuclear enrichment program, a step Israel deemed necessary to guarantee that Iran never acquire even the capacity to manufacture nuclear weapons. But the United States found itself distracted by events to the west of Iran, in Iraq.

The United States, desperate to achieve a semblance of international legitimacy for what was quickly becoming a nightmarish occupation, was scrambling at the U.N. Security Council to sway members to vote in favor of a resolution that would legitimize the occupation and the Interim Iraqi Governing Council. The U.S. had sought and gained compromise language from Russia, China, and Pakistan, and was looking for Russia to smooth over ruffled feathers that still existed with the French and Germans. The last thing the United States needed was to force a confrontation on Iran that would further alienate "old Europe," and risk losing the Russians and Chinese as well. David Kay, the former U.N. weapons inspector-turned CIA weapons sleuth in Iraq, had submitted a report to the U.S. Congress that underscored the fallibility of the Bush administration's case for war, namely the existence of weapons of mass destruction in Iraq. American soldiers continued to die in Iraq, the mission seemed far from accomplished, and no weapons were being discovered. American credibility was sinking fast, and as such October was not the time to push for another confrontation in the Middle East. The Security Council resolution was passed unanimously on October 16, but the United States still needed to tread lightly.

Into this void created by the distractions of Iraq on the United States stepped the European Union, or more specifically, what was to be known as the EU-3—the troika of Britain, France and Germany. Taking advantage of the opening created by the October 16 decision by Hassan Rowhani to "come clean" on Iran's nuclear program, and to move forward toward signing an Additional Protocol, the Foreign Ministers of Britain, France, and Germany flew to Tehran to help navigate Iran toward finalizing an agreement on bringing into force an Additional Protocol.

This led, on October 21, to what became known as the Tehran Declaration, where Iran capitulated to the IAEA demands put forward in its September resolution. According to the joint statement released after the agreement was concluded, Iran ". . . agreed on measures aimed at the settlement of all outstanding IAEA [International Atomic Energy Agency] issues with regards to the Iranian nuclear program and at enhancing confidence for peaceful cooperation in the nuclear field," and promised ". . . to engage in full cooperation with the IAEA to address and resolve through full transparency all requirements and outstanding issues of the Agency and clarify and correct any possible failures and deficiencies within the IAEA."

The Iranians, ". . . having received the necessary clarifications," declared their intent ". . . to sign the IAEA Additional Protocol and commence ratification procedures. As a confirmation of its good intentions the Iranian government will continue to cooperate with the Agency in accordance with the Protocol in advance of its ratification." Importantly, Iran noted that while it ". . . has a right within the nuclear non-proliferation regime to develop nuclear energy for peaceful purposes it has decided voluntarily to suspend all uranium enrichment and reprocessing activities as defined by the IAEA."

The EU-3, in its turn, ". . . welcomed the decisions of the Iranian government," and recognized ". . . the right of Iran to enjoy peaceful use of nuclear energy in accordance with the nuclear Non-Proliferation Treaty." The EU-3 acknowledged that the ". . . Additional Protocol is in no way intended to undermine the sovereignty, national dignity or national security of its State Parties," and that the Iranian decisions to cooperate should clear the way for the "immediate situation" to be resolved by the IAEA Board. The EU-3 stated that they believed the Iranian cooperation would ". . . open the way to a dialogue on a basis for longer term cooperation which will provide all parties with satisfactory assurances relating to Iran's nuclear power generation program." The EU-3 noted that "Once international concerns, including those of the three governments, are fully resolved Iran could expect easier access to modern technology and supplies in a range of areas."

This was a tremendously important document, one that fundamentally placed the European Union, through the commitments made by the EU-3, at odds with the United States. The EU-3 had basically acknowledged Iran's rights under Article IV of the NPT, and promised to help facilitate Iran's access to the technologies needed to bring its nuclear energy program to fruition.

Despite the breakthrough achieved by the October 21 Tehran Declaration tensions still ran high. The United States fretted over Iran's lack of information supplied regarding traces of highly enriched uranium, and warned that it may lead to a declaration of a violation of the NPT if not cleared up by the November 20 IAEA Board of Governors meeting. Once back home in Europe, the EU-3 quickly came under pressure from the United States concerning the scope of its agreement with Iran. To counter this, the EU-3 foreign ministers urged Iran to meet its pledge to stop uranium enrichment and allow inspections of its nuclear program, expressing concern that Iran had still not set solid dates for these steps.

The Iranians, ever sensitive to any sign of backtracking, picked up on the subtle change in the EU-3 position. On October 28 the Iranian president Khatami reminded the EU-3 that they needed to stick by their original commitment to help Iran acquire nuclear technology for peaceful purposes, regardless of the pressure being brought to bear by the United States.

On October 31, the date of the deadline set by the IAEA Board of Directors in its September resolution, a senior Iranian cleric, Ayatollah Ahmad Jannati, stated that although Iran had agreed to sign the additional protocol, ". . . Our 'red lines' still exist," adding that "If the European party fails to live up to its commitments, the commitments that we made should be in return regarded as canceled."

On October 31, in an inspection of the PFEP facility at Natanz, IAEA inspectors observed that no UF6 gas was being fed into the 164-machine cascade that had been installed there, but that construction and installation work continued. This observation created a controversy of sorts as to what actually defined Iran's ceasing all enrichment activities as required by the IAEA. The Iranians contend that the fact they had stopped inserting uranium hexafluoride into the centrifuges in and of itself constituted the cessation of enrichment activity. However, the IAEA held that the ongoing assembly and construction of centrifuge cascades at Natanz likewise constituted activities related to enrichment, and as such must be halted if Iran were to be in compliance with its obligations. Complicating the discussions about what constituted enrichment cessation was the public release by the CIA, in a report to Congress on November 7, of a U.S. intelligence assessment that held that Iran had vigorously pursued nuclear weapons production activities in the first half of 2003.

According to the CIA, the United States ". . . remains convinced that Tehran has been pursuing a clandestine nuclear weapons program." The absurdity of the CIA position was underscored by the fact that the CIA claimed that its satellites showed Iran actively trying to bury the centrifuge enrichment facility at Natanz, despite the fact that this facility was under the total monitoring of IAEA inspectors, who reported back that the Natanz plant was still very much under construction, and engaged in no activity whatsoever. Members of Congress who received the CIA briefing were alarmed at what they had been told. Clearly, the lessons of Iraq had not yet sunk in.

The CIA's report was timed to pre-empt a November 8 meeting in Vienna between Hassan Rowhani and Mohammed El-Baradei, in which the Iranians and the IAEA worked toward the signing of the Additional Protocol and reaching a precise definition of what constituted the cessation of nuclear enrichment activities by Iran. At the end of October, El-Baradei had written a letter to Iran in an attempt to clearly define the activities that required suspension. The first request, apparently undisputed, involves putting a stop to testing or operating gas centrifuges, a halt to the installation of centrifuges at Natanz, and ceasing all laser enrichment and plutonium reprocessing activities. However, the Iranians appeared to balk at El-Baradei's contention that Iran must likewise cease the production and assembly of centrifuges or centrifuge components at locations in Iran other than at Natanz, and that Iran must halt equipment imports relevant to the program.

In the face of all of this turmoil, Mohammed El-Baradei released his report on the status of the IAEA's investigations into Iran's nuclear programs to the IAEA Board of Governors on November 10. In this report, which provided an exhaustive look into the minutia of Iran's nuclear programs, El-Baradei concluded, "The recent disclosures by Iran about its nuclear program clearly show that, in the past, Iran had concealed many aspects of its nuclear activities, with resultant breaches of its obligation to comply with the provisions of the Safeguards Agreement. Iran's policy of concealment," El-Baradei wrote, "continued until last month, with cooperation being limited and reactive, and information being slow in coming, changing and contradictory." He went on:

While most of the breaches identified to date have involved limited quantities of nuclear material, they have dealt with the most sensitive aspects of the nuclear fuel cycle, including enrichment and reprocessing. And although the materials would require further processing before being suitable for weapons purposes, the number of failures by Iran to report in a timely manner the material, facilities and activities in question as it is obliged to do pursuant to its Safeguards Agreement has given rise to serious concerns.

To date, there is no evidence that the previously undeclared nuclear material and activities . . . were related to a nuclear weapons program. However, given Iran's past pattern of concealment, it will take some time before the agency is able to conclude that Iran's nuclear program is exclusively for peaceful purposes.

Iran's President Khatami, responding to the IAEA report, stated that the report proved Iran's innocence regarding its alleged nuclear weapons program, noting that "Iran will never go to enrichment of uranium over the 3.5 percent [mark] which is weapons-grade," and that the Iranians ". . . understand the world's concern in this respect."

The Iranians moved quickly to comply with their obligation to shut down their enrichment efforts. On November 10, 2003 Iran announced that it had decided to suspend all enrichment and reprocessing activities. On November 12, all centrifuges located in the cascade hall of the PFEP were shut down, and the feed cylinders removed. IAEA seals were applied to all enrichment equipment, and all uranium hexafluoride stocks were likewise placed under seal by the inspectors.

In the mindset of the Iranians, they were doing everything possible to comply with the demands of the IAEA, all the while preserving their right under the NPT to possess the full range of nuclear technologies relating to energy production. In discussions between the European Union and the Iranian Foreign Minister, Kharazzi, held on November 12, the Iranians reiterated their point of view that the IAEA's report proved Iran's lack of a nuclear weapons program. The European Union President, Italian Foreign Minister Franco Frattini, praised the Iranian progress toward transparency on its nuclear program, which had encouraged the European Union to cooperate with Iran on a variety of issues, including its nuclear program.

Under pressure from the United States, however, the EU-3 waffled, stating that it was not clear in their minds that Iran had fully responded to the requirements of the IAEA, noting that despite Iran's statement regarding temporary cessation of uranium enrichment activity, the Iranian definition of enrichment may be too narrow. The U.S. Undersecretary of State for Arms Control, John Bolton, dismissed the IAEA's report on Iran, saying that it was "impossible to believe." The report, according to Bolton, underscored the U.S. position that Iran was engaged in a "massive and covert" effort to acquire nuclear weapons.

Echoing the U.S. position, the head of Israel's Mossad stated that Iran was close to the "point of no return" on its nuclear weapons program, and that this program represented the greatest threat to the security of Israel since its inception. The fact that the IAEA, based upon some of the most intrusive inspections in the history of nuclear arms control, had determined that there was no nuclear weapons program in Iran was irrelevant. Both Bolton and the Mossad Chief were playing the game of perceptions, not reality. Both were pushing for Iran to be referred by the IAEA to the U.N. Security Council, where the United States would seek to put the nails in the coffin of the Iranian nuclear program once and for all.

Countering the U.S.–Israeli position, the E.U. Foreign Policy Chief Javier Solana said on November 7 that Iran had been honest about its nuclear program, and should not be reported to the U.N. Security Council for potential sanctions. The European Union, given its role in bringing about the Tehran Declaration, had taken the lead on drafting the IAEA Board's November resolution. U.S. Secretary of State Colin Powell called Solana's evaluation "premature," and on November 18 met with twenty-five current and future E.U. members in Brussels to discuss whether Iran's nuclear program should be declared in violation of the NPT. Powell failed to persuade his counterparts on this matter, and the next day, November 19, the E.U. foreign ministers reaffirmed Europe's commitment to the October 21 Tehran Declaration, and looked forward to Iran's prompt and full implementation of that agreement.

On November 20–21 the thirty-five-nation IAEA Board of Governors considered the recent IAEA report on Iran, and the E.U. draft resolution. The United States and Israel urged the European Union to adopt a tougher stance against the Iranians in order to rein in the nuclear ambitions of Tehran. However, in the face of European unity on the matter, the United States was compelled to drop its insistence that Iran be found in non-compliance with the NPT, and as such ended any chance of the Iranian case being referred to the Security Council. The Israelis responded to this news by having Israel's Defense Minister, the Iranian-born Shaul Mofaz, again emphasize Israel's intent to undertake unilateral military action toward Iran if the IAEA failed to halt Iran's nuclear weapons development.

On November 24, the U.S., France, Germany, and Britain finally agreed on tougher language for an IAEA resolution that condemned Iran for hiding its nuclear program in the past, but at the same time encouraged its new policy of honesty. The thirty-five-member board of the IAEA agreed on November 26 on a resolution that condemned the Iranian clandestine nuclear program, but refrained from reporting it to the U.N. Security Council where it could face sanctions. The head of the IAEA, El-Baradei, said any future failure to comply on the part of Iran would not be tolerated.

The IAEA's resolution strongly deplored Iran's past failures and breaches of its obligations to comply with the provisions of its Safeguards Agreement, and decided that should any "further serious failures come to light," it would meet immediately to consider "in the light of the circumstances and of advice from the Director General, all options at its disposal, in accordance with the IAEA Statute and Iran's Safeguards Agreement."

The IAEA also recognized Iran's decisions to conclude an Additional Protocol and to voluntarily suspend all enrichment and reprocessing activities. The Board pushed for Iran to move "swiftly to ratification" of the Protocol, and requested that Iran suspend all of its enrichment-related activities in a "complete and verifiable manner." The language of the Board's resolution on this matter was critical—in requesting, and not demanding, Iranian cooperation on the issue of cessation of enrichment activity, the Board recognized that Iran had the right to enrich. However, this right seemed to get swept aside given the emphasis placed on complete cessation of all enrichment.

Even the Board's referral to the October 21 Tehran Declaration (or as the Board referred to it, the Agreed Statement) between the Foreign Ministers of France, Germany, and the United Kingdom and the Secretary of the Iranian Supreme National Security Council was a way of welcoming Iran's concurrence to sign the Additional Protocol and to suspend its uranium enrichment activities, and not the EU-3's commitments to respect Iran's right to pursue peaceful nuclear technology, or its promise to help Iran acquire nuclear technology.

The IAEA's resolution seemed to have something in it for everyone. Europe, especially the EU-3, took the lion's share of the credit not only for drafting the resolution, but also facilitating the October 21 Tehran Declaration that made it all possible.

The United States, while stymied in its effort to get Iran referred to the Security Council, also saw a silver lining. Secretary of State Colin Powell, commenting afterward, pointed out that the IAEA resolution "notes that Iran has been in breach of obligations," and highlighted the fact that "there is one particular paragraph in the resolution which makes it very, very clear that if Iran does not now comply with obligations and the other agreements it's entered into, then this will be a matter that will be immediately referred to the IAEA Board of Governors for action, as appropriate under the various statutes." The United States had not given up on its campaign to get the Iranian case moved to the U.N. Security Council. Colin Powell had left no doubt that this was the ultimate end game for U.S. policy regarding Iran.

The Iranian Ambassador to the IAEA noted that while the resolution offset attempts "to create a crisis about Iran's peaceful nuclear program," and that the report focused "disproportionately on the past" and "did not fully and distinctly reflect the turn of policy and action in Iran on the 21st of October," the resolution proved Iran's point that it did not have a nuclear weapons program.

For Mohammed El-Baradei, the beleaguered IAEA Director General, the Board's resolution marked "a good day for peace, multilateralism and non-proliferation." However, El-Baradei knew that much work remained in the field of verification before Iran's nuclear program could be certified as exclusively peaceful in nature. In this, El-Baradei placed the burden of responsibility firmly on the shoulders of Iran.

But El-Baradei was wrong. The burden was not Iran's exclusively. The much-heralded October 21 Tehran Declaration required certain commitments from the European Union regarding Iran's rights afforded by the NPT, and facilitating Iran's peaceful pursuit of nuclear energy. In the rush to a resolution, these commitments seemed to be thrown to the side, never referred to by any party except Iran. On December 8 this uncomfortable fact was pointed out by the Iranian Foreign Minsitry, which noted that although uranium enrichment is within Iran's rights, and a total cessation of enrichment was not part of the Tehran Declaration, Iran would prove its goodwill by volunteering to temporarily suspend its enrichment activities. But this was only a temporary measure, in place until which time the IAEA had certified Iran's peaceful intent, and the EU-3 delivered on its promise of political and material support.

On December 10, after much debate, the Iranian government agreed to sign an Additional Protocol binding it to snap inspections of its nuclear facilities. The Foreign Ministry of Iran was given permission by the Iranian cabinet to instruct the Iranian ambassador to the IAEA to sign the Additional Protocol to the NPT. Final entry into force would be dependent upon the Iranian Parliament ratifying the bill, but the Iranians made it clear that they would implement the Additional Protocol in the interim as if it were already in force. The actual agreement was signed in Vienna on December 18, 2003, between Ambassador Salehi of Iran and Director General Mohammed El-Baradei. After the struggle and drama of the past eleven months, the signature ceremony passed with little attention from the rest of the world.

As if to underscore the incomplete nature of the IAEA–Iranian accord, Israel again threatened to take action against Iran's nuclear facilities, prompting Iran's president, Khatami, to reply that Israel would be making a huge mistake if it bombed Iran. The Iranian Air Force Commander, General Seved Reza Pardis, noted that should Israel attack Iran, it would be "digging its own grave."

The rumblings of political discontent soon gave way to the real rumblings of the earth when, on December 26, 2003, a magnitude 6.6 earthquake struck the Iranian city of Bam. Anywhere between 31,000 to 43,000 lives were lost out of a population of about 142,000 in Bam and surrounding areas; the surviving inhabitants were rendered homeless. Talk of a military strike gave way to the reality of military flights being used to dispatch international aid. Even the United States buried the sword, so to speak. On December 30, 2003 an eighty-one-member emergency response team comprising search and rescue specialists, medical support personnel, and humanitarian aid coordinators, flew into Iran aboard U.S. military aircraft. For a moment in time it appeared as if human compassion could triumph over political differences as Americans and Iranians worked side by side in a common cause.

But it was not to be.

Four
The Rational Actor

ON MARCH 9, 2004, RUSSIAN President Vladimir Putin appointed the veteran diplomat Sergei Lavrov as the Minister for Foreign Affairs, replacing Igor Ivanov. Ivanov was appointed as the Secretary of the Russian National Security Council. Prior to his appointment, Lavrov had served for ten years as the Permanent Representative of Russia to the United Nations, during which time he managed from the Russian perspective such crises as the breakup of Yugoslavia and Iraq.

Born in 1950, Lavrov graduated from the Moscow State Institute of International Relations before starting his career as a junior staffer at the Soviet Embassy in Sri Lanka 1972. From that posting Lavrov moved on to the field of international organizations, or the United Nations, working in turn the Soviet end of the problem from Moscow as a member of the Department of International Organizations within the Ministry of Foreign Affairs (MFA) from 1976 to 1981, and then as the First Secretary to the Soviet Mission at the United Nations in New York, from 1981 to 1988. From 1988 to 1992 Lavrov served in positions of increasing responsibility within the MFA, before being appointed as the Deputy Minister of Foreign Affairs of the Russian Federation in 1992.

Sergei Lavrov understood the United Nations, international law, and more importantly the reality of the role played by the five permanent members of the Security Council in overseeing issues pertaining to international peace and security. As a veteran diplomat whose career successfully straddled service in the Ministry of Foreign Affairs of both the former Soviet Union and the present-day Russian Federation, Lavrov had extensive first-hand experience in managing the delicate balance between national interests, global interests, and the interests manifested through being a veto-wielding member of an elite power-center, the Security Council, which in addition to the above-mentioned responsibilities, had its own vested interests to protect.

Iran would come to be the issue that would dominate the first years of Sergei Lavrov's tenure as Minister of Foreign Affairs, just as Iraq had dominated his time as the Permanent Representative to the United Nations. And it was this Iraq experience that colored much of Lavrov's perspectives regarding the interaction between Russia, the United States and the United Nations.

Lavrov became the Russian Ambassador to the United Nations in 1994, at a time when the issue of economic sanctions and Iraq was being strongly debated. In the ongoing struggle between U.N. weapons inspectors and the government of Iraq, the people of Iraq were paying the price. Russia, which initially supported the work of the inspectors in Iraq, believed that the sanctions regime had gone on far too long, and that with U.N. inspectors speaking of moving toward a monitoring phase of their work (as opposed to engaging in an active search for proscribed weapons), the time had come to ease the burden placed on the Iraqi people back in August 1990, when the comprehensive economic sanctions were first imposed.

The Russians worked to bring about the so-called Oil for Food program, where Iraq was permitted to sell its oil and, under U.N. supervision, use the proceeds to procure food, medicine, and other humanitarian relief supplies. The Russians worked with the United States to help craft compromise after compromise, all in an effort to ease the burden of sanctions on the Iraqi people while seeking to compel the government of Saddam Hussein to more fully cooperate with U.N. inspectors and as such comply with its obligation to disarm.

However, by 1997 it had become apparent to Lavrov and the Russians that the United States had no intention of ever lifting the U.N. sanctions against Saddam Hussein's regime, at least not until which time the Iraqi dictator was removed from power. The Russian Ambassador watched in frustration as the U.N. weapons inspection process was hijacked by the United States as a facilitator for the continuation of economic sanctions against Iraq, and then as the weapons inspection process itself was used as justification for the initiation of military action against Iraq, first in December 1998, as part of Operation Desert Fox, and again in March 2003, as part of Operation Iraqi Freedom. The 2003 war was a bitter pill for Lavrov, as he had invested a significant amount of time and personal prestige in trying to avert war through effective diplomacy as carried out within the framework of the United Nations, only to watch the United States mock both the United Nations and Russia by invading Iraq void of any justification or legitimacy brought on by U.N. Security Council concurrence.

As the war in Iraq turned into the occupation of Iraq, and the United States increasingly turned its sights on Iran, Sergei Lavrov had reason to be concerned; to him, the situation vis-à-vis Iran seemed like déjà vu, with the United States engaging in the same pattern of deceit and abuse of power in an effort to implement a unilateral policy of global hegemony under the smokescreen of disarmament. Russia held that there could be no talk of imposing economic sanctions against Iran, and that war was simply out of the question. As long as the Iranian issue could be contained within the framework of the IAEA in Vienna, as opposed to the Security Council chambers in New York, Russia believed that it could forestall any bold moves by the United States against Iran. This was to be Lavrov's task.

Lavrov's appointment came at a critical juncture in the ongoing effort by the IAEA to come to grips with the scope and intent of the Iranian nuclear program. Within a week of his taking the helm at the Russian Ministry of Foreign Affairs, Lavrov had to confront an emerging crisis with Iran over an IAEA Board of Governors' resolution issued on March 16. The IAEA expressed great concern over what it deemed to be a lack of transparency on the part of Iran on a number of issues, first and foremost of which were new revelations about a new generation of gas centrifuges used in the enrichment of uranium, the so-called P-2. Like almost every aspect of the Iranian-IAEA relationship, the P-2 program was complicated, especially considering that its roots lay not in the ongoing IAEA investigation in Iran, but thousands of miles away, in the Mediterranean waters off the coast of Libya.

On December 19, 2003, the government of Libya announced its decision to eliminate all materials, equipment and programs leading to the production of internationally proscribed weapons—including nuclear weapons. The official Libyan announcement proclaimed that Libya had been working with the CIA and MI-6 over the course of several years in order to reach an agreement about how best to proceed with turning over Libya's WMD programs. While the Libyan announcement noted that the current cooperation dated back to March 2003, and had been formalized in September 2003, it hinted at the reality that Libya had been working hand in glove with the U.S. and British intelligence services for many years prior to that time.

According to a European intelligence official, Libya had in fact initially agreed to turn over to the United States and the British its decrepit chemical warfare program, and nascent biological weapons program, neither of which remained viable. Libya, as part of an overall framework developed in the aftermath of the Lockerbie airline explosion in 1988, had cooperated with the investigation of that act of terrorism, and agreed to enter into various arms control and non-proliferation agreements, in exchange for a lifting of economic sanctions and the welcoming of Libya by the United States and Great Britain back into the fold of the international community.

But the CIA and MI-6 had bigger fish to catch. The United States wanted Libya to time the announcement of its new stance so that the Bush administration could make a public link between Libya's "surrender" and the American decision to move against Iraq. According to the thinking in the Bush administration White House, linking Libya with Iraq would create the weapons of mass destruction tie-in with the decision to invade, even if no WMD were discovered in Iraq.

But the British intelligence services had an even grander scheme in mind. They wanted to take advantage of the new-found Libyan willingness to cooperate in order to set up a sting operation that would bring down an even larger threat than aged Libyan WMD programs. The target was the father of the Pakistani nuclear bomb, A. Q. Khan, and the Pakistani nuclear weapons industry, which had for some time been involved in illicit trafficking of nuclear-enrichment technologies, and even nuclear weapons-related designs, to other nations.

Rumors of the involvement of A. Q. Khan in selling nuclear enrichment and nuclear weapons technology and information had been circulating among the intelligence services of the world for some time. In 1995, in the aftermath of the defection of Saddam Hussein's son-in-law, Hussein Kamal, to Jordan, when the Iraqi government turned over to U.N. weapons inspectors hundreds of thousands of pages of documents and drawings concerning its past proscribed weapons programs, one of the documents received by the inspectors dealt with an approach made by A. Q. Khan to Iraq in 1989 to sell to Iraq technology and information related to the manufacture of highly enriched uranium and a nuclear device.

A. Q. Khan used as bait some highly technical information concerning a weapons-only related matter which, he thought, proved his bona fides. According to Iraqi government documents concerning this approach, which were included in the files turned over to the U.N. weapons inspectors, the Iraqi Intelligence Service, or Mukhabarat, which had received the original approach from A. Q. Khan, viewed the approach as being part of a Western sting operation, and instructed all of its offices to avoid any interaction with the A. Q. Khan network.

The IAEA, which was responsible for the assessment of all nuclear-related activity in Iraq, turned over the entire cache of documents to Israeli intelligence for further evaluation. The Israelis felt that the involvement of A. Q. Khan was quite real, but noted that the Iraqis did not appear to enter into any arrangement. Indeed, in discussions with the Iraqis, U.N. weapons inspectors also came to the conclusion that the A. Q. Khan approach never materialized into anything real.

But what shocked the Israelis was the fact A. Q. Khan was shopping not just nuclear enrichment technology on the black market, but also nuclear weapons design information. The design information provided to the Iraqis was associated with the proper functioning of an implosion devise, and represented a level of understanding which could have cut months, if not years, off of any Iraqi bomb program, given the fact that usually a number of tests were required before this particular level of technical understanding was reached.

The Israelis shared their concerns with the British and Americans, and all three parties agreed that the A. Q. Khan activity was a top target in terms of intelligence and interdiction. The Israelis also worked closely with German intelligence on this matter. The Germans had a long history of close cooperation with the Israelis on intelligence matters, especially technical intelligence. This included joint exploitation of Soviet-bloc military equipment as well as assistance in uncovering efforts by nations hostile to Israel to acquire technology which could be used in manufacturing WMD. German companies had been deeply involved in assisting Saddam Hussein's Iraq when it came to WMD. Germany had been especially embarrassed when it became clear that German companies had facilitated the Iraqi efforts to extend the range of its SCUD missiles. Some forty-one modified SCUD missiles were fired by Iraq against Israel during the 1991 Gulf War. Many of these missiles carried German-made parts, or were manufactured using German machine tools and technical know-how.

In the aftermath of the 1991 Gulf War, and in concert with U.N. weapons inspectors, the Germans carried out extensive investigations into the role played by German companies in assisting Saddam's WMD programs. During the course of these investigations, the Germans were surprised to find that oftentimes the German companies being investigated for their work with Iraq had similar files showing a parallel level of cooperation with Iran. Most of these efforts dated back to the time of the Iran–Iraq War, but some showed evidence of activity well into the 1990s. Germany, alarmed by these findings, cooperated closely with the CIA, British Intelligence and the Israelis to track down the extent of the German cooperation with Iran for the purposes of interdicting and terminating these efforts.

It was the German government that led some of the initial investigations into the transfer of technology related to the enrichment of uranium, specifically centrifuge-associated technology, from Europe to nations like Iraq, Iran, and Pakistan. European technology also made its way to South American nations such as Brazil. But the Germans were hampered by domestic German law concerning what they could do, especially if the activity involved German citizens and companies. This is where the U.S. and British intelligence services came into play. For years the CIA had been pushing the notion of a broad intelligence sharing operation between nations which would serve as the basis for interdiction operations involving the shipment of WMD-related materials, in particular those affiliated with ballistic missiles. This operation had been extensively discussed by the CIA, through its London Station, with counterparts in the British MI-6. It was MI-6, according to a knowledgeable source, which came up with the idea to use Libya as a "float" for the purposes of exposing, and subsequently shutting down, the A. Q. Khan nuclear proliferation effort.

The British had, for some time, been tracking the activity of a Sri Lankan businessman named Buhary Seyed Abu Tahir. Abu Tahir ran a Dubai-based company, SMB Group, Dubai, which was involved in computer and information technology work. Sometime in the mid- to late 1980s, Abu Tahir became involved in a variety of business relations in Pakistan. It was during the course of these business activities that Abu Tahir first met A. Q. Khan. Through A. Q. Khan, Abu Tahir was put in contact with a number of European business contacts, including several from Germany, who had assisted Khan in the past with procuring specific components used in the manufacture of gas centrifuges for the enrichment of uranium.

In 1994–1995 Abu Tahir served as a facilitator for overseeing the shipment from A. Q. Khan in Pakistan to Iran of dozens of used P-1 gas centrifuges which were no longer needed by the Pakistani Kahota enrichment facility. The Pakistanis had moved on up to an improved gas centrifuge design, the P-2. With the P-1 centrifuges, based upon the original URENCO designs pilfered by A. Q. Khan, now considered excess, the decision was made to sell them to Iran. Abu Tahir's success in concluding the transaction with Iran opened the door up for additional business opportunities, including the Libyan deal.

In 1997 Abu Tahir met with Libyan officials, on behalf of A. Q. Khan, and began negotiations about the shipment from Pakistan to Libya of nuclear-related material and technology. Libya was reeling under U.N. and U.S. economic sanctions, and there was a genuine concern within the inner circle of the Libyan leader, Muhammar Khadafi, that the United States was actively seeking to remove him from power. A decision was made that perhaps the best way to secure the survival of Khadafi would be for Libya to acquire nuclear weapons. The cheapest and quickest route toward this end was deemed to be through the A. Q. Khan network out of Pakistan.

But even as Libya was looking to nuclear weapons to serve as a buffer of protection from the regime change policies of the United States, events were occurring that would compete for the strategic direction Libya was willing to take. In 1998 the Clinton administration let it be known that if Libya were to agree to turn over two Libyans accused of involvement in the 1988 bombing of Pan Am Flight 103 over Lockerbie, Scotland, and pay reparations to the families of those who lost their loved ones on that flight, then consideration might be given to the lifting of U.N. sanctions. In April 1999 the Libyan government turned over the two suspected bombers, Abdel Basset Ali Megrahi and Al Amin Khalifa Fhimahto, to an international court in the Netherlands, prompting the easing of U.N. economic sanctions. Great Britain normalized relations with Libya in November 1999, and in December of that same year gave Libya diplomatic recognition.

Starting in 2000, the British worked very hard with their Libyan counterparts to find a way to convince the United States to lift its own economic embargo of Libya, and restore diplomatic relations. During these initial meetings, the British made the Libyans aware of the fact that Libya's nuclear dealings with Pakistan were not unknown in London, and that Libya would gain considerable ground diplomatically with the United States if it were willing to give up not only its nuclear ambition, but all WMD, including long-range missiles.

Libya agreed that this would be a wise course of action. However, the British convinced their Libyan counterparts that there would need to be a dramatic demonstration of Libya's new stance. For this, the British proposed Libya assist in uncovering the A. Q. Khan nuclear black market network.

Libya had continued to receive shipments of nuclear-related material from Pakistan, including P-1 centrifuges, uranium hexafluoride gas, and design drawings, including that of a Chinese-style nuclear device. With the assistance of British intelligence, the Libyans expanded their cooperation, seeking from Pakistan new-style P-2 centrifuge designs, as well as access to Pakistan's black market suppliers. MI-6, according to a knowledgeable source, helped develop the idea of creating a special workshop in Libya, Workshop 1001, which would become a high-precision machine shop for the manufacture and assembly of P-2 centrifuges. Through the Workshop 1001 concept, MI-6 was able to gain direct access to Abu Tahir's procurement network, including his Malaysian manufacturing plants and Dubai shipping networks. MI-6 actually provided Abu Tahir with component drawings, and facilitated the acquisition of precision machine tools. Several shipments were sent to Libya, and received, as part of this process.

After September 11, 2001, the British took advantage of America's Global War on Terror to introduce Libya to the United States, this time not as an enemy, but rather an ally. Libya, having much experience in the world of international terror, was able to supply the CIA with a great deal of information about Al Qaeda and other international Islamic terror groups. The CIA found the Libyan information to be of considerable utility.

The British exploited the inroads made in Libyan-American relations by further suggesting that Libya make a deal with the United States, in which Libya would trade its WMD programs, including its so-called nuclear weapons program, in exchange for improved U.S. relations. Initial discussions on this matter were started in March 2003, on the eve of the U.S. invasion of Iraq.

The United States was looking for something dramatic in the way of nonproliferation. For some time, the United States had pushed the idea of a broad international coalition against the proliferation of WMD. The Proliferation Security Initiative, or PSI, fit this bill. The PSI was in effect a giant intelligence sharing mechanism, in which the involved nations exchanged data about the illicit shipment of WMD-related materials. It was also a facilitating agreement, in which the involved nations would work with one another to interdict shipments of interest. President Bush announced the PSI during a visit to Kracow in May 2003. The actual agreement was signed in Paris in September 2003. The White House praised the initiative as ". . . a new environment to combat trafficking to and from states and non-state actors of proliferation concern of weapons of mass destruction, their delivery systems, and related materials. The commitment of the countries currently participating—Australia, France, Germany, Italy, Japan, The Netherlands, Poland, Portugal, Spain, the United Kingdom, and the United States—emphasizes the need for proactive measures to combat the threat from the proliferation of weapons of mass destruction."

But, according to sources familiar with the PSI, the adoption of the agreement was delayed until September for a more specific reason: the Bush administration wanted a dramatic demonstration of the effectiveness of its new initiative. By early October 2003 the British–Libya sting operation was well advanced. MI-6 had removed all traces of technical drawings from the Malaysian manufacturer, and the parts produced were loaded onto a German-flagged ship, the *BCC China*, for transit to Libya. The United States Navy was tasked with intercepting the *BCC China*, which was in turn diverted to an Italian port. On board were found containers holding thousands of parts for use in assembling P-2 gas centrifuges.

Of note, the parts involved constituted only some of the total parts needed to assemble a centrifuge. None of the parts shipped represented high-tech materials. This was, according to a source, because British law prohibits its intelligence services from the facilitation of complete WMD-related material, even if part of a sting operation. In any event, the MI-6-Libyan sting was a tremendous success. Libya got what it wanted—an entrée into improved relations with the United States. The British and Americans got what they wanted—unambiguous evidence of the role played by A. Q. Khan in shipping nuclear technology abroad.

Mohammed El-Baradei and the IAEA were quick to gain access to the Libyan nuclear-related cache. They were stunned by the quantity and quality of the material provided by Libya, and were quick to note that there were similarities between markings, packaging, and company names on the crates observed in Libya, and similar crates they had seen earlier in Iran. The IAEA had been pressing Iran for some time now on the specific identity of its foreign suppliers; something Iran had assiduously resisted doing. Now, thanks to the Libya sting, the IAEA had the identities of not only the intermediary companies, but also the country of origin of the material in question: Pakistan.

In a stunning sequence of events, the Pakistani government, confronted by the overwhelming amount of data that implicated personnel and companies operating inside Pakistan, and seemingly with the official consent of the Pakistani government, launched an immediate investigation. Pakistan dispatched a team of experts to Libya and Iran to review the allegations presented, apprehended nearly a dozen officials inside Pakistan, and then, on February 24, put the father of the Pakistani nuclear bomb himself, A. Q. Khan, on national television, where he confessed to selling Pakistan's nuclear secrets to both Libya and Iran. Iran was quick to dismiss any linkage between A. Q. Khan's activities and the Iranian nuclear program, stating that it had received all of its material, the totality of which had been declared to the IAEA, through intermediaries.

Thanks to the Libya escapade, the IAEA now had an opening for which to confront Iran on, namely the issue of the P-2 centrifuges. The IAEA approached Iran about the issue in mid-January 2004, expressing concern that Iran had kept this aspect of its nuclear program a secret at a time when Iran was professing complete transparency about its nuclear program.

Iran, for its part, was somewhat perplexed by the IAEA's focus on the P-2 centrifuge, namely the IAEA's insistence that Iran had kept the program a secret. The Iranians had shown El-Baradei and the other IAEA officials samples of the P-2 rotors at the Natanz exhibition hall in February 2003. Furthermore, Iranian experts had discussed Iran's research into centrifuge rotors of different dimensions than the P-1 as early as the summer of 2003, and through to the fall of 2003. But the main argument, and a legally justifiable one, was that Iran was not obligated to declare the P-2 centrifuge to the IAEA.

The October 21 declaration provided by Iran to the IAEA, and which the IAEA cited as being the document in which Iran should have declared the P-2 program, was only intended to deal with insufficiencies with Iran's safeguards responsibilities. Iran would have had to declare the P-2 under the Additional Protocol, but that was not signed until December 18, 2003, and even then had not come into force. Iran had agreed to act as if the Additional Protocol were in place, pending its ratification by the Iranian Parliament, and as such had promised to deliver additional reports in accordance with a timeline agreed upon by the IAEA, which called for the initial declarations to be submitted by June 18, 2004. Iran claimed to have had every intent of declaring the P-2 project at that time. The fact that the IAEA raised the issue of the P-2 before that timeline (i.e., January 2004) had passed did not reflect negatively on Iran's intentions, or so Tehran believed.

In any event, the P-2 was strictly in the nascent stage of development, involving low-level research and development. The centrifuge Iran was using for its enrichment program was the P-1, and had been fully declared to the IAEA. To the Iranians, the entire P-2 saga was much ado about nothing.

In addition to its concerns over the P-2 centrifuge issue, the IAEA had other issues that it felt needed clarification. One of these involved an Iranian effort to extract polonium from irradiated bismuth metal. The IAEA had first become aware of this activity in September 2003, when Iran had provided documents and records relating to undeclared irradiation experiments involving uranium. Although bismuth is not a material subject to declarations under safeguards, the IAEA inspectors were concerned because polonium, in conjunction with beryllium, could be used as a neutron generator for some nuclear weapons designs.

Polonium is a radioactive alpha-emitting isotope that has legitimate civilian applications, such as in radioisotope thermoelectric generators, a sort of nuclear battery. The Iranians had informed the IAEA in November 2003 that the bismuth irradiation had been part of an old feasibility study for the production of polonium for use in such a nuclear battery. Iran was somewhat confused by the IAEA interest in polonium. The experiments in question took place in 1991, and involved two samples being irradiated, of .5 and 1.5 grams, respectively. The attempt to extract polonium from the first sample failed, and the effort was terminated. The Iranians had written down these experiments in logbooks made available to the IAEA for years, and no interest was ever expressed. Iran stated that it never procured beryllium, additional proof that the experiments were not related to nuclear weapons. In any event, the polonium extraction effort was terminated in 1991, never to be repeated.

Why the IAEA placed so much emphasis on polonium puzzled the Iranians. The answer of course was that the United States, which knew much about the design of nuclear weapons, posited an intent (i.e., neutron generator for weapons purposes) void of any evidence thereof. The polonium issue was clear evidence that the United States was exerting a tremendous amount of pressure on the IAEA to leave no stone unturned, and no accusation unspoken, when it came to Iran's nuclear program. The polonium issue was a red herring, and everyone knew it. But the IAEA raised it, and soon the critics of Iran's nuclear program were citing it as clear-cut proof as to the ill-intent of Iran.

The IAEA was also concerned with Iran's past effort to extract plutonium from irradiated uranium. Iran had provided the IAEA with a full accounting of this matter, and yet in doing so had misrepresented the amount of plutonium eventually extracted (in the form of liquid plutonium) as being 2 micrograms. The IAEA, in doing its own calculations, felt that the amount of plutonium that should have been extracted was more along the lines of 2 milligrams. In either event, the material in question had been turned over to the IAEA, and represented such a small amount of material as to barely warrant comment. However, the IAEA chose to present the discrepancy between the Iranian calculations and those done by the IAEA as being significantly different. This was a highly charged and extremely misleading statement, again representing a bias among those writing IAEA reports toward characterizing the Iranian nuclear program in as negative a light as possible. The production of 2 milligrams of pluto-nium is more in keeping with the declared Iranian goal of making plutonium for use in medical applications, than it would be for weapons production.

Other matters were raised by the IAEA Director General, none of which was representative of anything major in terms of weapons pro-duction. The IAEA was concerned about Iran's plans to construct a heavy water research reactor at Arak, which the Iranians claimed would be for the production of medical isotopes. The IAEA was concerned that the Arak reactor could be used for the production of plutonium.

Another major issue of concern was Iran's laser enrichment program. The Iranians had already declared a laser-enrichment effort that had failed to reach fruition. This laser enrichment effort, which had been subsequently canceled, was the primary reason behind Iraq's efforts to acquire and manufacture uranium metal (laser enrichment processes require the use of uranium metal). However, according to some within the IAEA, as well as the positions taken by the United States and Israel, there was no other explanation available than Iran's desire to use uranium metal as a reflective damper to increase the yield of a nuclear weapon. But the facts argued otherwise.

In a biting resolution adopted on March 13, 2004, the IAEA Board of Governors stated that it "Deplores that Iran, as detailed in the report by the Director General, omitted any reference, in its letter of October 21, 2003, which was to have provided the 'full scope of Iranian nuclear activities' and a 'complete centrifuge R&D chronology,' to its posses-sion of P-2 centrifuge design drawings and to associated research, man-ufacturing, and mechanical testing activities—which the Director General describes as 'a matter of serious concern, particularly in view of the importance and sensitivity of those activities.' "

The Board also echoed ". . . the concern expressed by the Director General over the issue of the purpose of Iran's activities related to experiments on the production and intended use of polonium-210, in the absence of information to support Iran's statements in this regard." Finally, the Board called on Iran ". . . to be pro-active in taking all necessary steps on an urgent basis to resolve all outstanding issues, including the issue of LEU and HEU contamination at the Kalaye Electric Company workshop and Natanz; the issue of the nature and scope of Iran's laser isotope enrichment research; and the issue of the experiments on the production of polonium-210."

The Iranians were enraged over the IAEA Board's report, believing that it did not reflect the reality of the level of cooperation taking place between Iran and the IAEA. The Iranians showed their anger by refusing to allow IAEA inspectors, operating under Iran's voluntary adherence to the Additional Protocol while the matter of ratification was being discussed before the Iranian Parliament, to enter Iran for inspections planned for mid-March, and threatened that Iran might cease cooperating with the IAEA altogether.

One of Sergei Lavrov's first tasks was to nip this crisis in the bud, reminding the Iranians that the only path out of the current situation ran through the IAEA, and that Iran would have to fully cooperate and comply with the requests and requirements of the IAEA Board. Iran backed off, and at the end of March, allowed the IAEA inspectors to return to Iran and continue their work.

But in a critical move, the Iranian government held off on submitting to the Iranian Parliament the bill for ratification of the Additional Protocol. In February the Iranians held a controversial election for Parliament, in which religious conservative parties achieved a majority. The new Parliament was scheduled to convene in June. By holding off on submitting the Additional Protocol for ratification, the Iranians were making the point that while they had agreed to act as if the Additional Protocol was in force, they did so voluntarily, since without ratification the Additional Protocol had no legal standing.

Iran had a lot at stake beyond national pride. At risk if Iran walked away from the IAEA were lucrative trade talks ongoing with the European Union. The EU-3 continued to work with Iran in an effort to hammer out an agreement, but in the end everything hinged on Iran's level of cooperation with the IAEA. Russia, too, had several projects under way, the largest and most controversial being the Bushehr nuclear reactor, which was under construction and scheduled to come on line sometime in 2005. Despite considerable pressure placed on Russia by the United States, the Russians refused to budge on their insistence that the Bushehr project was totally related to the pursuit of peaceful energy, and had no relation whatsoever to a nuclear weapons program. However, as Lavrov made clear, Russian assistance was linked to Iran's continuing to cooperate with the IAEA.

The IAEA Board of Governors had instructed El-Baradei to prepare a report by May 2004, so that the Board could consider the Iranian matter at its meeting in June. In order to help facilitate this process, El-Baradei and a team of senior IAEA officials, including Pierre Goldschmidt and Olli Heinonen, traveled to Tehran on April 6 for meetings with senior Iraqi officials, including President Khatami, Gholamreza Aghazadeh, the head of the AEOI, Hassan Rohani, the Secretary of the Supreme National Security Council, and K. Kharrazi, the Minister of Foreign Affairs. All parties agreed to accelerate the program of work so as to clear up the IAEA's outstanding issues in time for the June meeting of the Board of Governors.

Concerning the matter of the P-2 centrifuges, the Iranians provided the IAEA with a detailed accounting of the program, including the locations and affiliations of several sites around Iran involved in P-2 related activities. While Iran facilitated access to every civilian-related site, the IAEA and Iran could not agree upon modalities for inspection of three workshops that carried out sensitive research work on behalf of the Defense Industries Organization (DIO).

While negotiations continued regarding access to the DIO facilities, the IAEA was able to conduct numerous other inspections of locations in Iran associated with declared nuclear-related activities. Iran continued to prepare its initial declaration in accordance with the Additional Protocol. These declarations were originally scheduled to be submitted on June 18, but El-Baradei had requested that, in the interest of full disclosure and facilitating the work of the IAEA in preparation for the June Board of Governors meeting, that Iran accelerate the process. The initial Additional Protocol declarations were delivered almost one month ahead of schedule, on May 21. The Iranians noted, in submitting the declaration, that although it was done within a shortened time period, nonetheless ". . . every reasonable effort has been made to provide the Agency with the information to the extent that it is relevant to and compatible with the provisions of the Protocol" and that the declarations were "open to further clarification and amplification if needed."

Iran had made it very clear to all parties that its suspension of enrichment activities was voluntary, and linked to the EU-3 abiding by its commitments undertaken in the October 21, 2003, Tehran Declaration. The March IAEA Board of Governors resolution, assessed by many in Iran as being a product of U.S.-based pressure, was seen as trying to turn the voluntary temporary suspension of nuclear enrichment into a permanent situation. On April 29 the Iranians, in order to demonstrate that they had not given up on the issue of enrichment, informed the IAEA that it planned to carry out so-called hot tests of the uranium hexafluoride production line at the Uranium Conversion Facility in Isfahan.

The IAEA protested, stating that the planned hot tests would constitute the production of uranium hexafluoride, and as such equate to the manufacture of feed material for enrichment purposes, thereby violating the ban on enrichment activity. On May 18, Iran informed the IAEA that "the decision taken for voluntary and temporary suspension is based on clearly defined scope which does not include suspension of production of uranium hexafluoride." Once again Iran was heading for a confrontation with the IAEA over what it considered its inalienable right to develop technology related to peaceful energy related programs.

On the issue of uranium hexafluoride itself, the Iranians provided additional clarification concerning the missing 1.9 kilograms of Chinese-procured uranium hexafluoride. Originally, the Iranians had stated that the missing material had leaked from the storage vessel. Later, Iran admitted using the 1.9 kilograms in undeclared P-1 centrifuge tests carried out at Kalaye. However, IAEA environmental testing had detected trace elements of uranium hexafluoride in the roof of the building holding the Chinese uranium hexafluoride, prompting the Iranians to declare that they had also stored some indigenously produced uranium hexafluoride at that facility, and it had, indeed, leaked out.

In an effort to clarify the remaining outstanding issues, the IAEA conducted an intensive program of work extending from the end of May into the first week of June, where they were finally granted access to the three DIO workshops, and provided with new information about the P-2 program, including new details about the importation from foreign suppliers of magnets associated with the P-2 (previously the Iranians had denied any foreign manufacture), and the identification of a new DIO site that had been involved in the manufacture of the rotors used on the P-2 centrifuge (and which the IAEA was provided access to).

The IAEA was thrown off when the Iranians produced a private commercial contractor who stated that he had held discussions with a supplier of magnets, asking for 4,000 sets to be provided. This was in contrast to earlier declarations by Iran that the P-2 program was a small research and development effort. The private contractor told the IAEA that he had come up with the 4,000 figure on his own, hoping to get a lower price from the supplier. However, this answer did not seem to satisfy the IAEA, who now took the position that the P-2 program was potentially bigger than what Iran had declared, and as such the IAEA could not guarantee that there were no secret centrifuge facilities operating in Iran outside of the monitoring currently being conducted by the IAEA inspectors.

Something else was bothering the IAEA experts. The chronology presented by Iran, which had initial technical drawings related to the P-2 being acquired in 1995, and then no work being done until 2001, and mechanical testing taking place only in 2002, was too short in the minds of the experts.

Another unresolved issue was that of HEU samples collected at the Kalaye workshop, and on a machine tool that had, at one time, been located at the Kalaye workshop. These samples, consisting of 36 percent HEU, were unexplainable under the current Iranian declaration that held that all contamination not associated with the limited Iranian centrifuge tests had to be as a result of cross-contamination from used P-1 centrifuge parts and associated equipment purchased from Pakistan. The 36 percent HEU, however, was Russian in origin (certain Russian research reactors use uranium fuel enriched to 36 percent). The Iranians continued to insist that all contamination came from Pakistan, something that made the IAEA experts nervous. If the Iranians were using HEU enriched at 36 percent as their feedstock for a centrifuge cascade operating highly efficient P-2 centrifuges (or even the less efficient P-1 design), the period of time required to make weapons grade HEU would be drastically reduced.

These two main issues of the P-2 centrifuges and the HEU contamination could not be resolved in time for the June IAEA Board of

Governors meeting. However, Iran was confident that the amount of cooperation it had exhibited to date, combined with the fact that, in its opinion, all that was required to clarify the two outstanding issues was more time for the IAEA to study, and as such comprehend, the data it had available, meant that the June report should move Iran very close to being able to resolve its position vis-à-vis the IAEA, and as such open the way toward not only the resumption of its enrichment program, but also improved trade with the European Union, in accordance with the Tehran Declaration of October 21, 2003.

It was not to be. In a strongly worded resolution, the IAEA Board of Governors stated that ". . . as indicated by the Director General's written and oral reports, Iran's cooperation has not been as full, timely and proactive as it should have been, and, in particular, that Iran postponed until mid-April visits originally scheduled for mid-March—including visits of Agency centrifuge experts to a number of locations involved in Iran's P-2 centrifuge enrichment program—resulting in some cases in a delay in the taking of environmental samples and their analysis." The United States was quick to cite the IAEA resolution—which it helped draft—in condemning Iran for conducting a secret nuclear weapons program.

The U.S. actions came on the heels of a dramatic escalation in tension between the United States and Great Britain on the one hand, and Iran on the other, over the situation in Iraq. The United States faced a complete meltdown of the security situation inside Iraq in April, with large-scale revolts taking place in Falluja, Najaf, and elsewhere. The United States and the United Kingdom were quick to blame Iran for interfering with the internal situation in Iraq. The animosity drawn from the Iraq situation easily spilled over into the nuclear question, as demonstrated by a speech made by President Bush at a NATO gathering in Istanbul at the end of June where he condemned Iran as a "terrorist state" seeking to acquire nuclear weapons.

In the midst of the fallout from the June IAEA Board of Governors meeting, yet another controversy emerged, this one dealing with a site in Tehran called Lavizan-Shian. This site first came to public attention in May 2003 when the Iranian opposition group, National Council for Resistance of Iran, announced that the Lavizan-Shian Technical Research Center was associated with biological weapons research for the Iranian Ministry of Defense.

By May 2003 the NCRI's days were numbered; in August 2003 the U.S. Justice Department shut down the activities of the NCRI, stating that the NCRI was a known terrorist group. However, no arrests were made by the Justice officials, and many of the personnel involved simply reorganized to create a buffer between the NCRI/MEK affiliation and the ongoing work they were conducting in Iran.

Despite the efforts of many, including members of Congress and elements of what has come to be known as the Israeli Lobby, to have the NCRI and its parent organization, the MEK, removed from the State Department's list of terrorist organizations, in the end the complexity of the U.S.–MEK relationship—which may include a classified aspect set forth in a top secret Presidential National Security Directive pertaining to U.S. policy objectives in Iran—could not withstand the inherent contradictions of a stated terrorist group providing press briefings which in turn put into the public domain intelligence on Iran which, unlike that of another well-known opposition group, the Iraqi National Congress, turned out to be for the most part accurate. There was also concern that the NCRI–Israeli relationship was starting to call the shots concerning Iran by dictating the pace of the confrontation. The NCRI had done its job, placing the Iranian nuclear program on the world stage. Now it was time for it to simply slip into the background, and let U.S. policy formulators take control.

The Israeli intelligence services, again the source of the NCRI information, imparted upon the IAEA the importance that they placed on the site. However, there was no hook for the IAEA to justify requesting access to a location that did not have a reasonably defined link to nuclear activity. The Israelis kept pressing the issue, however, especially in the aftermath of the Libya conundrum in December 2003–January 2004. The Israelis were able to gain access to sensitive communications between the Iranians and Pakistanis that indicated that the Iranians were seeking to keep quiet about naming Pakistan directly as a source of Libya's P-2 centrifuge program. While the language used in the intercepts was apparently vague and non-specific, it did hint at some sort of cover-up activity by the Iranians. Some familiar with this information believe that it only relates to an agreement by the Iranians not to divulge politically sensitive aspects of the government-to-government relationships behind the A. Q. Khan network; others believe that the cover-up goes deeper, and deals with undeclared secret nuclear weapons-related work. One of the locations believed to be involved in such a cover-up was the Lavizan-Shian facility.

Lavizan-Shian had been reported to be a Ministry of Defense facility with biological warfare associations, placing it outside the purview of the IAEA. The facility had a long history of sensitive military work. During the time of the Shah, Lavizan was the headquarters of the Imperial Guard. Later it became a central hub of the new Islamic Republic's military research activity, and many of Iran's most sensitive military projects, including several ballistic missile-related activities, were managed from Lavizan. The Lavizan-Shian facility, adjacent to the larger Lavizan base, was involved in physics research activities.

In 1989 the Iranians established the Physics Research Center at Lavizan-Shian. Originally intended to be a biological research activity, the facility was converted into a civil defense-related activity, which had the responsibility of developing technologies and methodologies that would help detect and protect Iran from either WMD attacks from foreign powers, or accidental nuclear releases domestically. In this context, two so-called Whole Body Counters (WBC), which had originally been procured by Iraq from the United States in the early 1990s (the WBCs were produced by Connecticut-based Canberra Industries Inc.), were installed at the Lavizan-Shian facility. Work on civil defense continued until 1998, at which time ownership of the site came into dispute between the Iranian Ministry of Defense and the municipality of Tehran. Sometime in December 2003 the Iranians began dismantling Lavizan-Shian, removing the buildings and scraping away the topsoil, so that by May 2004 the site had been totally razed. The combination of the NCRI–Israeli reporting, satellite imagery showing the removal activity at the site, and information that showed the two WBCs being located at the site, led the IAEA to request an inspection of Lavizan-Shian in June 2004.

The visit was granted, and the inspectors given access to the WBCs and associated equipment, but the extensive earth removal activity that had transpired at Lavizan-Shian prior to the arrival of the IAEA inspectors made the environmental sampling techniques used by the IAEA previously nearly useless. Some have contended that this was a deliberate ploy on the part of the Iranians, although documents provided to the IAEA by Iran tend to support the Iranian claim that all of this was simply part of the efforts undertaken by the municipality of Tehran to convert a former Ministry of Defense-affiliated site into a city park, work on which pre-dated the May 2003 NCRI briefing and as such makes any cause-effect analysis based upon chronology moot.

The dramatic imagery of the reduction of the Lavizan-Shian site, when showed out of context, makes an impressive (and yet misleading) case for the concealment by Iran of something sinister at that location. The media hyped the Lavizan-Shian concealment, giving it more emphasis than even the IAEA thought it deserved. According to Iran, the purpose of Lavizan-Shian had been "preparedness to combat and neutralization of casualties due to nuclear attacks and accidents (nuclear defense) and also support and provide scientific advice and services to the Ministry of Defense." Iran provided the IAEA with a list of the eleven activities conducted at Lavizan-Shian, but, citing security concerns, declined to provide the IAEA with a list of the equipment used there. Iran told the IAEA categorically that "no nuclear material declarable in accordance with the Agency's safeguard[s] was present" and that "no nuclear material and nuclear activities related to fuel cycle [were] carried out in Lavisan-Shian." The IAEA was not able to contradict any aspect of the Iranian declaration about Lavizan-Shian.

As a result of the continued fall-out from Iran's ire at the June Board of Governors report, the Iranians made good on their threat to suspend earlier commitments regarding "expanded voluntary measures" concerning the cessation of manufacturing and testing of centrifuge components. The IAEA urged Iran to "continue to build international confidence" by continuing to adhere to the voluntary halt in centrifuge work, but Iran went ahead with its threats, removing IAEA seals from material associated with the centrifuge manufacture activities. By August Iran had assembled approximately seventy new centrifuges as a result of this resumption of activity. All of the work was conducted under IAEA supervision.

Iran had also gone forward with its promise to conduct hot tests of the uranium conversion facility. One test, done in May–June 2004, produced some 30–35 kilograms of uranium hexafluoride. Other tests, involving the conversion of some 35 tons of yellowcake, took place in early September 2004.

None of this boded well for Iran in the upcoming IAEA Governor's Board meeting scheduled for September. While IAEA Director General Mohammed El-Baradei was able to report that Iran was providing good access to facilities, and that no evidence of ongoing enrichment had been detected, he continued to note that Iran had not adequately answered the two most outstanding issues facing the IAEA—the traces of LEU and HEU that were discovered at Natanz and Kalaye, and matters pertaining to the P-2 centrifuge program. This, on top of the Lavizan-Shian issue, the questions about polonium and plutonium, and Iran's continued intransigence on the matter of a heavy water reactor being constructed at Arak, all provided fuel for those powers that were pushing to have Iran declared to be in violation of the Non-Proliferation Treaty, namely the United States.

The Arak question was typical of the kind of event that made the Iranians question the IAEA's commitment to allowing Iran to proceed with its nuclear energy program along the lines permitted it under Article IV of the Non-Proliferation Treaty. There was considerable concern on the part of several interested parties, the United States and Israel foremost, that Iran's plans for a heavy water reactor had less to do with research and more to do with creating a source of weapons grade plutonium. Israel knew all too well what the potential of a small heavy water reactor was—its own "research reactor" at Dimona, a heavy water design, served as the centerpiece of its clandestine nuclear weapons program. As far as Iran was concerned, Israel in many ways was imprinting its own past pattern of behavior, including motivations, onto the Iranians.

Iran was permitted to build the heavy water reactor, and indeed had submitted the required drawings to the IAEA for review as required by the safeguards agreement and the NPT. However, experts at the IAEA, in reviewing the Iranian plans, questioned the absence of so-called hot cell windows and manipulators, in the drawings. One would normally expect to see the presence of these items if one was seeking to extract radioisotopes for research purposes, as Iran claimed. Without these, it would be easy to conclude that Iran was simply looking to extract plutonium. The Iranians provided the IAEA with documentation which showed that the Iranians had, indeed, factored in hot cell windows and manipulators in the original 1977 plans, but that these had been dropped from the current plan due to procurement problems. Once a source of hot cell windows and manipulators were found, then the design drawings would be updated taking into consideration the new technical information. Void of these, however, there was nothing to declare.

Another sticky issue remained the matter of Iran's continued refusal to ratify the Additional Protocol. The failure of Iran to accomplish this task left the door open for criticism from the United States, typified by comments made in mid-August by John Bolton, the Undersecretary of State for Nonproliferation, when he told a conservative American think-tank that ". . . impetus behind the Iranian quest for nuclear weapons is so great it has caused Iran to renege on its commitments to the IAEA to ratify the Additional Protocol and fully cooperate with inspectors, and renege on its commitment to the Europeans to suspend uranium enrichment activities."

The Iranians, of course, took a different approach. The newly elected conservative Parliament was a strong advocate of Iran's legal right to enrich uranium, and had been trying to pass its own bill instructing the Iranian government to resume the enrichment of uranium. This seemed to be the opposite direction that needed to be taken if ratification of the Additional Protocol was the objective. It was clear in the minds of the Iranians that ratification of the Additional Protocol could only come about when the IAEA recognized Iran's inherent right to nuclear energy, inclusive of an enrichment program. According to a senior Iranian parliament member, the "Majlis [Parliament] certainly will not approve the additional protocol in view of the [IAEA] Board of Governors current record, but the Board can pave the way for Iran to join the protocol if it attempts to close Iran's nuclear dossier in its next [September 13, 2004] session."

The September meeting of the IAEA Board of Governors brought together three differing points of view regarding the Iranian issue— Russia, the European Union and the United States. Russia, more than anything, viewed its support for Iran from a geo-strategic imperative. The Russians had over the course of several years watched as the United States orchestrated the expansion of NATO right up to the borders of Russia, and then the transformation of NATO from a defensive pact into one capable of conducting offensive warfare (witness Serbia and Kosovo).

The U.S.-led invasion of Iraq was yet another example of American hegemony left unchecked. Russia had significant economic interests in Iran, to be certain. The military sales and nuclear energy markets were both lucrative for the Russians. But more than anything else, Iran was where Russia intended to draw the line when it came to what it viewed as the naked abuse of power being wielded by the United States. Of course, Russia needed to maintain an aura of legitimacy and respectability on the Iranian issue, and would not actively support or endorse an Iranian nuclear weapons program. As such, Russia would continue to support the IAEA's demands that Iran answer with full transparency its requests for continued access and information concerning Iran's nuclear program. Russia even supported the freeze on enrichment. But as for economic sanctions, the Russian position was quite clear: No.

An adjunct of the Russian position was that of fellow Security Council member China. In March of 2004 China had signed a twenty-five-year deal to import 110 million tons of liquefied natural gas (LNG) from Iran. By the time of the IAEA Board meeting in September, China was on the verge of closing an even bigger deal, worth some $100 billion, which had the Chinese importing another 250 million tons of LNG from Iran over a twenty-year period. Under this deal, China would also be able to import 150,000 barrels of crude oil per day during the twenty-five-year period. China, in one fell swoop, was about to become Iran's oil market.

In addition to the impressive levels of LNG and crude oil importation, China was also going to invest huge amounts of money into Iran's oil and gas fields, both in terms of exploration and drilling, totaling another $100 billion over twenty-five years. China was in no mood to put this considerable investment at risk by supporting any referral of Iran to the Security Council. Furthermore, the growing Sino–Russian entente dictated a common national security posture, and on one issue the two former superpowers agreed: the United States needed to be checked, and Iran was the best place to do the checking.

The European Union, for its part, had to tread carefully. On the one hand, the European Union wanted to fully exploit the economic benefits of open trade with Iran, and as such was anxious for the nuclear issue to be resolved. They were fully aware of the Iran–Chinese oil and gas deals, and wanted to be able to engage in similar activities. On the other hand, the European Union could not simply ignore the position taken by the United States. Their stance was inherently contradictory, at once recognizing Iran's right to enrich uranium, while at the same time saying Iran could never be allowed to enrich uranium.

Iran recognized this, as well. Hassan Rowhani, in Europe ahead of the IAEA Board meeting for talks with European Union officials about Iran's nuclear program, noted that "If the Europeans do not respect their commitments or present an illogical or harsh resolution, Iran has already decided its response." Rowhani went on to say that "Iran will never compromise on its right to gain access to the complete nuclear fuel cycle." The European Union, in the form of the EU-3, responded by setting a two-month deadline for Iran to stop all enrichment activity. On the surface, this represented a harsh rebuke. In reality, however, it signaled that the European Union was not caving into pressure put on by the United States to immediately refer Iran to the Security Council.

The issue of the referral of the Iranian file to the Security Council weighed heavily on all parties. In its November 2003 resolution, the IAEA Board of Governors agreed to consider "all options at its disposal" should "any further serious Iranian failures" come to light. The spate of condemnations by the Board of Iran in every resolution passed since had created a situation where the IAEA was in danger of boxing itself into a corner. To elevate Iran's inability or unwillingness to not fully answer questions to the satisfaction of the IAEA on matters pertaining to the nuclear issue to the status of being a threat to international peace and security was a stretch. However, by continuously drawing lines in the sand that were ignored by Iran, the Board was put in the position of being found irrelevant. This, of course, was the whole approach of the United States when it came to Iran and the IAEA. It was never a question of "if" concerning Iran's being referred to the Security Council, but only "when."

The United States thought that the time was now. According to the U.S. way of thinking, the IAEA statute provides that the IAEA should notify the Security Council of questions that fall within the competency of the United Nations Security Council. Accordingly, the American position held, the IAEA needed to decide whether or not Iran posed a threat to international peace and security that warranted

Chapter VII intervention by the Security Council. The United States was pushing for IAEA referral of Iran because in November 2004 it would assume the Presidency of the Security Council, and as such have tremendous latitude on setting the agenda of the Council. Secretary of State Colin Powell made a public case that Iran had a nuclear weapons program, and that "this [Iran] is a matter that should go to the Security Council as quickly as possible."

Shortly before he traveled to Vienna for the September IAEA Governors Board meeting, John Bolton visited Israel, where he proclaimed that the United States "would not rule out an attack if peaceful diplomacy failed to stop Iran from getting atomic weapons." Bolton's choice of words, and location for uttering them, came at an inopportune time. That same month the FBI had acknowledged that it was investigating a serious case of espionage involving a Department of Defense official, the pro-Israeli Lobby AIPAC, and Israel itself. The case involved the unauthorized disclosure of classified information from the Department of Defense official to AIPAC, which then forwarded the information on to Israel. The intelligence in question dealt with Iran.

Bolton was to be joined in Vienna by Ambassador Jackie Sanders, who was the U.S. representative to the Geneva-based Conference on Disarmament. Bolton and Sanders were representing the United States in the place of the regular intermediary, Ambassador Stephen Brill. The presence of Bolton and Sanders underscored the seriousness in which the United States placed getting Iran referred to the Security Council at this time. But Bolton's rhetoric and grating manner undermined any benefit that might have been accrued by having such a senior delegation present in Vienna. No matter how hard he pressed, the IAEA Board would not cave in to Bolton's insistence that the IAEA set an October 31 deadline for referral of Iran to the Security Council.

Up until this time the IAEA Board of Governors had passed all of its resolutions on the basis of unanimous consent; the last thing the IAEA wanted was to present Iran with anything less than a solid front. The Bolton initiatives were threatening to force any IAEA resolution to a vote, where the Board might be presented with numerous no votes, or abstentions. Sensing deadlock, the EU-3, with Russian support, pushed a compromise draft resolution that called for Iran to fully cooperate with the IAEA inspectors so that they could understand the full extent and nature of Iran's enrichment program before the Board's next meeting in November 2004. The outstanding issues continued to focus on the P-2 centrifuge issue and the sources of HEU and LEU contamination. The EU-draft also expressed the Board's deep regret that Iran reversed its decision to voluntarily suspend its enrichment and reprocessing activities, and again urged Iran to ratify the Additional Protocol to its NPT safeguards agreement.

The Bolton-led U.S. delegation attempted to derail the E.U.-draft resolution by once again demanding an October 31 deadline for Iran's full compliance, or else the matter would be referred to the Security Council. The United States also demanded that two critical paragraphs be removed from the draft. The first paragraph so targeted spoke of recognizing "the right of states to the development and practical application of atomic energy for peaceful purposes." This was a reference to Article IV of the NPT, something the United States had made clear did not apply in the case of Iran. The second was curious, and deeply troubling. The United States wanted the standard boiler-plate language that existed in all IAEA resolutions which expressed appreciation for the "professional and impartial efforts by the Director-General and the Secretariat to implement Iran's NPT safeguards . . . as well as to verify Iran's suspension of enrichment-related and reprocessing activities."

Officially, what vexed the United States most was El-Baradei's repeated statements that his inspectors had not detected any evidence of an Iranian nuclear weapons program. But from the perspective of the unapologetically pro-Israeli perspective of John Bolton, it was El-Baradei's tendency to criticize Israel's nuclear weapons program that was particularly disturbing (especially when El-Baradei, one month before the September 2004 IAEA Board meeting, stated that Iran had been much more forthcoming and cooperative about its nuclear program than Israel ever had).

In any event, the United States failed on all accounts. There was no referral, no deadline, and no eliminated paragraphs. Ambassador Sanders tried to put the best possible face on for the Americans, and she tipped off all parties as to what the ultimate endgame strategy was for the United States, by remarking that the IAEA Board's resolution ". . . sends an unmistakable signal to Iran that continuing its nuclear weapons program will bring it inevitably before the (U.N.) Security Council."

The September 18 IAEA Board of Governors resolution was seen by many as a welcomed respite, a chance for all parties to catch their respective breaths before moving forward concerning the Iranian nuclear file. But any settlement with Iran that preserved its right to carry out the enrichment of uranium was unacceptable to Israel, and as such the United States.

The Israeli point of view was summarized in a presentation made by Foreign Minister Silvan Shalom before the U.N. General Assembly on September 23, 2004. Shalom stated that "The international community now realizes that Iran—with missiles that can reach London, Paris, Berlin and southern Russia—does not only pose a threat to the security of Israel, but to the security and stability of the whole world. Indeed, Iran has replaced Saddam Hussein as the world's number one exporter of terror, hate and instability." Shalom's speech underscored an even more blunt statement made by Israeli Prime Minister Ariel Sharon, who stated that Iran was the greatest threat to Israel's existence, and that "Israel would not allow Iran to be equipped with a nuclear weapon."

Israel had defined nuclear weapon capability as having the means to enrich uranium. As such, the Israeli red line was the very same enrichment program that the Iranians believed they had an inalienable right to pursue under Article IV of the NPT. Given America's overwhelming pro-Israeli posture when it came to anything dealing with Middle East security, there could be no doubt in anyone's mind that Israel's red lines were also America's. Far from providing a respite designed to de-escalate tensions, the September 2004 IAEA resolution was nothing more than the calm before the storm.

Five

The War Party

FOLLOWING PASSAGE OF THE SEPTEMBER 2005 resolution by the IAEA in Vienna, Under Secretary of State John Bolton returned to Washington, D.C., deeply disappointed in the decisions made by the IAEA, the moderate stance being taken by the IAEA Director General, Mohammed El-Baradei, and by what he viewed as the overly compromising nature of the European Union. Bolton had come to Vienna charged with getting the Iranian account transferred from IAEA oversight to the purview of the United Nations Security Council. Given Bolton's history, it would seem at first blush quite strange to have a man who had spent much of his professional life deriding the United Nations, and the role played by the Security Council in particular, to be suddenly advocating the primacy of the Security Council when it came to Iran. But even a cursory review of Bolton's background clearly showed that when it came to the United Nations and Iran, nothing was as it might appear at first glance.

Being stymied by the IAEA was both a personal and professional defeat for John Bolton. As the Under Secretary for Nonproliferation, Iran was his account, his responsibility, and things weren't going well. But the Iran account represented much more than simply a professional responsibility for Bolton; it was also very personal. And given Bolton's background, separating personal from professional when it came to Iran was a very difficult thing to do. Before returning to government service in 2001 with the Bush administration, John Bolton had served as the senior vice president for the conservative think tank the American Enterprise Institute, as well as a director for the Project for a New American Century (prior to that Bolton had served as the assistant secretary of state for international organizations under George H. W. Bush). In both positions Bolton had the opportunity to make his personal opinions, especially on matters pertaining to the U.N. and U.S. national security, well known.

In October 1999, John Bolton, in his role as AEI vice president, authored an article, published in the conservative magazine *The Weekly Standard*, in which he took the U.N. Secretary General to task, along with the U.N. Charter and any American official who acceded to the belief that the United States was somehow beholden to the rule of international law. Bolton took particular affront to the position held by Kofi Annan regarding the U.S.-led NATO intervention in Kosovo. Bolton quoted Annan as saying "Unless the Security Council is restored to its preeminent position as the sole source of legitimacy on the use of force, we are on a dangerous path to anarchy." Bolton explained away America's reluctance to take the Kosovo case to the Security Council, noting that had the United States sought a U.N. resolution to intervene ". . . it would have almost certainly have been vetoed by Russia and China. Furthermore," Bolton wrote, "if the Security Council were considered the sole arbiter of just intervention, any use of force that lacked its imprimatur would be illegitimate." Bolton went on:

> Not only is the Annan doctrine limitless in its purported reach, it also greatly inhibits America's ability (and everyone else's, for that matter) to use force to protect and advance its vital national interests. Such a limitation was never seriously advanced, and certainly not accepted, when the Senate considered the U.N. Charter in 1945. Indeed, during the Cold War, Americans would have greeted such statements by a U.N. secretary general with derision.

Bolton rejected any notion of the United States seeking permission from the U.N. Security Council when addressing issues it deemed paramount to its own national security interest. The appropriate response, according to Bolton, would have been to announce that the United States ". . . did not need the Security Council's permission to act. Besides, the Security Council was paralyzed and therefore useless for our purposes." This particular passage warrants emphasis given Bolton's recent tirade in Vienna about the need to refer the Iran issue to the Security Council.

In his 1999 article Bolton cautioned about the threat from "emerging new international norms" which, in his opinion, ". . . will make it harder and harder for the United States to act independently in its own legitimate national interest." What Bolton, and his superiors in the Bush administration, believed to represent the legitimate national interest of the United States was not simply hypothetical, but rather set forth in great detail, both in terms of positions held prior to taking office (representative of foundational thought), and official positions as expressed in government documents published by the Bush administration.

In 2000, John Bolton, as a Director for the Project for a New American Century, helped prepare a document, "Rebuilding America's Defenses," or RAD, that had the imprint of many people who would go on to serve in senior levels of the administration of George W. Bush, including Paul Wolfowitz, Stephen Cambone, and "Scooter" Libby. The document was a straightforward, frank, and frightening look at the vision of how America would interface with the rest of the world under conservative Republican leadership.

"America's global leadership, and its role as the guarantor of the current great-power peace," the RAD document noted, "relies upon the safety of the American homeland; the preservation of a favorable balance of power in Europe, the Middle East, and surrounding energy-producing region, and East Asia; and the general stability of the international system of nation-states relative to terrorists, organized crime, and other 'non-state actors'."

A preview of President Bush's 2002 State of the Union Address was provided as well. "The current American peace will be short-lived if the United States becomes vulnerable to rogue powers with small, inexpensive arsenals of ballistic missiles and nuclear warheads or other weapons of mass destruction. We cannot allow North Korea, Iran, Iraq or similar states to undermine American leadership, intimidate American allies or threaten the American homeland itself. The blessings of the American peace, purchased at fearful cost and a century of effort, should not be so trivially squandered." And the consequences for any rogue power that dared to confront the United States was likewise spelled out: "American military preeminence will continue to rest in significant part on the ability to maintain sufficient land forces to achieve political goals such as removing a dangerous and hostile regime when necessary."

John Bolton's influence in shaping what has come to be known as neoconservative policy carried over from private life to official duty. He and his fellow neoconservative ideologues took the framework of policy inherent in their writings and, once ensconced inside the administration of President George W. Bush, turned it into formal doctrine, exploiting the fragile state of U.S. democracy in the form of a Congress paralyzed by fear in the aftermath of the terrorist attacks of September 11, 2001, to turn their visions into a National Security Strategy that was promulgated one year after the events of 9/11, in September 2002.

The 2002 National Security Strategy of the United States represented a sweeping transformation of how America under President Bush saw its position vis-à-vis the rest of the world. For anyone fearful of any notion of an unrestrained hyper-power, the document was disturbing, for the new document was nothing less than a road map for global hegemony on the part of the United States of America, at once endorsing the notion of unchecked power, pre-emptive war (and perpetual war, as well, in the form of imminent threat), unilateralism in disregard for international law, and regime change. A careful reading of key passages from the 2002 National Security Strategy shows just how influential neoconservative ideologues such as John Bolton were in shaping the policies of the Bush administration:

The United States possesses unprecedented—and unequaled—strength and influence in the world. Sustained by faith in the principles of liberty, and the value of a free society, this position comes with unparalleled responsibilities, obligations, and opportunity. The great strength of this nation must be used to promote a balance of power that favors freedom.

America is now threatened less by conquering states than we are by failing ones. We are menaced less by fleets and armies than by catastrophic technologies in the hands of the embittered few. We must defeat these threats to our Nation, allies, and friends.

However, this campaign need not be sequential to be effective;

the cumulative effect across all regions will help achieve the results we seek. We will disrupt and destroy terrorist organizations by:

- Direct and continuous action using all the elements of national and international power. Our immediate focus will be those terrorist organizations of global reach and any terrorist or state sponsor of terrorism which attempts to gain or use weapons of mass destruction (WMD) or their precursors;
- Defending the United States, the American people, and our interests at home and abroad by identifying and destroying the threat before it reaches our borders. While the United States will constantly strive to enlist the support of the international community, we will not hesitate to act alone, if necessary, to exercise our right of self defense by acting preemptively against such terrorists, to prevent them from doing harm against our people and our country; and
- Denying further sponsorship, support, and sanctuary to terrorists by convincing or compelling states to accept their sovereign responsibilities. We will also wage a war of ideas to win the battle against international terrorism. This includes:

  — Using the full influence of the United States, and working closely with allies and friends, to make clear that all acts of terrorism are illegitimate so that terrorism will be viewed in the same light as slavery, piracy, or genocide: behavior that no respectable government can condone or support and all must oppose;
  — Supporting moderate and modern government, especially in the Muslim world, to ensure that the conditions and ideologies that promote terrorism do not find fertile ground in any nation;
  — Diminishing the underlying conditions that spawn terrorism by enlisting the international community to focus its efforts and resources on areas most at risk; and
  — Using effective public diplomacy to promote the free flow of information and ideas to kindle the hopes and aspirations of freedom of those in societies ruled by the sponsors of global terrorism.

For centuries, international law recognized that nations need not suffer an attack before they can lawfully take action to defend themselves against forces that present an imminent danger of attack. Legal scholars and international jurists often conditioned the legitimacy of preemption on the existence of an imminent threat—most often a visible mobilization of armies, navies, and air forces preparing to attack.

We must adapt the concept of imminent threat to the capabilities and objectives of today's adversaries. Rogue states and terrorists do not seek to attack us using conventional means. They know such attacks would fail. Instead, they rely on acts of terror and, potentially, the use of weapons of mass destruction—weapons that can be easily concealed, delivered covertly, and used without warning.

The targets of these attacks are our military forces and our civilian population, in direct violation of one of the principal norms of the law of warfare. As was demonstrated by the losses on September 11, 2001, mass civilian casualties is the specific objective of terrorists and these losses would be exponentially more severe if terrorists acquired and used weapons of mass destruction.

The United States has long maintained the option of preemptive actions to counter a sufficient threat to our national security. The greater the threat, the greater is the risk of inaction—and the more compelling the case for taking anticipatory action to defend ourselves, even if uncertainty remains as to the time and place of the enemy's attack. To forestall or prevent such hostile acts by our adversaries, the United States will, if necessary, act preemptively.

The United States will not use force in all cases to preempt emerging threats, nor should nations use preemption as a pretext for aggression. Yet in an age where the enemies of civilization openly and actively seek the world's most destructive technologies, the United States cannot remain idle while dangers gather. We will always proceed deliberately, weighing the consequences of our actions. To support preemptive options, we will:

- build better, more integrated intelligence capabilities to provide timely, accurate information on threats, wherever they may emerge;
- coordinate closely with allies to form a common assessment of the most dangerous threats; and
- continue to transform our military forces to ensure our ability to conduct rapid and precise operations to achieve decisive results.

The purpose of our actions will always be to eliminate a specific threat to the United States or our allies and friends. The reasons for our actions will be clear, the force measured, and the cause just.

The 2002 National Security Strategy of the United States represented a frontal assault on the basic framework of international law that had held the world together, however tenuously, since the end of World War II. It also codified the doctrine of global hegemony on the part of the United States, replete with notions of preemptive war, unilateralism, and regime change. When one compares and contrasts the positions staked out in the 2002 National Security Strategy, and the positions espoused by the Bush administration, through the vehicle of John Bolton, at the IAEA concerning Iraq, there is an inherent contradiction at work. Rather than seeking genuine consensus based upon a common framework designed to peacefully resolve the situation with Iran, the United States appeared rather to be forcing conditions which would paralyze the Security Council into inaction, thereby freeing up the United States to act independently in its own national interest.

When it came to defining what constituted the national interest, John Bolton, like many of his neoconservative colleagues, seemed to possess a decidedly split personality, especially when it came to matters involving the state of Israel. Bolton's pro-Israeli proclivities entered the spotlight when, in 1991, as the State Department's official responsible for international organizations, he helped orchestrate a repeal of a controversial U.N. resolution from the 1970s which equated Zionism with racism. Bolton does not come to his pro-Israeli stance based upon religious union with Israel—he is not Jewish, but rather Christian, the kind of Christian that had the arch-conservative, former Republican Senator from North Carolina, Jesse Helms, proclaim in January 2001: "John Bolton is the kind of man with whom I would want to stand at Armageddon, if it should be my lot to be on hand for what is forecast to be the final battle between good and evil in this world." But Bolton has developed a strong relationship with Israel, one that had him undermine official U.S. policy by keeping policy papers critical of Israeli actions from crossing the desk of the Secretary of State as Bolton did early on in his tenure in the administration of George W. Bush, blocking a memo which suggested that Israel had violated American laws with its July 23, 2000, assassination of Salah Shehada, a senior Hamas activist in Gaza City. Israel reportedly used an American-made F-16 fighter-bomber to drop a bomb on a house in the Gaza strip, killing Shehada and fourteen others (including women and children), and injuring more than 100 others. In his position as undersecretary of state, Bolton has engaged in numerous one-on-one meetings with Israeli officials without getting prior country clearance from the relevant offices within the State Department. Bolton frequently travels to Israel, where he has developed a strong relationship with Israeli intelligence officials, again outside of official bureaucratic channels.

In fairness, Bolton's unorthodox approach to diplomacy does not extend solely to Israel. Bolton has long been a strong force for anti-communism, and for promoting a Cold War-era point of view that pushes U.S. supremacy around the globe. He has a history of forcefully backing the cause of an independent Taiwan, while denigrating Sino–U.S. relations. Not surprisingly, Bolton is vociferously anti-United Nations, having been famously (or infamously) quoted as saying that "there is no such thing as the United Nations," and that "if the U.N. Secretariat building in New York lost ten stories, it wouldn't make a bit of difference" (both comments were made in the mid-1990s, when Bolton was a private citizen). Again, it seems quite curious that an individual possessing such strong anti-U.N. sentiments would be advocating U.S. policy positions at a U.N. forum such as the IAEA, unless the goal and objective was to undermine and/or discredit the U.N. process as a whole, thereby freeing up U.S.-centric unilateralism on the part of the Bush administration per the National Security Strategy of the United States.

Almost immediately upon his return to Washington, John Bolton sought to undermine the sense of normalcy and calm represented in the September IAEA resolution. Reinforcing the American contention that Iran was pursuing a covert nuclear weapons program in parallel with its declared nuclear energy efforts, Bolton orchestrated a series of leaks to the U.S. media, acting on Israeli-provided information, that Iran was pursuing illicit nuclear technology at a military site near Parchin. The Israelis had already passed this information on to the IAEA, who had initially requested that the Iranians facilitate access to Parchin back in June 2004. Iran, seeking to minimize IAEA intrusion into matters not dealing with nuclear activity, and which were sensitive to Iran's legitimate national security interests, were dragging their feet on the Parchin visit request. However, when U.S. newspapers started running stories based upon the Bolton leaks, accusing Iran of having illegal nuclear weapons programs operating at Parchin and other sites, the Iranians publicly denounced the stories, saying that the IAEA could visit the site if it wanted to.

Bolton continued to pour fuel on the flame, suggesting to his contacts in the U.S. media that the IAEA was too timid when it came to Iran and its nuclear program, and that the Parchin matter should be pursued more forcefully. Parchin, however, wasn't the target. Bolton, as the point man for U.S. policy on Iran, wanted the Iran case sent to the Security Council. He recognized that the United States faced an uphill struggle to convince the IAEA to agree to such a move. However, by keeping the pressure up on Iran and the IAEA, Bolton was convinced that the United States would eventually either find incontrovertible evidence of Iranian wrong doing or, failing that, simply wear down European opposition by betting on the fact that in the long run Europe would ultimately side with the United States in any stand-off involving Iran.

Despite his reputation as a maverick, Bolton was not acting on his own volition when it came to Iran, but rather as part of a larger U.S. policy to force a confrontation with Iran. Bolton had provided a hint as to the ultimate objectives of such a strategy when, shortly after the fall of Saddam Hussein's government in April 2003, he visited Israeli Prime Minister Ariel Sharon and assured him that with Iraq cleaned up, the United States would move forward to take care of other problem nations, such as Iran and Syria. With the considerable problems that stemmed from the ongoing occupation of Iraq serving as a brake for any bold extension of the politics of confrontation in the months following Saddam's fall from power, Iran had been put on the back burner. Now, with a transition of sovereignty (on paper at least) taking place in Baghdad in June 2004, and upcoming elections scheduled for January 2005, many in the Bush administration felt the time was ripe to push the Iranian agenda up to front burner status. This included the President himself, who hinted at the possible course of policy direction he was navigating towards regarding Iran in an interview with Fox News' conservative talk show host Bill O'Reilly in late September 2004.

> **O'REILLY**: Iran said yesterday: Hey, we're going to develop this nuclear stuff, we don't care what you think. You ready to use military force against Iran if they continue to defy the world on nuclear?
>
> **BUSH**: My hope is that we can solve this diplomatically.
>
> **O'REILLY**: But if you can't?
>
> **BUSH**: Well, let me try to solve it diplomatically, first. All options are on the table, of course, in any situation. But diplomacy is the first option.
>
> **O'REILLY**: Would you allow Iran to develop a nuclear weapon?
>
> **BUSH**: We are working our hearts out so that they don't develop a nuclear weapon, and the best way to do so is to continue to keep international pressure on them.
>
> **O'REILLY**: Is it conceivable that you would allow them to develop a nuclear weapon?
>
> **BUSH**: No, we've made it clear, our position is that they won't have a nuclear weapon.
>
> **O'REILLY**: Period.
>
> **BUSH**: Yes.

John Bolton was quick to capitalize on the President's public assertion, which opened up the possibility of U.S. military action against Iran during a question and answer period following a presentation at the American Enterprise Institute the day after the Bush–O'Reilly interview, noting that President Bush had said ". . . we don't take options off the table. And that we are determined that Iran not possess nuclear weapons. And that is the fundamental point of policy. U.S. Secretary of State Colin Powell reiterated the point this week. While stating that the United States had no immediate plans to attack Iran, he pointedly added: 'Every option, though, of course remains on the table.' " Earlier, in his prepared remarks, Bolton had questioned the role being played by the IAEA when it came to Iran, noting that there was no role for a technical agency when it came to international security issues, and that the Iranian case needed to be moved quickly to the arena of the Security Council.

The "every option remains on the table" rhetoric began to dominate the news cycle, in stark contrast to the calm language of the IAEA resolution. There was a definite reason for this strong posturing. The last thing the Bush administration wanted was to have the U.S. public pondering the possibility that Iran might not, after all, be pursuing a nuclear weapons program, but rather only a peaceful nuclear energy program. By elevating the discussion to the realm of conflict potential, and boldly stating that Iran would never be allowed to possess nuclear weapons, the Bush administration bypassed any debate as to the relative merits of its arguments as to whether or not any such weapons program existed, instead creating an environment that simply assumed that such a program was already in place in Iran.

Presidents do not speak idly when it comes to national security issues, and Bush's hints about all options being on the table represented the tip of the iceberg when it came to the issue of military strikes against Iran. U.S. military plans against Iran were being dusted off and updated. Furthermore, given the close linkage that existed between the policies of the Bush administration regarding Iran, and the state of Israel, the not-so-hidden hand of Israel was often found to be involved in such deliberations. Israel was a strong proponent of an Osirak-type strike against Iran, in effect carrying out a replay of its 1981 air strike against an Iraqi nuclear reactor Israel suspected of being tied into an Iraqi nuclear weapons program. Israeli officials were warning the United States, in public and in private, that Iran was coming dangerously close to crossing the red line of nuclear technological awareness and capability. In short, the Israelis contended that soon Iran would have all the know-how and technical capability to enrich uranium to levels required for nuclear weapons.

Once they possessed this, Iran posed a threat even if it stopped its research efforts in the nuclear arena. Iran, according to Israel, had to be stopped before it was too late.

U.S. military and intelligence officials had reviewed the possibility of a decapitating strike against Iran's nuclear program. The results were not encouraging. Iran did not possess a single target, such as Iraq's Osirak nuclear reactor, that could be bombed and in doing so defeat the nuclear program. There were numerous targets, spread out over a vast territory, which would require a massive effort to interdict that not only lacked certainty of mission success, but escalated conflict with Iran so rapidly that there was no way to contain the violence. In short, according to U.S. military planners, an attack on Iran, even if it was limited in scope to Iran's nuclear activities, would rapidly spin out of control into a regional conflict that could not be contained.

While the media buzzed with news of increased U.S. military planning for an attack against Iran, an even more explosive story emerged which had the United States selling to Israel some 500 "bunker buster" bombs, along with thousands of other precision munitions of the sort that would be needed if Israel were to attack Iran. The Iranian reaction was swift, and predictable. Not only did Iran restate its position that it would strongly retaliate against any military attack on its soil, it invoked the specter of an Iranian policy of preemption, with Iran's defense minister, Ali Shamhani, warning, "We will not sit and wait for what others will do to us." As if to prove the point, the Iranian military, during its annual military parade in October 2004, showed off its long-range ballistic missiles draped in anti-U.S. and anti-Israeli slogans.

Iran was not to be intimidated. Shortly after the IAEA resolution passed in September, Iran decried the result as illegal, and soon after announced that it would begin to convert some 37 tons of uranium oxide, or yellowcake, into hexafluoride gas for use as a feedstock for enrichment of uranium through the centrifuge process. The Iranians also hinted that they would pull out of the NPT if the IAEA referred the Iranian case to the Security Council during its November 2004 meeting.

The Bush administration found, however, that it might have pushed too hard and too fast on the issue of confronting Iran. The president was in the midst of a contentious presidential election race with the Democratic senator from Massachusetts, John Kerry. The war in Iraq was not going well, and the President was under increasing criticism from the fact that the U.S. intelligence case made for justifying the invasion of Iraq, namely that Saddam Hussein posed a threat warranting military action because of massive stocks of undeclared weapons of mass destruction, had turned out to be a false one. Selling another military adventure based upon a hyped up threat at a time when the country was already sharply divided over the first war was not deemed to be politically wise.

Further dampening any rush toward conflict with Iran was the fact that the military itself was ambivalent about the feasibility (and viability) of such a move, especially if it were to be limited in scope to neutralizing Iran's nuclear program. The cycle of escalation of any such action was such that the United States would rapidly find itself embroiled in another land war for which it lacked the resources to sustain. Any military strike against Iran, the military believed, would quickly become a fight to the finish, with the ultimate outcome in doubt.

Clearly a quick military strike against Iran was not on the books. Neither was any military action focused solely on Iran's nuclear capabilities. The targeting of any such strike was proving problematic at best. Thanks to the IAEA inspections, the United States (and Israel) had extremely detailed intelligence on Iran's nuclear enrichment program, at least in so far as it had been declared to the IAEA. However, both Israel and the United States contended that there existed in Iran a secret military program dedicated to the manufacture of nuclear weapons. If these sites existed, they were located outside the net thrown by the IAEA inspections. Both Israel and the United States were carrying out a full-court press to try to identify and locate these secret facilities. Israel made heavy use of its connections in Iraqi Kurdistan and in Azerbaijan to set up covert intelligence cells inside Iran, whose work was allegedly supplemented with specially trained commandoes entering Iran disguised as local villagers.

The United States was conducting similar operations, using Iranian opposition forces, in particular the MEK (whose political action front, the NCRI, had recently been shut down inside the United States, accused of being a terrorist front), to conduct cross-border operations under the supervision of the CIA. The United States also made use of its considerable technical intelligence collection capabilities, focusing the attention of its imagery and electronic eavesdropping satellites, as well the aerial armada of aircraft the U.S. military was operating all along Iran's periphery. The problem was, neither the Israelis nor the United States could detect any activity whatsoever that could point to a definitive location on the ground inside Iran where covert nuclear weapons activity was taking place.

Both the Israelis and the United States had collected significant communications between Iran and Pakistan, which showed a conspiracy upon both parties to try and hide the true nature of their cooperation on nuclear matters. However, the intelligence was ambiguous at best. Were the Iranians and Pakistanis simply trying to keep secret their commercial dealings in an attempt to avoid further embarrassment (a finding many both in Israel and the United States found plausible), or were they hiding something more nefarious, and simply exercising extreme caution when discussing it? The Israeli proclivity towards konseptsia, which led to a huge intelligence failure on their behalf regarding Iraq, was still very much a factor when it came to Iran.

Israel, rightfully fearful of a nuclear-armed Iran, boxed itself into a corner by interpreting any activity on the part of Iran related to nuclear material, whether or not it was for peaceful purposes, as being involved in a nuclear weapons program. The Israelis had already convinced themselves that there was an Iranian nuclear weapons program. They now simply had to keep searching for the definitive proof of the existence of such. Void of any information regarding Iranian nuclear activity in the northern and western reaches of Iran, the Israelis postulated that the Iranians must have relocated their program to the eastern provinces, thereby increasing the distance Israeli aircraft would have to fly to strike them. Again, there was absolutely no hard intelligence that pointed Israel in this direction, only analysis based upon a pre-conceived konseptsia that these facilities existed.

While the United States was carrying out extensive operations inside Afghanistan, and to a lesser degree Pakistan, the CIA and U.S. Special Operations Command had yet to organize any effort to conduct cross-border operations into eastern Iran in any meaningful way.

Until such targeting data was acquired, any talk of a military strike was premature. This reality, as difficult as it was for the proponents of bombing Iran to accept, actually was greeted with some relief by many in Washington, D.C. The need for the military and CIA to get their respective acts together in eastern Iran meant that there was a period of time in which the rest of U.S. policy could catch up.

In mid-October the White House called together its Iran policy team, and with the President presiding, a new roadmap was laid out. First, the United States would continue pressuring the IAEA to transfer the Iranian case to the Security Council. However, this was not seen as being likely to happen until at least the June IAEA Board of Governors meeting. The goal of the U.S. team in Vienna would be to shape the debate in such a way as to facilitate a positive vote for transfer in June 2005. The decision was made to expand the focus of U.S. concern in Iran to be inclusive of human rights, democracy, and terrorism, not simply nuclear weapons. The CIA was tasked with carrying out operations designed to influence public opinion in Iran, especially with presidential elections coming up in June 2005. The Iranian theocracy's crack down on reformists in the last parliamentary elections had resulted in numerous demonstrations. Indeed, from September 15 to October 15, 2004, more than 150 separate demonstrations had taken place in Iran, not only in big cities like Tehran or Isfahan, but throughout the country, including in the holy city of Qom. The United States would dramatically increase its funding of pro-West democracy groups, as well as work with Israel to increase the level of anti-regime broadcasts into Iran.

By broadening the scope of its campaign against Iran, the Bush administration was doing its best to shift the focus of any impending confrontation with Iran away from a simple United States versus Iran equation, to one that was more akin to Iran versus the world. Iran had been trying to get the United States to engage in direct one-on-one talks since the immediate aftermath of the 2003 invasion of Iraq, even going so far as to propose, via a two-page letter sent through a Swiss intermediary, peace with Israel (indirectly stated in the form of acceptance of the principle of land-for-peace, which builds on a March 2002 declaration in Beirut, supported by such staunch American allies as Egypt and Saudi Arabia, which seeks a comprehensive peace with Israel in return for Israel's withdrawal to the territory it had controlled before the 1967 war). The Iranians also proposed to cut off funding to Hamas and the PLO, and to seek a halt to terrorist attacks against civilians within the 1967 borders. And, from the nuclear point of view, Iran agreed to abide by the 93+2 formulation of safeguard inspections, which included signing an Additional Protocol. In return, Iran sought an end to all sanctions, and security assurances from the United States, including the re-establishment of relations.

The Bush administration never publicly reacted to the Iranian initiative, in large part because its basic policy formulation was one of regime change in Iran, not negotiating the continued existence of that regime. The Bush administration knew that its policies regarding Iran were not acceptable at face value to the international community. Direct talks with Iran would fatally complicate U.S. regime change plans by highlighting the true objectives of the Bush administration's policies, which sought regime change even if it required the unilateral application of military force that resulted in increased violence and destabilization in the Middle East. From the Bush administration's point of view, the rest of the world, in particular the European Union, Russia, and China, needed to be inserted as a buffer between the United States and Iran, and the nuclear issue pursued to the point that the entire world viewed the Iranian effort in a negative light, thereby making the U.S.–Iranian struggle an Iranian–international community struggle.

The Bush administration likewise had to contend with domestic American politics. Direct negotiations with Iran were not considered viable, given the heavy anti-Iran sentiment that existed in Congress, and the fact that any opening towards Iran along such lines would simultaneously open a window of opportunity for the Democratic Party in the November 2004 presidential race. The White House could neither take for granted electoral victory in the November 2004 presidential race, nor congressional support for tougher action on Iran. In May 2004 the House of Representatives passed House resolution 398, which expressed "the concern of Congress over Iran's development of the means to produce nuclear weapons." Opponents of this resolution charged that it led the United States down the road to war against Iran, in so far as it calls upon all state parties to the Nuclear Nonproliferation Treaty—including the United States—to use "all appropriate means to deter, dissuade, and prevent Iran from acquiring nuclear weapons." The resolution also "calls on the

President to use all appropriate means to prevent Iran from acquiring nuclear weapons," thereby creating a precedent for future escalation of the use of force against Iran, similar to legislation endorsing regime change in Iraq back in 1998. Clearly this was the direction the President and his conservative allies in Congress were trying to head. In July 2004 the Senate passed a watered-down version of the House resolution, Senate resolution 81, which called upon the use of "appropriate means" to prevent Iran from acquiring nuclear weapons.

While the language of the Senate resolution may have been toned down, the intent of the resolution, or at least the underlying policies it purported to support, was very hawkish indeed. Senator Sam Brownback, an influential Republican from Kansas who sits on the Senate Foreign Relations Committee, made these comments following passage of the Senate resolution:

> Just as it was an important rhetorical step for President Reagan to dub the Soviet Union an "Evil Empire," so too it is important for us to recognize the current regime in Iran for what is—an illegitimate, ruling elite that stifles the growth of genuine democracy, abuses human rights and exports terrorism.

> To the Iranian people, I offer my continued support. This is how history is made—one brave act at a time. The battle for your freedom will be long and hard. Stay strong, and know that America supports you, and will be there to help you rebuild your beautiful land. Hopefully, next July—as America again celebrates its independence, we can rejoice with you in celebrating a free Iran as well.

If the Bush administration were able to hold onto the White House in November 2004, many proponents of regime change in Tehran firmly believed they would be able to orchestrate the demise of the Mullahs by the summer of 2005. Congress, so they believed, was already on their side. They simply needed to move the Iranian case to the Security Council, force a showdown where the paralysis of the international community was readily demonstrable to Congress and the American public, and then move on Iran militarily, and unilaterally so if required.

In keeping with this line of thinking, the President, in late October 2004, instructed the Pentagon to be prepared by June 2005 to initiate, on the President's orders, a sustained military aerial campaign designed not only to take out Iran's nuclear capabilities, but also to facilitate regime change by decapitating the mechanisms of governance used by the Mullahs to retain control. The CIA's role in this regard was to increase the flow and quality of intelligence on both Iran's nuclear capabilities and the strength of the internal opposition. Iran was planning on elections for the presidency in June 2005. The White House believed that it could create a nexus of sorts, in which the IAEA transferred the Iranian file to the Security Council, the Iranian internal situation explodes over the presidential election, and the U.S. military is prepared to act immediately once the Security Council balked at taking decisive action. June 2005 was envisioned as being a month of decisive confrontation with Iran, a confrontation that the White House was planning on hiding behind a smokescreen of diplomacy.

All of this activity was not going unnoticed around the world. The European Union took to heart the threat of war between the United States and Iran. The European Union was Iran's main trading partner, with around 35 percent of total market share of Iranian global trade amounting to some 57.2 billion euros. Iran was a big supplier of energy to the European Union, and its oil-based economy imported a large amount of European technology and hardware. In the midst of the American conundrum over Iran, the European Union was undergoing some internal turmoil of its own. E.U. Commission President Romano Prodi, who had assumed office with the vision of creating a unified, strengthened European foreign policy, indicated that he was stepping down as Commission President in order to resume his political career in Italy, where he was planning on making a run at Prime Minister Silvio Berlusconi. The European Union tapped the former Portuguese Premier, Jose Manuel Durao Barroso, as Prodi's successor.

Where Prodi had been a force of opposition to the United States, opposing the war in Iraq and pushing for greater European independence in foreign and security policies, Barroso had been an active supporter of the U.S.-led invasion of Iraq (hosting a pre-war summit in the Azores between the United States, Great Britain and

Spain). Upon receiving his nomination as E.U. Commission President, Barruso immediately pledged to unite Europe and heal the wounds created by the Iraq war. "It is true the Iraq question divided Europe," he said in his remarks. "It is important that we concentrate on what unites us."

In a move that reflected the deft hand of Romano Prodi, the European Union also unanimously selected former Spanish Prime Minister Javier Solana as the High Representative for foreign policy, with his assumption of office as Europe's first foreign minister once the European Constitution came into force (anticipated to occur sometime in 2007). Solana, acting in accordance with the wishes of Prodi, had been very active in getting the European Union engaged on the issue of Iran. However, the lack of unity within Europe made it virtually impossible for the European Union to act in any cohesive, decisive fashion when it came to implementation of its agreements with Tehran. The so-called Tehran Declaration of October 2003 floundered almost immediately in the face of American opposition to any notion of legitimacy to Iran's nuclear ambitions, even if limited to peaceful uses. The European Union continued to proceed as if Iran had rights under Article IV of the NPT, whereas the United States wanted to limit these rights (or indeed eliminate them altogether). Unwilling to stand up to the United States, Europe had negotiated an agreement it was unable, or unwilling, to see through. Iran's obstinacy in breaking its commitment to cease enrichment activity was driven largely by Europe's unwillingness to negotiate in good faith.

A key aspect of the EU-3 intervention was the schizophrenic nature of the three nations that had come together on the issue. Two of the three—Great Britain and France—already held positions on the Security Council of the United Nations. The third—Germany—very much desired to join them there in the future. As such, there was a strong will among the EU-3 to be seen as operating in a strong, yet balanced manner when it came to Iran and its nuclear program. Great Britain, having sold its soul in joining the United States in invading Iran, was keen on re-establishing a sense of credibility within the European Union, and of exploiting its close relations with America to help moderate the hawkish policies of the Bush administration. France, strongly opposed to the U.S.-led invasion of Iraq, wanted to move away from being the perennial European "dove" on international security issues, and likewise was keen on seeing Europe emerge as a foreign policy counter to the United States.

Germany held an even more complicated position. Its political leadership continued to oppose the U.S.-led actions in Iraq, and was not inclined to stand by idly in the face of any precipitous move against Iran. And yet Germany had a hidden factor in its foreign policy considerations, one not readily visible to the rest of the world—Israel. For many years, dating back to the 1960s, Germany had sought to atone for its past sins vis-à-vis its treatment of Jews by accommodating Israeli foreign policy, defense and intelligence concerns. German intelligence was particularly close with the Israelis'. Technical exchanges had been arranged over the years in which Soviet-bloc equipment had been made available to Israeli intelligence personnel so that the Israelis could gain special insight into the weapons systems of its potential enemies. It was not an uncommon sight throughout the 1980s and '90s to have Israeli personnel wandering around any number of secretive German military installations, poring over equipment and diagrams with their German counterparts. The Germans also sought to atone for the support they had provided to Saddam Hussein's Iraq, where German companies had sold technology that had enabled Iraq to modify its SCUD missiles so that thirty-nine were able to strike Israel in the 1991 Gulf War. Unlike their civilian masters, German military and intelligence officials had a very pro-Israeli posture, and were inclined to be extremely hawkish when it came to the defense of Israel.

Many Germans secretly supported the Israeli position concerning the need for a preemptive strike. German intelligence agents, operating under economic cover, had been inside Iran for years, oftentimes in support of joint German–Israeli mission objectives (for instance, Germany had taken a lead role in covert operations designed to determine the fate of the Israeli pilot, Ron Arad, shot down over Lebanon and long believed by Israel to be held by the Iranians). These Germans reported back about a number of economic and political matters, including any signs of dissent in Tehran. It was German reporting on increased unrest in Iran, passed on to Israel, and in turn from Israel to the Bush White House, which helped shape the new American policy position that Iran could be taken down from the inside. So even while German diplomats negotiated in support of an incentives-based approach towards resolving the Iranian nuclear crisis, German intelligence officials secretly hedged their bets towards an American-backed effort to undermine and overthrow the regime of the Mullahs.

There was no real consensus among the EU-3 on the issue of Iran. Each nation had its own reasons for wanting to broker a deal with Iran, and none of the reasons coincided with one another other than a desire (shared by all except some German intelligence officials) to prevent the United States from stumbling into yet another Middle Eastern disaster. But the war-like rhetoric coming out of the United States made it difficult to contain the situation.

Surprisingly, it was Great Britain that seemed most anxious to stave off U.S. military action against Iran. In a show of defiance to the American talk of war, in October 2004 the Iranian Parliament, to shouts of "Death to America," unanimously approved the outline of a bill that would compel the Iranian government to resume uranium enrichment. However, at the same time the bill outline was being voted on, Iran's delegation to the IAEA was keeping open the door of negotiated settlement, noting that there was a good chance Iran could reach a compromise deal with the European Union.

The European Union was quick to jump at the opening, and soon found itself engaged in direct talks with Iran on the issue of trade incentives in exchange for Iran agreeing to suspend indefinitely its nuclear enrichment activities. The British Foreign Minister, Jack Straw, made it clear that diplomacy, and not war, was the only way forward regarding Iran. "I don't see any circumstances in which military action would be justified against Iran, full stop," Straw said. By early November 2004 it had become clear that President Bush had won a second term in office, creating an opening for the world to make new progress in the Middle East, including Iran. "Not only is that [war] inconceivable but I think the prospect of it happening is inconceivable," Straw told reporters. For its part, Iran appeared ready to negotiate, continuing its pledge not to build nuclear weapons, while insisting on its right to pursue peaceful nuclear technology.

With the deadline of the November IAEA Board of Governors meeting looming, the EU-3, with the help of the E.U. foreign policy advisor, Javier Solana, hammered out an agreement with Iran that came to be known as the "Paris Agreement." Signed in Paris on

November 15, the Paris Agreement was a sweeping document that tightened up the definitions concerning what Iran was obligated to do regarding the suspension of enrichment, while noting that the agreement was voluntary and not legally binding. In it the EU-3 recognized "Iran's rights under the NPT exercised in conformity with its obligations under the Treaty, without discrimination," while Iran reaffirmed that "in accordance with Article II of the NPT, it does not and will not seek to acquire nuclear weapons," adding that Iran "commits itself to full cooperation and transparency with the IAEA." Iran also promised to "continue to implement the Additional Protocol voluntarily pending ratification."

But the clincher in the agreement, at least as far as the EU-3 were concerned, was the part of the deal that specified that Iran, in order to build further confidence, decided ". . . on a voluntary basis, to continue and extend its suspension to include all enrichment related and reprocessing activities, and specifically: the manufacture and import of gas centrifuges and their components; the assembly, installation, testing or operation of gas centrifuges; work to undertake any plutonium separation, or to construct or operate any plutonium separation installation; and all tests or production at any uranium conversion installation. The IAEA will be notified of this suspension and invited to verify and monitor it. The suspension will be implemented in time for the IAEA to confirm before the November Board that it has been put into effect. The suspension will be sustained while negotiations proceed on a mutually acceptable agreement on long-term arrangements." The EU-3, in return, recognized that ". . . this suspension is a voluntary confidence building measure and not a legal obligation." The document went on:

Sustaining the suspension, while negotiations on a long-term agreement are under way, will be essential for the continuation of the overall process. In the context of this suspension, the E3/EU and Iran have agreed to begin negotiations, with a view to reaching a mutually acceptable agreement on long-term arrangements. The agreement will provide objective guarantees that Iran's nuclear program is exclusively for peaceful purposes. It will equally provide firm guarantees on nuclear, technological and economic cooperation and firm commitments on security issues.

A steering committee will meet to launch these negotiations in the first half of December 2004 and will set up working groups on political and security issues, technology and cooperation, and nuclear issues. The steering committee shall meet again within three months to receive progress reports from the working groups and to move ahead with projects and/or measures that can be implemented in advance of an overall agreement.

In the context of the present agreement and noting the progress that has been made in resolving outstanding issues, the E3/EU will henceforth support the Director General reporting to the IAEA Board as he considers appropriate in the framework of the implementation of Iran's Safeguards Agreement and Additional Protocol.

The E3/EU will support the IAEA Director General inviting Iran to join the Expert Group on Multilateral Approaches to the Nuclear Fuel Cycle.

Once suspension has been verified, the negotiations with the EU on a Trade and Cooperation Agreement will resume. The E3/EU will actively support the opening of Iranian accession negotiations at the WTO.

With the Paris Agreement inked, the IAEA Board of Governors had a green light to issue the most mildly worded resolution since the Iran crisis began back in early 2002. In addition to the Paris Agreement, the IAEA Board of Governors had received an upbeat report from the IAEA Director General, Mohammed El-Baradei, about the status of work between the IAEA and Iran. It appeared as if the IAEA was close to closing the books on the Iranian nuclear program, especially when considering the two primary outstanding issues of LEU/HEU contamination, and the P-2 centrifuges.

Concerning the contamination issue, El-Baradei reported ". . . the Agency's current overall assessment is that the environmental sampling data available to date tends, on balance, to support Iran's statement about the origin of much of the contamination. However," the Director General reported, "while contamination due to imported components and equipment is one possible explanation, other possible explanations continue to be investigated by the Agency, including the possibility of the contamination having resulted from undeclared enrichment activities conducted by Iran, from imported uranium not declared to the Agency and/or from contaminated equipment imported from sources other than those known to the Agency." The IAEA report concluded that its ". . . current overall assessment with respect to this issue is that the environmental sampling data available to date tends, on balance, to support Iran's statement about the foreign origin of much of the observed contamination."

On the issue of the P-2 centrifuges, the IAEA stated it had ". . . reiterated its previous requests for further information from Iran, along with supporting documentation, on the procurement of magnets for the P-2 centrifuges (in particular, on the sources of all such magnets), including attempted procurement and enquiries about procurement, and the procurement of any other relevant components, with a view to facilitating completion by the Agency of its assessment of the P-2 experiments said to have been carried out by the private contractor . . . Iran finally provided the Agency with copies of the contract and the report, which had been informally translated by Iran in April 2004. These documents appear to confirm the Iranian statements about the nature of the work requested of and carried out by the contractor between 2002 and 2003."

Perhaps most significant was El-Baradei's overall conclusion, which held that "All the declared nuclear material in Iran has been accounted for, and therefore such material is not diverted to prohibited activities. The Agency is, however, not yet in a position to conclude that there are no undeclared nuclear materials or activities in Iran. The process of drawing such a conclusion, after an Additional Protocol is in force, is normally a time consuming process. In view of the past undeclared nature of significant aspects of Iran's nuclear program, and its past pattern of concealment, however, this conclusion can be expected to take longer than in normal circumstances. To expedite this process, Iran's active cooperation in the implementation of its Safeguards Agreement and Additional Protocol, and full transparency, are indispensable."

One could not blame Iran for reading between the lines of the IAEA report and thinking that the end was almost near. Negotiations with the European Union on following up on the Paris Agreement began soon after the IAEA report was issued. The EU-3 sent a powerful delegation to Iran to carry out the discussions, including Great Britain's Jack Straw, France's Michel Bernier, and Germany's Joshka Fischer, accompanied by the E.U. foreign policy advisor, Javier Solana. The senior Iranian negotiator was the Secretary of the National Security Council, Hassan Rowhani. Mohammed El-Baradei also took part in the meeting.

The major problem with the Paris Agreement, however, lay not in the details covering Iran's obligations to suspend its enrichment programs, but rather with the duration of the suspension. The Paris Agreement recognized that the Iranian suspension is non-binding, temporary, and voluntary. What it failed to address was Iran's position that the suspension of enrichment activities could only go on for so long. The Chairman of the Iranian Expediency Council, former President Hashemi Rafsanjani, put the world on notice as to Iran's position on how long any suspension could be expected to last for when he said, "I do not think the ceiling of this period should be more than six months to prove to them that Iran is not seeking military applications." Rowhani stated clearly, "The duration of the suspension will only be for the duration of the negotiations. And as I said before, when we say the duration of the negotiations, we are talking about a few months. There is no talk of years."

Israel and the United States had made clear their respective red lines when it came to Iran's nuclear ambitions: no enrichment. But Iran had red lines of its own, as pointed out by the Supreme Leader, Ayatollah Khamenei, who stated, "The Islamic Republic of Iran will definitely not abandon its nuclear activities, and this is our red line. The diplomatic efforts and talks with the Europeans and the International Atomic Energy Agency were conducted by observing this red line."

The bottom line was that the Paris Agreement was only a stopgap measure which, unless either Iran or the United States (and Israel) were willing to alter their respective positions, was doomed to fail. This, more than anything, explains the stance the Bush administration took in the wake of the signing of the Paris Agreement and the positive IAEA report, in which the United States proclaimed its wary support of the EU-3 initiative. More than anything the United States knew that this agreement was stillborn. It would undoubtedly fail of its own accord in six months at best. This gave the Bush administration, which in the aftermath of the November 2004 victory in the polls was undergoing a major shake-up of its foreign policy team, time to regroup and reorganize, with an eye on June 2005 as being the decisive month—a time period that just so happened to roughly coincide with the anticipated floundering of the Paris Agreement.

The United States made an effort in December 2004 to further streamline its effort to get Iran referred to the Security Council when it undertook efforts to deny El-Baradei a third consecutive term in office. El-Baredei was a very popular Director General, and had established a sound reputation for fairness and toughness in handling not only the Iraqi, Iranian and North Korean issues, but also in standing up to the United States on the issue of Iraq's nuclear program. When the United States encountered difficulty in generating any enthusiasm among even its closest of allies to dump El-Baradei, John Bolton himself took the unusual move to personally order and review communications intercepts involving El-Baradei and Iran, in an effort to find some evidence of wrong doing. None was discovered, and El-Baradei was confirmed for his third term without issue. However, the bad blood between the IAEA Director General and the United States continued.

While the United States and the EU-3 were focused on the intricacies of the Paris Agreement, other nations sought to expand their interaction with Iran in other ways. China, which had already inked multibillion-dollar deals with Iran involving oil and gas, signed an even larger deal at the end of October 2004, solidifying Iran's role as key player in China's ambitious economic growth plan for the next twenty-five years. This was not a trivial event. Beyond the massive size of the Chinese-Iranian economic interaction from a financial standpoint is the significance of such a binding agreement from the political perspective. The scale of the Chinese deal, when combined with Iran's stated objective of establishing an oil exchange (or bourse) which would make use of the petroeuro as opposed to the petrodollar represented a direct challenge to the supremacy of the U.S. dollar when it comes to the global oil market. The monopoly enjoyed by the U.S. dollar when it comes to oil trading has kept its value at inflated rates, especially when one considers the level of the U.S. national debt. Any major shift away from the petrodollar to petroeuros would result in a lessening of global demand for the dollar, with the likely result being a calamitous drop in value of the dollar. Such a collapse could very well damage the U.S. status as a world economic leader.

The Chinese–Iranian oil and gas deal suddenly provided China with a tremendous amount of leverage when it came to U.S.–Iranian relations. China holds over $600 billion in U.S. currency reserves, meaning that China would loose tremendously if the dollar collapsed. As such, China found itself in a strategic swing position vis-à-vis U.S.–Iranian relations. The size of the Chinese–Iranian energy relationship is such that Iran could not set up a meaningful petroeuro bourse without Chinese participation, and Chinese participation is doubtful so long as China holds such vast U.S. currency reserves. The potential of China to abandon its propping up of the U.S. dollar through its extensive purchasing of U.S. debt presented a new reality that the Bush administration simply could not ignore. By leveraging so much of its future economic growth in Iranian energy, China had, in effect, drawn its own red line around Iran. Any effort by the United States to act precipitously against Iran would be seen by China as a direct attack against its vital economic interests. Europe had surpassed the United States as China's number one trading partner, and as such made the euro a much more desirable currency for trade. The real prospect of China shifting its holding of U.S. bonds and dollars over to euros threatens the viability of the U.S. economy in a way that nothing comes close to in modern times. The combined effects of China dumping the U.S. dollar and a crisis in oil availability brought on by a U.S. invasion of Iran would result in the simultaneous devaluation of the dollar while at the same time creating hyper-inflationary trends brought on by extremely high oil prices that would impact the ability of the U.S. government to fund even basic programs, yet alone the massive deficit-driven budgets the Bush administration had been operating under. In short, China alone possessed the ability to collapse the U.S. economy if the United States invaded Iran.

While some would argue that there would be no incentive for China to behave in such an aggressive manner, one needs to only look to the actions of the U.S. Congress, which in January 2005 passed a resolution condemning the European Union for pledging in December 2004 to work to lift the arms embargo against China that had been in effect since 1989. The fact is that many in Washington, D.C., view China as a threat to the United States of America, and define the threat not only in economic terms, but also military. The Bush administration, together with its allies in the U.S. Congress, seemed driven to push Europe and China as far away from the embrace of the United States as possible. While such policies might play well at home, with a domestic constituency ignorant of world affairs, they did not go over well in either Brussels or Beijing.

There was some hope that diplomacy would take on a new prominence in a second Bush administration. While President Bush spoke confidently about having received a "mandate" from the American people in the November 2004 election, the fact was that America remained a much-divided nation, largely because of the Iraq war. The lack of clarity concerning the future direction the newly elected transitional government of Iraq, voted in on January 30, 2005, would take only further muddied the picture. As the reality emerged that Iraq had, through a democratic process heavily influenced by the United States, elected a pro-Iranian Shi'a theocracy, it became clear that U.S.–Iranian affairs were no longer simply defined by the nuclear issue, but also by what the Bush administration increasingly referred to as Iranian meddling in the internal affairs of Iraq.

However, by the end of January 2005 the Iraqi election results were still unclear, and when the question of Iran was raised at the confirmation hearings of Condoleezza Rice, President Bush's choice to replace Colin Powell as Secretary of State, the former National Security Advisor put Congress on notice that she had no intention of softening the hard line towards Iran. "At some point, Iran has to be called to account for its failure to meet its international obligations," she stated.

Condi Rice's confirmation as Secretary of State paved the way for President Bush to carry out a charm offensive in Europe designed in part to mend fences over Iraq, and to set a course for improved European–American relations, albeit on terms almost exclusively favorable to the United States. However, media reports about a potential U.S. military attack against Iran, and the refusal of the Bush administration to reject such speculation outright (the President and his staff called such reports ridiculous, but then noted that "all options remained on the table") incensed many European politicians who believed that the best path towards peace with Iran lay through diplomatic discourse of the sort set out in the Paris Agreement. German politicians called the American threats ". . . a shot across the bow for the European Union's policy of negotiation." Many Germans viewed the U.S. statements on Iran as simply reflecting a decision by the United States to expand upon its Iraqi policies, rather than reign in such excessiveness. "We need diplomatic solutions, not threats of force," another German politician noted. German politicians appealed to the U.S. President to support, not hinder, the E.U.'s diplomatic initiatives. "We would move forward much faster, if the Americans didn't just stand with their arms folded watching the Europeans," said another member of the German parliament.

But the fact was that no German politician had the wherewithal or political courage to stand up to the United States. Germany, Britain and France were behaving in a manner that was strikingly similar to the behavior of British prime minister Neville Chamberlain in 1938 when he backed down over Hitler's demands over the Sudetenland in Czechoslovakia. In an effort to forestall another American illegal war of aggression, the Europeans were negotiating with Iran to convince the Iranians to give up a nuclear program that operated demonstrably within the framework of international law. Europe committed to the principle of Iranian legal rights regarding the enrichment of uranium, all the while caving into pressure from the United States to deny Iran this right. The inherently contradictory policy position taken by Europe in this regard was clear to all, it seemed, except Europe. Iran refused to give up its right to pursue the nuclear fuel cycle, while the United States refused to give Europe any maneuver room in this regard.

The subordinate role expected by the United States of Europe was emphasized by President Bush himself, when during his initial speech to NATO and EU leaders in Brussels, he extolled the virtues of a revived transatlantic alliance while making veiled threats of new U.S. unilateralism. Bush sought to bury the hatchet over Iraq, noting that "Our strong friendship is essential to peace and prosperity across the globe, and no temporary debate, no passing disagreement of governments, no power on Earth will ever divide us."

But then Bush turned around and delivered a slap to the face of European diplomacy by reiterating that when it came to Iran, the United States reserved the right to resort to military action. "In safeguarding the security of free nations," he said, "No option can be taken permanently off the table."

While President Bush was in Europe, the Russian government was welcoming Iran's top nuclear negotiator, Hassan Rowhani. In statements meant to be heard by President Bush, Russian President Vladimir Putin stated that the Iranian nuclear program was exclusively for peaceful purposes. Following his meeting with Putin, Rowhani announced that Russia and Iran were to shortly sign an accord that had Russia providing Iran with nuclear fuel for its Bushehr reactor, and to send spent nuclear fuel from the Russian-built reactor in Bushehr from Iran to Russia for reprocessing. President Bush flew to Moscow for meetings with President Putin on this matter, but left empty-handed. Shortly after Bush flew home, Russia and Iran formally signed the nuclear fuel deal.

The Russian-Iranian nuclear deal set off an explosion of protest within the U.S. Congress. John McCain, a Republican senator from Arizona, called for Russia's exclusion from the July 2005 G-8 Summit meeting. Showing just how pre-inclined the U.S. Congress was to accept at face value the notion of a nuclear-armed Iran, Jane Harmon, the ranking Democrat on the House intelligence committee, joined McCain in condemning Russia, noting, "This is the time to be tough with Russia. Iran going nuclear is a danger for the entire world, including Russia."

The Congressional hand-wringing did not impress Europe, where the E.U. Commission commented that the Russia nuclear fuel deal was "compatible with our own approach," noting that the Russian-built reactors in Bushehr ". . . will operate under the close supervision of the IAEA."

If the Bush visit to Europe was meant to create a solid front against the Iranians over the issue of nuclear technology, it failed. In March 2005 the IAEA met once again to discuss Iranian compliance with its safeguards agreement, as well as the Paris Agreement. IAEA Director General El-Baradei delivered an upbeat assessment of the state of affairs between the IAEA and Iran, noting, "Iran has facilitated Agency access under its safeguards agreement and additional protocol to nuclear material and facilities, and has also provided access to other locations in the country, including a transparency visit to a military site [i.e., Parchin]."

> We have continued to implement the measures of the additional protocol by reviewing declarations made by Iran and conducting complementary access and other verification activities. The Agency has also continued its verification of Iran's voluntary suspension of enrichment and reprocessing related activities. The Agency has been making progress in two important issues, regarding the origin of the contamination on equipment at various locations in Iran in cooperation with the country concerned, and regarding follow-up on information provided by Iran on its centrifuge programmes.

However, when El-Baradei turned the stage over to the IAEA Deputy Director for Safeguards, Pierre Goldschmidt, the tone of the IAEA's report changed considerably. According to Goldschmidt, Iran failed to cooperate fully with the IAEA by not providing adequate information about its uranium-enrichment program. Iran also delayed IAEA access to some facilities suspected of playing a role in nuclear weapons research. Goldschmidt did note, as had El-Baradei, that Iran continued to observe its November pledge to suspend its enrichment program.

Goldschmidt's main bone of contention with Iran lay in the IAEA's efforts to establish a firm documentary trail concerning Iran's procurement of P-1 and P-2 centrifuges, either in complete form, as components, or in the form of design drawings, from the A. Q. Khan network. Iran had provided some documentation, but these were insufficient for the IAEA to have absolute certainty that there was not an undeclared program. Complicating this investigation was the fact that the IAEA was pursuing, in parallel, investigations in Malaysia, Pakistan, and Dubai, as well as Iran.

While nothing the IAEA collected directly contradicted what Iran was saying regarding their procurement efforts, inconsistencies in the four investigations, coupled with Goldschmidt's back-door access to Israeli intelligence which pointed to a covert centrifuge program in Iran, cast doubt in the minds of the IAEA investigators as to the veracity of the Iranian claims. The United States and Israel were focusing in on the initial 1987 meeting between Iran and A. Q. Khan, believing that the Iranians were not revealing the entire scope of what had been discussed at that time. The U.S. and Israeli concerns were fueled by ongoing communications intercepts between Iran and Pakistan that hinted strongly at a cover-up. That a cover-up was under way there was no doubt; whether it involved simply hiding details that would be embarrassing to both Iran and Pakistan, or whether it related to a covert nuclear program could not be ascertained. However, what was clear was that Iran was not in violation of its NPT obligations in any aspect of its ongoing interaction with the IAEA, regardless of the ire on the part of Pierre Goldschmidt. But this fact was seldom highlighted by the United States, Israel, or the IAEA inspectors.

Likewise, Goldschmidt was unhappy about delays in access to the Lavizan–Shian and Parchin facilities. Iran had granted the IAEA access to Lavizan–Shian earlier, but was denying any renewed visit, noting that the IAEA had already determined that environmental samples taken there had turned up negative. The IAEA contended that these results were irrelevant, given the fact that Iran had so thoroughly altered the site prior to the sampling campaign. Iran held firm. Likewise, at the military facility in Parchin, the IAEA had indicated that it was interested in four locations. The Iranians, stating that the facility was a sensitive military installation, said the IAEA could pick one location for a visit. The IAEA did, and nothing was found. Goldschmidt again viewed the Iranian actions in a negative light. However, because these sites are not safeguarded, the IAEA has limited authority to visit them without evidence that Tehran is conducting nuclear activities there, evidence that Goldschmidt, despite his Israeli intelligence contacts, was unable to provide.

The report by Pierre Goldschmidt, rather than the one delivered by El-Baradei, more accurately reflected the underlying reality concerning the state of affairs between the European Union and Iran when it came to negotiating the specifics of the Paris Agreement. Since negotiations began back in December 2004, there had been no significant progress. Under increasing pressure from the United States, the EU-3 pressed Iran hard for a commitment to permanently suspend its nuclear enrichment programs. This the Iranians refused to do.

Europe tried to soften the Iranians by offering a number of economic incentives, and had their hand strengthened in mid-March when the new U.S. Secretary of State, Condoleezza Rice, indicated that the United States was willing to suspend its objections to Iran joining the World Trade Organization, as well as suspend specific economic sanctions concerning the sale of spare parts for aircraft, if Iran would give up its enrichment programs. Iran refused on all counts.

From the Iranian perspective, the cessation of enrichment activity was a temporary confidence building measure that would stay in place until the IAEA could confirm the peaceful nature of Iran's nuclear program, at which time the freeze would be lifted and Iran would proceed with the full scope of nuclear activity permitted under the NPT, and under full IAEA monitoring. However, it was becoming clear to Tehran that, regardless of what the Europeans had signed up to in the Paris Agreement, the EU-3 had no intention of allowing Iran to possess an indigenous enrichment capability, and in effect had subordinated European diplomacy to U.S. policy objectives.

The Iranians were bending over backward to find some common ground. In March the Iranians tabled a deal in which they would agree to limit the scope of their enrichment program to a single facility housing only 3,000 centrifuges, versus the 50,000 they had originally envisioned. This plant, the Iranians noted, would be under full IAEA monitoring. Iran also promised to ratify the Additional Protocol, and to allow the IAEA "intrusive inspection access" to other facilities throughout Iran, including military sites. The United States rejected the Iranian initiative, noting that it would still provide Iran with the personnel and expertise that could be used in a secret centrifuge facility.

The Iranian intransigence only reinforced the concerns of hardliners in both the United States and Israel that Iran had intent to develop nuclear weapons. Indeed, during a visit to President Bush's Crawford, Texas, ranch in mid-April 2005, Israeli Prime Minister Ariel Sharon presented Bush with fresh Israeli intelligence, inclusive of Israeli satellite photography, which Sharon said reinforced the Israeli contention that Iran not only possessed a nuclear weapons program, but that the program was well advanced. This information had also been shared with Pierre Goldschmidt and Olli Heinonen at the IAEA, further entrenching their hard-line position vis-à-vis Iran. The combined pressure brought to bear behind the scenes by the IAEA, United States and Israelis pushed the EU-3 negotiators to harden their own line concerning Iran's cessation of enrichment activities. By the end of April the Iranians were threatening to walk out of the Paris Agreement negotiations altogether, and resume enrichment activities. In a near panic, the EU-3 proposed a meeting in mid-May in which the framework would be set for a sweeping EU-3 proposal to be presented to Iran by August. Mollified, Iran agreed to continue the negotiations.

The United States was biding its time, confident that the EU-3 negotiations with Iran would eventually break down. Meanwhile, preparations were under way for a big showdown with Iran in June. President Bush surprised almost the entire world when, in March 2005, he nominated the primary architect of America's Iran policy, John Bolton, to be the next U.S. Ambassador to the United Nations. Bush could not have sent a stronger signal about his ultimate intentions than sending to the U.N. a man who had, throughout his career, openly mocked the world organization. The goal was simple—to put in place a no-nonsense representative who would aggressively push the Bush agenda at the Security Council, up to and including forcing a showdown over Iran when that issue was finally referred by the IAEA. Because when it came to the issue of Iran, the Bush administration ultimately had only a single policy objective: regime change, at any cost.

Six
Endgame

IN THE MINDS OF MANY of his followers, he was a living Martyr, having narrowly escaped death when, in June 1981, a bomb hidden inside a tape recorder exploded, causing permanent injury, yet leaving him alive. His religious studies took him from Mashhad, in Azeri northern Iran, to the Shi'a holy city of Najaf, in Iraq, and then on to the Iranian holy city of Qom, where he studied under the Ayatollah Khomeini. As the influence of the Ayatollah Khomeini rose, so did his, and in the autumn of 1979 he was elevated to the highly visible and important post of leader of the Friday Prayers in Tehran. In 1981 he was elected as President of Iran, the first cleric to hold the position, and in 1985 he was re-elected. A close associate of the Ayatollah Khomeini, he ensured that the policies pursued by the Iranian government were conservative in nature, and in keeping with the ideals and vision of the Iranian revolution and Islamic law. When the Grand Ayatollah Khomeini died in 1989, he was elected as Khomeini's successor as Supreme Leader of Iran. Holding staunchly anti-Western views, including publicly advocating for the elimination of Israel in 2000, he is seen as an extremely conservative leader who is a staunch advocate of Islam. And yet, despite all of this, the Ayatollah Ali Hossayni Khamenei may represent the best hope for a diplomatic resolution of the Iranian nuclear crisis.

Ever since the Iranian revolution published its December 1979 constitution (amended in 1989 to pave the way for the legitimacy of Ali

Khamenei as the heir to the Ayatollah Khomeini), the political, economic, and social policies of the Islamic Republic of Iran have been governed by the principles of Islamic, or Shari'a, law as interpreted by the Jaafari sect of the Shi'a faith, which serves as the official religion of Iran. The Iranian constitution calls for a Supreme Leader to be selected by eighty-six "virtuous and learned men" known as the Assembly of Experts, elected by the people of Iran. The Supreme Leader then appoints a Guardian Council of the Constitution, comprised of twelve members, six of whom are selected by the Supreme Leader, and six of whom are selected by the Iranian judiciary. The Guardian Council has the responsibility of interpreting the Iranian constitution, as well as determining the qualification (based upon compatibility with the ideals and values set forth in the constitution) of anyone running for elected office, especially the presidency or parliament (and even the Assembly of Experts). The Guardian Council can veto any legislation of the Iranian Parliament, or Majlis. If the Parliament votes to override the veto of the Guardian Council, then the matter is referred to the Expediance Council, which then resolves the dispute in consultation with the Supreme Leader. The Supreme Leader is the commander in chief of the Iranian military, and has absolute powers over all military, intelligence and security operations, and is the only person empowered within Iran to declare war. The Supreme Leader's powers are only limited by the Assembly of Experts, which can vote to remove the Supreme Leader from office at any time.

Since the inception of the IAEA-Iran stand-off of Iran's nuclear programs, the Ayatollah Khamenei, had been following the issue closely. His decision to have the Secretary of Iran's Supreme National Security Council, Hassan Rowhani, serve as the overseer of the nuclear negotiations with the IAEA demonstrated the seriousness in which Khamenei holds the matter. In September 2004, in an effort to guide the Iranian Parliament in an ongoing debate on whether or not to pass legislation banning nuclear weapons in Iran, Khamenei issued a fatwa, or religious edict, during Friday Prayers in which he stated that the production, stockpiling, and use of nuclear weapons were forbidden under Islam and that the Islamic Republic of Iran would never acquire these weapons. Despite the fatwa, the Iranian parliament was deadlocked on passing legislation that made such a bold statement. The decision of the parliament had everything to do with domestic politics, and nothing to do with Iran's national security, since the Supreme Leader holds supreme on that issue. Iranian parliamentarians were loath to legislate away a nuclear option when Israel and other regional powers, including Pakistan and India, had nuclear weapons programs. Unfortunately, many Western observers have looked at the inaction of the Iranian parliament as indicative of the true direction being taken by Iran. However, Khamenei reigns supreme when it comes to such issues, and having codified his decision in the form of a fatwa, Khamenei wrapped policy with Islam, making any deviation from the stated course as set forth in the fatwa reasons for removal from office by the Assembly of Experts.

Khamenei understood the domestic political sensitivity of Iran's nuclear program, and the ease in which it could be hijacked by those willing to exploit mass sentiment. Any effort by the West, especially the United States and Israel, to use the nuclear standoff as a vehicle to foment internal unrest inside Iran was doomed to fail. The Iranian people had, by and large, rallied around the nuclear issue as a matter of national pride. It was Khamenei's intent, however, to make sure these nationalistic sentiments did not go overboard and manifest themselves into a public cry for Iran to pursue a nuclear weapon. In June 2005, at the height of a bitterly contested presidential election, the Ayatollah Khamenei went out of his way to pound this point home in a speech he delivered on the occasion of the anniversary of the death of the Ayatollah Khomeini, June 4, 2005. "The world and the countries that want to secure their future are all against the monopoly of nuclear technology by a few countries," Khamenei said. "To say that no country has the right to have access to nuclear technology means that in twenty years' time, all of the countries of the world will have to beg certain Western or European countries to meet their energy demands. They will have to beg for energy in order to run their lives. Which country, nation, or honest official is ready to take that? Today, our nation has taken a step forward in this road. It has become the pioneer and stands courageously by this end. Iran is not a threat to any country and everyone knows this fact about Iran. We have not threatened neighboring countries."

Khamenei then turned his sights on the Bush administration. "We are not a threat whatsoever to the world and the world knows it. The

Americans, with their shameless propagandas, want to influence world public opinion. However, they haven't yet managed to do so and will not be able to do so in the future either . . . their other issue is that Iran seeks a nuclear bomb. It is an irrelevant and wrong statement, it is a sheer lie. We do not need a nuclear bomb. We do not have any objectives or aspirations for which we will need to use a nuclear bomb. We consider using nuclear weapons against Islamic rules. We have announced this openly."

Khamenei had no desire to pursue a conflict with either the United States or Israel. In the wake of the overthrow of Saddam Hussein, he had been the one behind the reaching out, via Switzerland, to the United States in April 2003, and had authorized his representative to put peace with Israel on the table. The fact that the Bush administration had failed to respond in any fashion to the initiative (other than to formally criticize the Swiss ambassador for even forwading such a communication in the first place) did not sway Khamenei from continuing to articulate a moderate approach towards resolving the differences between Iran and the United States. But Khamenei had a very uphill struggle to convince the United States that he was sincere. The United States, in the form of the Bush administration, seemed more determined than ever to force an ultimate confrontation with Iran.

John Bolton's nomination as the U.S. Ambassador to the United Nations coincided with an increased effort by the CIA to influence the upcoming Iranian Presidential elections in June 2005. Rather than actually trying to pick a winning candidate, the CIA was simply trying to foster public discontent which would manifest itself in public demonstrations and other forms of civil dissent. If enough instability could be generated, the Iranian regime of the Mullahs just might, in the minds of those formulating policy in Washington, D.C., fall of its own volition. And if not, then it would be so weakened as to make it vulnerable to a major air strike operating in concert with civil unrest. The feeling in some circles in Washington, D.C., was that if the United States demonstrated its resolve by bombing Iran in a decisive fashion, striking not just nuclear targets but an entire range of governmental and national security targets, then the people of Iran might be emboldened enough to take matters into their own hands and drive the Mullahs from power.

There were a number of problems with the U.S. strategy. First of all, there was tremendous dissatisfaction within the U.S. Congress over the selection of John Bolton as U.S. Ambassador. The goal was to have him confirmed and in his office in New York by April or May at the latest. June came and went, and Bolton had still yet to be confirmed. Second, the IAEA was unable to produce any smoking gun evidence that could prove that Iran had a covert nuclear program. This made any hope of referring the Iran case from the IAEA to the Security Council in June 2005 unlikely. Third, the EU-3 negotiations with Iran were still viable. Finally, and perhaps most critically, the U.S. had failed miserably in its effort to influence the Iranian presidential election. In a shock result, the arch-conservative mayor of Tehran, Mahmoud Ahmadinejad, was elected President. Ahmadinejad immediately declared that his election marked a major victory for Islam, and the dawn of a new era. "Thanks to the blood of the martyrs, a new Islamic revolution has arisen and the Islamic revolution of 1384 [the current Iranian year] will, if God wills, cut off the roots of injustice in the world," he said. "The wave of the Islamic revolution will soon reach the entire world."

Almost as soon as his victory was declared, the White House, in a move carefully choreographed with the news media, identified Ahmadinejad as one of the hostage takers when the U.S. Embassy was overrun by Iranian revolutionaries back in 1979. The U.S. claims, based upon the personal recollections of some of the surviving hostages, and backed up by unconvincing grainy photographic images which were said to show Ahmadinejad leading the hostages away, quickly fell apart. But in making these claims the Bush administration was firing the initial salvo of what would become a war of words and fiery rhetoric between two extremely conservative opponents.

June also brought with it an escalation in tension between the Iranians and the EU-3 over the status of the Paris Agreement negotiations. The Iranians remained committed to the suspension of its enrichment activities, but needed the EU-3 to make progress. The EU-3, under pressure from the United States, was pushing Iran to cease its enrichment program altogether, something Iran refused to consider. At the same time, Iran, working with Russia, was considering a Russian offer to enrich Iranian uranium. The Russian deal was unclear as to whether it would involve lightly processed Iranian uranium ore, or Iranian produced uranium hexafluoride. In any event, the Russian offer added another twist in the ongoing negotiations. In order to help create movement with the EU-3, Iran offered to limit its centrifuge operations to a few hundred centrifuges, backing down from the earlier offer to limit centrifuge operations to some 3,000. However, the United States had made its position clear: Iran had to totally dismantle its enrichment facilities. Not a single centrifuge would be allowed to operate, under the U.S. position. While the EU-3 did not formally convey their position in such stark terms, they viewed dismantlement of the facilities a logical step once Iran agreed to a complete suspension of enrichment. No one seemed to be listening when Iran said that nothing could make it give up its enrichment efforts.

The June 2005 IAEA Board of Governors meeting went by without issue, with both the IAEA Director General, Mohammed El-Baradei, and the Deputy Director for Safeguards, Pierre Goldschmidt, restating their reports from March 2005, with only a few technical changes. Both El-Baradei and Goldschmidt expressed dissatisfaction with the pace and level of cooperation on the part of Iran, although neither could provide any information to sustain any notion of any undeclared nuclear-related activity inside Iran. However, there was a disturbing trend taking place within the IAEA reporting. Rather than emphasizing what was being found in Iran, and putting that in context, the IAEA was beginning to head down the analytical path of assessing what was not being found, and assessing that in the context of what other parties were speculating might exist in Iran. In short, the Iranian government was, more and more, being asked to prove a negative. And, as had been the case in Iraq years before, the more the Iranians cooperated, the more speculation ran rampant in the IAEA and elsewhere. It seemed that the world was very much in danger of repeating the same mistakes all over again, allowing genuine non-proliferation to be subordinated to a policy of regime change. Iran was becoming increasingly fed up with the IAEA/EU-3 process, and on August 1, 2005, brought the issue to a head by informing the IAEA that it intended to resume uranium conversion operations at the Isfahan facility, in short resuming operations to convert uranium oxide into uranium tetrafluoride, and then to uranium hexafluoride. The Iranian announcement also put the IAEA and the EU-3 on notice that Iran would not brook continued affronts to its dignity and national security by acceding to a total freeze on enrichment activities indefinitely.

"Iran has worked closely with the Agency [IAEA], during the course of the last two years, to deal with the issues and questions raised about its peaceful nuclear program," the Iranian letter stated. "All significant issues, particularly those related to the sources of HEU, have now been resolved. Indeed, except for few questions, mostly speculative, nothing more remains to close this Chapter."

The Iranians had harsh words for the IAEA. "Regrettably, Iran received very little, if anything, in return and instead has repeatedly expanded its voluntary confidence building measures only to be reciprocated by broken promises and expanded requests. The October 2003 promises of the E3 on nuclear cooperation and regional security and non-proliferation have yet to be even addressed . . . the E3/EU has yet to honor its recognition, in the Paris Agreement of November 2004, of 'Iran's rights under the NPT exercised in conformity with its obligations under the Treaty, without discrimination.' "

"After over three months of negotiations following the Paris Agreement," the Iranians noted, "it became evident the E3/EU simply wanted prolonged and fruitless negotiations, thereby prejudicing the exercise of Iran's inalienable right to resume its legal enrichment activities, and did not have the intention or the ability to present its proposals on objective guarantees on peaceful nature of Iran's nuclear program, as well as firm guarantees on economic, technological and nuclear cooperation and firm commitments on security issues."

"It is now self-evident," the Iranians concluded, "that negotiations are not proceeding as called for in the Paris Agreement, due to E3/EU policy to protract the negotiations without the slightest attempt to move forward in fulfilling their commitments under the Tehran or Paris Agreements. This protracted continuation is solely geared to serve the purpose of keeping the suspension in place for as long as it takes to make the cessation a *fait accompli*. This is contrary to the letter and spirit of the Paris Agreement and is not in line with principles of good faith negotiations."

Then the Iranians dropped their bombshell, in effect calling the bluff of the EU-3 and the IAEA:

"As the IAEA Board of Governors has underlined, suspension 'is a voluntary, non-legal binding confidence building measure'. When the Board itself explicitly recognizes that suspension is 'not a legally-binding obligation', no wording by the Board can turn this voluntary measure into an essential element for anything. In fact the Board of Governors has no factual or legal ground, nor any statutory power, to make or enforce such a demand, or impose ramifications as a consequence of it. In light of the above, Iran has decided to resume the uranium conversion activities at the UCF in Esfahan on 1 August 2005."

In a near panic, the EU-3 on August 5, 2005, rushed to get out its much-delayed concrete proposal regarding how to go forward vis-à-vis the Paris Agreement. As the Iranians had predicted, the document represented nothing new. In fact, it not only largely repeated a proposal put forward by the EU-3, and which had been rejected by Iran, prior to the acceptance by all parties of the Paris Agreement, but it also incorporated in its entirety the U.S.–Israeli position that Iran could not have a nuclear enrichment program in any way, shape or form. It also called upon Iran to accept conditions that went well beyond anything required of the NPT (one especially bold recommendation was that Iran would accept ". . . a legally binding commitment not to withdraw from the NPT and to keep all Iranian nuclear facilities under IAEA safeguards under all circumstances," and to allow ". . . IAEA inspectors to visit any site or interview any person they deem relevant to their monitoring of nuclear activity in Iran." In short, the EU-3 incentives package said that there would be one standard for Iran when it came to the NPT and nuclear energy, and another standard for the rest of the world.

Not unexpectedly, Iran rejected the EU-3 proposal outright. In its angry letter responding to the EU-3 proposal, Iran held back no punches. "The proposal presented by the E3/EU on August 5, 2005," the Iranian letter read, "is a clear violation of international law and the Charter of the United Nations, the NPT, Tehran Statement and the Paris Agreement of November 15, 2004."

> The proposal self-righteously assumes rights and licenses for the E3 which clearly go beyond or even contravene international law and assumes obligations for Iran which have no place in law or practice.
> The proposal incorporates to a series of one sided and self serving extra-legal demands from Iran, ranging from accepting infringements on its sovereignty to relinquishing its inalienable rights.

- It seeks to intimidate Iran into accepting intrusive and illegal inspections which go well beyond the Safeguards Agreement or the Additional Protocol as well as the provisions of the IAEA Statute and its mandate;
- It asks Iran to abandon most of its peaceful nuclear program;
- It also seeks to establish a subjective, discriminatory and baseless set of criteria for Iranian nuclear program.
- Such criteria would effectively dismantle most of Iran's peaceful nuclear infrastructure;
- Criteria that if applied globally, would only monopolize the nuclear industry for the Nuclear Weapon States.

"The proposal," the Iranians concluded, "not only violates the Paris Agreement, but in fact makes a mockery of that agreement . . . the proposal is extremely long on demands from Iran and absurdly short on offers to Iran and it shows the lack of any attempt to even create a semblance of a balance. It amounts to an insult on the Iranian nation, for which the E3 must apologize."

Far from apologizing, the EU-3 released a statement that might as well have been drafted in Washington, D.C., or Tel Aviv. In high-handed tones void of any foundation in law as set forth by either the NPT or any IAEA resolution, the EU-3 noted that many questions still existed about the exclusively peaceful nature of Iran's nuclear program, and hinted at the existence of a nuclear weapons effort by noting that ". . . we do not believe that Iran has any operational need to engage in fissile material production activities of its own, nor any other reason to resume activity at Esfahan, if the intentions of its nuclear program are exclusively peaceful . . . any such resumption of currently suspended activities, including uranium conversion, will only further heighten international concern about the real objective of Iran's nuclear program."

The Iranian actions, precipitous as they appeared, were born out of an increasing frustration on the part of the Ayatollah Khamenei that the United States was using the EU-3 negotiations as a vehicle to perpetuate a freeze of Iran's nuclear enrichment program. The Iranians had invested considerable resources into developing such a capability, and had thousands of highly trained technicians standing by, doing nothing, while the freeze was in effect. With no serious movement underway on the part of the Europeans, Iran had no choice, from the standpoint of Khamenei, other than to resume operations, if even on a limited scope.

Needless to say, the Iranian actions did not go over well, either in Europe or with the IAEA. President Bush appeared on Israeli television, and reiterated the position of his administration that "all options remained on the table" when dealing with Iran.

Mohammed El-Baradei, the IAEA Director General, immediately stepped forward and stated that the only way to resolve the situation with Iran was through diplomacy. El-Baradei was in an unenviable position. He had just survived a bid by the United States to block his appointment to a third term as IAEA Director General. The United States, spearheaded by John Bolton, was not happy at what it perceived to be El-Baradei's weak stance on both the North Korean and Iranian issues, as well as the much publicized position El-Baradei took before the invasion of Iraq in March 2003, in which he directly contradicted the Bush administration's position that Iraq had a nuclear weapons program (El-Baradei had been proven correct). El-Baradei was up for the Nobel Peace Prize, and did not want to be seen by anyone as being controversial in any way. As such, he needed to bend with the political winds that were howling in Vienna about Iran, refusing to show any softness to the Iranian position while not endorsing anything other than diplomacy when it came to resolution of the problem.

The United States wasn't going to make it easy for El-Baradei. In August President Bush, sidestepping growing discontent in the U.S.

Senate with his nomination for U.S. Ambassador to the United Nations, John Bolton, made a recess appointment that put the hard-line neoconservative right back into the Iranian issue, at a time when the United States was aggressively pushing for the Security Council to be taking over the Iran file. This meant Bolton would be well placed to push the Bush administration's agenda.

Fortunately for El-Baradei, he had some powerful allies when it came to pursuing a diplomatic solution. German Chancellor Gerhard Schroeder, likewise responding to President Bush's words, said, "Let's take the military option off the table. We have seen it doesn't work." Russia, a veto wielding member of the U.N. Security Council, also came down strongly on the side of diplomacy, issuing an official statement that said: "We favor further dialogue and consider the use of force in Iran counter-productive and dangerous, something which can have grave and hardly predictable consequences . . . We consider that problems concerning Iraq's nuclear activities should be solved through political and diplomatic means, on the basis of international law and Tehran's close cooperation with the International Atomic Energy Agency."

El-Baradei was a thorn in the side of the Bush administration, especially when it came to the issue of Iran's nuclear programs. The Bush administration believed that the Iranian case should be open and closed, and that El-Baradei's diplomatic demeanor was not only out of line for a technical agency, but more importantly being used by Iran to buy time until it could solidify its nuclear weapons program. But El-Baradei was not one to roll over. He had long criticized what he believed to be the hypocritical position taken by the United States and others when it came to pursuing restrictive non-proliferation policies abroad while expanding their own nuclear weapons programs at home. "We must abandon the unworkable notion that it is morally reprehensible for some countries to pursue weapons of mass destruction," El-Baradei said, "yet morally acceptable for others to rely on them for security—and indeed continue to refine their capacities and postulate plans for their use." El-Baradei was in particular concerned about the March 15, 2005, U.S. Department of Defense policy paper, "Doctrine for Joint Nuclear Operations," which made permissible the employment of nuclear weapons by the United States preemptively, in non-nuclear environments, either to defeat overwhelming conventional opposition, or simply to assure U.S. victory.

However, there are two sides to every coin, and El-Baradei had likewise to address the concerns in Europe and the United States over the Iranian actions of August 2005. Under the growing threat of war, on September 2, 2005, Mohammed El-Baradei reported to the IAEA Board of Governors that he was unable to conclude, "there are no undeclared nuclear materials or activities in Iran." It didn't matter that El-Baradei could not point to any evidence that suggested there was in fact any undeclared material or activities existent inside Iran. The nature of the investigation had been, thanks to U.S. pressure, changed into becoming a search designed to prove a negative, versus any real search for the truth. El-Baradei recognized the extra-legal aspects of his investigation, stating that Tehran alone held the key to solving the problem, but that this would require Iran to provide the IAEA with documents and access to facilities for which Iran had no legal obligation to do. Rather than clearing up any remaining out-standing issues (although El-Baradei pretty much closed the door on the questions surrounding the sources of HEU and LEU detected in Iran; it appeared that the Iranian version of events—that the material in question was cross-contaminated with nuclear material from Pak-istan—was in fact correct), El-Baradei started digging deeper into the history of Iran's nuclear programs, asking questions about activities that dated back to 1985.

As a result of El-Baradei's report, the IAEA Board of Governors engaged in a heated debate over what to do with Iran. The United States, this time joined by the European Union, argued strongly for a referral to the Security Council. Russia and China, along with the non-aligned nations, resisted such a referral, and demanded more time for diplomacy. In a compromise, the Board declared that "Iran's many failures and breaches of its obligations to comply with its NPT Safeguards Agreement . . . constitute non compliance," and that "the history of concealment of Iran's nuclear activities . . . the nature of these activities, issues brought to light in the course of the Agency's verification of declarations made by Iran since September 2002 and the resulting absence of confidence that Iran's nuclear program is exclusively for peaceful purposes have given rise to questions that are within the competence of the Security Council, as the organ bearing the main responsibility for the maintenance of international peace and security." However, rather that referring Iran to the Security Council immediately, an act that Russia and China would have opposed, the IAEA decided to address the timing and content of any report to the Security Council at a later date.

The IAEA Board's resolution sent a strong signal to Iran that it needed to cooperate, but it also reinforced Iran's point that what the IAEA asked of it was above and beyond that which was required by law. In its resolution, the IAEA noted that its continued efforts to "follow up on information pertaining to Iran's nuclear program and activities that could be relevant to that Program" were hampered by the fact that the IAEA's legal authority to pursue such issues were limited. In order to get around these issues, the IAEA, in its resolution, endorsed Iran as a special verification case requiring Iran to submit to restrictions above and beyond that required by the NPT.

El-Baradei was "encouraged" that the resolution provides an opportunity for continued diplomacy, remarking that "the ball now is with Iran to continue to cooperate with the agency as early as possible." However, in Tehran the decision of the IAEA's Board was condemned. The Iranians threatened to end its voluntary adherence to the Additional Protocol, and cancel the remainder of what it called its "voluntary and temporary concessions," such as its suspension of enrichment activities, unless the IAEA reversed its decision. Noting the implicit threat of referral to the Security Council, the Iranian Foreign Ministry likewise threatened that Iran might respond to any such referral by withdrawing from the NPT altogether. The representatives of Ayatollah Khamenei, however, offered a more diplomatic response, stating that Iran would continue to adhere to the NPT, and that the extent of Iran's response would be determined by what the EU-3 offered next.

Even while controversy swirled around the IAEA Board's resolution, Mohammed El-Baradei was pushed even more into the international spotlight by being awarded the 2005 Nobel Peace Prize. Even Iran felt that El-Baradei deserved the award. But while El-Baradei's awarding of the Nobel Peace Prize added increased credibility to the cause of diplomacy, there were those who continued to push aggressively for a military response. In the immediate aftermath of the IAEA vote, a delegation of Israeli members of parliament traveled to the United States, warning that America and its allies must act to stop, by force if necessary, Iran's nuclear weapons program. Israel, the Israeli lawmakers said, would act unilaterally if nothing were done.

The Israeli parliamentarian's words, combined with similar rhetoric in Washington, D.C., as well as growing speculation in the American media concerning a U.S. or Israeli military strike against Iran, only further radicalized Iran's firebrand President Ahmadinejad, who in October 2005 publicly declared that Israel should be "wiped off the face of the earth." It didn't matter that Ahmadinejad had no power whatsoever when it came to using force against any threat, domestic or foreign (all power resided with the Supreme Leader, Khamenei), or that the Ayatollah Khamenei directly contradicted Ahmadinejad a scant ten days later, noting that Iran "will not commit aggression toward any nations. We will not breach any nation's rights anywhere in the world." It was Ahmadinejad's statement that caught the world's attention, elevating Iran as a genuine threat in the mind of much of the public, in America and elsewhere.

Ahmadinejad's verbal gaffe opened the door for the Bush administration, which knew that the way ahead was paved towards a referral to the Security Council. All the United States needed to do was feign interest in diplomacy. The new Secretary of State, Condoleezza Rice, met with her counterparts in Russia to encourage the Russians to work with the EU-3 to come up with creative solutions in resolving the IAEA-Iran standoff. This was done not from any interest in diplomacy, but rather in co-opting the Russians by having them buy into a process (E.U.-based economic incentives in exchange for Iran's dropping completely its nuclear enrichment program) that was doomed to fail because the United States had no intention of ever seeing it succeed.

Reality likewise tempered the American decision to appear diplomatic. While Europe had acted with a united front in pushing for the IAEA to refer Iran to the Security Council in September, the fact that the Russians and Chinese had abstained from the vote meant that any such referral would be meaningless. Moving forward precipitously would only threaten to break apart international consensus. The failure of Russia and China to block the IAEA resolution meant that there was an opening that could be exploited, the Europeans believed, and they lobbied hard for American support of the diplomatic track.

Washington concurred, even going so far as to support a European initiative that allowed Iran to produce uranium hexafluoride, so long as it was processed outside Iran. The European proposal mirrored one being made by the Russians, indicating that the European approach of wooing the Russians in through diplomacy was working. The Europeans believed that should Iran reject a joint European–Russian approach, the Russians would have no choice but to support referral to the Security Council.

But even as the United States publicly supported a diplomatic posture vis-à-vis Iran, behind the scenes it was redoubling its effort to poison the well by hyping the threat of an Iranian nuclear weapons program. Since the summer of 2005, the United States had been pushing new intelligence it had, in the form of a laptop computer that had materialized from mysterious sources. The laptop contained files and drawings that the United States claimed linked the Iranian nuclear program to military use, including drawings of what the United States claimed to be a nuclear warhead. The existence of the laptop and its contents was leaked to the press, setting off a storm of public debate about the threat posed by Iran.

The laptop was a product of a joint cooperation between the Israeli intelligence service and its German counterparts. Using sources developed from inside Iran, the Germans were apparently able to gain access to certain internal computerized working files related to ongoing research and development on a tri-conic re-entry vehicle for the Iranian Shahib-3 missile. The Shahib-3 missile had a longer range than the SCUD missile upon which it was based, and as such had a much greater re-entry speed as it neared impact. This higher speed was too much for the conventional warhead design to handle, and as a result the warhead would tumble and spin, either failing to detonate or missing its intended target by many miles. The use of a tri-conic design would enable the Shahib-3 warhead to remain relatively stable during re-entry, increasing the reliability and accuracy of the missile.

The United States misrepresented the tri-conic warhead design material as evidence of an Iranian nuclear warhead design. Likewise, the laptop made reference to a Green Salt project in Iran, which linked the manufacture of uranium tetra fluoride (sometimes referred to as green salt) to the Iranian military. Other documents dealt with alleged high-explosive tests that were said to be related to an Iranian nuclear weapons program. While the warhead files might have had some relation to actual ongoing projects inside Iran, however peripheral, the green salt documents were extremely dubious, raising the specter of a falsification of data. The high-explosive test data likewise was so general as to provide nothing of substance towards linking it to any nuclear-specific activity. What made this particular data somewhat suspicious, however, was that the Israelis had been telling the IAEA, in particular Olli Heinonen, about high explosive tests being conducted at the Parchin military facility. The link between the laptop data and Israel's earlier intelligence could be viewed as coincidence, but some European intelligence officials believe that there is a link, and that link is Israel, and as such the whole package of intelligence that is included in the laptop is questionable in terms of its overall veracity. The Iranians, for their part, called the laptop intelligence "total fabrication." However, in private meetings with the IAEA, the Iranians did indicate that there were aspects of reality woven throughout the entire laptop story. Some point to these Iranian admissions as proof that the laptop data is credible; others say it only reinforces their concern that the Israelis built an overall story about military involvement in a nuclear weapons program using as seed-stock a few verifiable facts.

The laptop controversy was brewing at the same time the IAEA was making progress in getting to the bottom of the A. Q. Khan procurement network. Pakistan had agreed to make certain individuals who had been involved in the procurement process available to the IAEA, and the IAEA was also able to access the Malaysian citizen involved in both the Libyan and Iranian shipments. The IAEA was also able to gain access to the facilities in Dubai where components had been stored awaiting shipment. A key development was the fact that the A. Q. Khan network had delivered identical packages of components to Iran and Libya. The IAEA was therefore able to refer to the totality of the Libyan package, and compare and contrast it to the Iranian claims. Faced with this new information, Iran provided to the IAEA documents, which included instructions on the manufacture and molding of uranium metal into hemispherical shapes, needed for any implosion-type weapon.

While on the surface such documents appeared damning, the Iranian officials claimed that the A. Q. Khan network had provided the documents on its own, and that Iran was only interested in the centrifuge enrichment-related documents. While a source within the A. Q. Khan network claimed it was Iran that had originally requested the documents, the IAEA could not verify these claims, and noted that it had observed nothing in Iran which indicated the Iranians had ever taken any action in relation to the activities referred to in the documents. However, the IAEA remained concerned that there might be an undisclosed uranium enrichment program, which in turn could point to an undisclosed nuclear weapons program.

The IAEA continued to focus on Iran's procurement of both P-1 and P-2 centrifuges, and sought data dating back as far as 1985. However, in its own internal technical assessment, the IAEA recognized that Iran had serious shortcomings with its P-1 program, and that the centrifuges were not operating at full capacity, nor were the Iranians able to produce them in the numbers needed to fulfill their strategic objectives. The inconsistency in holding Iran accountable for the genesis of a program that was not achieving the desired technological achievement was apparently lost on the IAEA.

The IAEA, in November 2005, finally gained access to all buildings it was interested in the Parchin military camp. Nothing prohibited was found, but the IAEA did observe a high-speed camera, which among its many utilities can be used in high-explosives tests related to nuclear weapons. As such, a negative finding in the form of an inspection was now turned into a renewed effort against Iran based upon un-sustained allegations.

The same held true concerning the Lavizan–Shian facility. No data linking the site to a nuclear weapons program (or even nuclear enrichment program) had been uncovered. However, the IAEA continued to pursue the presence at Lavizan–Shian of two whole-body counters, believing that these represented evidence of potential involvement of the site in the manufacture of nuclear material. However, the whole-body counters detected gamma particles, while the manufacture of enriched uranium produced alpha and beta particles. As such, the whole-body counter theory was baseless, void of any other data linking the whole-body counters to nuclear weapons work.

Another area being pursued by the IAEA involved the Iranian uranium mine at Gchine. The IAEA questioned why Iran would stop work to develop the Gchine mine in favor of the less-promising

Shagand mine. U.S. and European intelligence speculated that the Gchine mine was evidence of the involvement of the Iranian military in uranium exploration and mining. However, the Iranians had provided documents to the IAEA that refuted such a link. Under pressure from the United States, the IAEA refused to accept the Iranian story without additional documentation.

The IAEA pressed Iran to provide more information about these and other issues throughout October and November 2005. In late January, during IAEA visits to Iran over the course of a week, Iran responded to most of the IAEA's requests, including providing data concerning the Green Salt allegations. However, the window of opportunity for diplomacy was slammed shut, not by the Iranians, but by the IAEA, operating under considerable pressure from the United States.

With the atmosphere of trust regarding Iran so poisoned by the U.S. whisper campaign, and its refusal to stop its work at the uranium conversion facility, it was not difficult for the United States to finally achieve what it had wanted all along when it came to Iran and the IAEA—referral to the Security Council. Following a statement to the IAEA in late January 2006 by the new Deputy-Director General for Safeguards, Olli Heinonen (Pierre Goldschmidt had departed the post in the fall of 2005), the IAEA Board of Governors voted, on February 4, 2006, to refer the Iranian case to the Security Council. The IAEA resolution reiterated its litany of complaints against Iran, and noted that it was prevented by the limits of authority provided under the NPT to pursue the matter further. In the end, the IAEA, while making note that ". . . Article IV of the Treaty on the Non Proliferation of Nuclear Weapons stipulates that nothing in the Treaty shall be interpreted as affecting the inalienable rights of all the Parties to the Treaty to develop research, production and use of nuclear energy for peaceful purposes without discrimination and in conformity with Articles I and II of the Treaty," also pointed out that Iran was, to use El-Baradei's own words, a "special verification case," directed the Director General to "report to the Security Council of the United Nations that these steps are required of Iran by the Board and to report to the Security Council all IAEA reports and resolutions, as adopted, relating to this issue."

The Iranian reaction was swift, and predictable. "Issue as many resolutions like this as you want and make yourself happy. You can't prevent the progress of the Iranian nation," President Ahmadinejad told the Iranian press. "In the name of the IAEA they want to visit all our nuclear facilities and learn our defense capabilities, but we won't allow them to do this," he added.

The Iranian government sent the IAEA a letter, which put the IAEA on notice that from February 6, 2005, Iran's ". . . commitment on implementing safeguards measures will only be based on the NPT Safeguards Agreement between the Islamic Republic of Iran and the Agency," and that ". . . all voluntarily suspended non-legally binding measures including the provisions of the Additional Protocol and even beyond that will be suspended." The IAEA was requested to limit the presence of IAEA staff in Iran only to work relevant under the existing safeguards agreement, and that the IAEA should remove all "containment and surveillance measures" beyond normal IAEA safeguard measures be removed." The days of Iran's voluntary cooperation were over, at least for the time being.

The Bush administration had scored a major diplomatic victory. However, the IAEA referral to the Security Council was not a green light for military action. Russia and China, in agreeing to vote in favor of the referral, insisted that the Security Council hold off on taking any action until after the March 2006 IAEA Board of Governors meeting. This opened the door for Russia to press forward with its bi-lateral discussions with Iran over a compromise solution on the question of enrichment. Moscow had proposed giving Tehran part-ownership of a gas centrifuge plant located in Russia that would enrich Iranian-produced uranium hexafluoride, thereby allowing Iran to keep in operation the uranium conversion facility at Esfahan. This facility had been in operation since the Iranian decision in August 2005 to resume operations.

On the surface, the Russian proposal contradicted the U.S.–Israeli red line over any enrichment-related activity. But the reality was that the Russians were giving the Iranians permission to pursue a technology that they had not yet perfected. The Iranian uranium mines produced ore that was heavily contaminated with the element molybdenum. Iran had yet to perfect a technique to remove this containment from the ore during processing, meaning that Iranian uranium hexafluoride, if inserted into a centrifuge, would destroy the centrifuge shortly after operations began, either by clogging up pipes and tubes, or throwing off the balance of the centrifuge enough to cause it to destroy itself. Until which time the Iranians perfected the purification of uranium ore, resulting in molybdenum-free uranium oxide, the Russian offer failed to advance the Iranian program, while creating the perception of a concession. A key sticking point to the Russian deal was whether or not Iran would be able to retain a small research and development capability in centrifuge enrichment. Russia would not commit one way or another, instead asking Iran to resume dialogue with the European Union. Iran refused.

While Russia and Iran talked, the United States began to make its move in the Security Council. U.S. diplomats envisioned a multiphased approach towards dealing with Iran in the Council. First would be to get a Presidential Statement encouraging the Iranians to cooperate. Failing that, the United States would push the Security Council to adopt a Chapter VII resolution which would increase the IAEA's rights when it came to inspections in Iran (thus certifying El-Baradei's description of Iran as a special verification case), and make Iran's cooperation with such legally binding. If after this Iran still refused to cooperate, the United States would push for an increasing level of stringent sanctions which, if they did not work, would prompt a demand by the United States that the Security Council undertake even more stringent diplomatic efforts, perhaps even a resolution authorizing the use of force.

Russia and China would not likely go along with the U.S. proposals, especially at the latter stages, but the United States was prepared for this eventuality. Ambassador John Bolton's appointment was not an idle one. Shortly after the IAEA referred the Iranian case to the Security Council, newly appointed Ambassador Bolton put the Security Council on notice: "This is a real test for the Security Council. There's just no doubt that for close to 20 years, the Iranians have been pursuing nuclear weapons through a clandestine program that we've uncovered. If the U.N. Security Council can't deal with the proliferation of nuclear weapons, can't deal with the greatest threat we have with a country like Iran—that's one of the leading state sponsors of terrorism—if the Security Council can't deal with that, you have a real question of what it can deal with."

Iran during this time was not standing idle. On February 11, Iran began conducting enrichment tests, feeding uranium hexafluoride gas into a single P-1 centrifuge. On February 15, Iran fed uranium hexafluoride into a 10-centrifuge cascade, following that act a week later by doing the same with a 20-centrifuge cascade. These tests were designed to work out the kinks in terms of technical protocols, as well as determining whether the P-1 centrifuges were functional. By all accounts the Iranians considered all tests to be successful.

On February 27, 2006 Mohammed El-Baradei delivered a report to the IAEA Board of Governors in which he reiterated his past position that although the IAEA had not seen indications of diversion of nuclear material to nuclear weapons or other nuclear explosive devices, there remained uncertainties with regard to both the scope and the nature of Iran's nuclear program. The IAEA Board considered El-Baradei's report, and decided not to issue a resolution, since the matter of Iran's nuclear program was already referred to the Security Council.

On March 20, 2006 the United States met in Berlin with the new working group on Iran, the so-called "P-5 plus Germany" (signifying the permanent five members of the Security Council and Germany) in order to draft a Presidential Statement from the Security Council. Already there were signs of a split within the "P-5 plus Germany" group, with the United States and the EU-3 pushing for tough language, including a deadline, and Russia and China taking a softer approach. In the end, the Russians and Chinese, in order to present a solid front to the Iranians, agreed on a thirty-day deadline.

On March 29, the Security Council issued its Presidential Statement, in which it called upon Iran to undertake the measures required by the IAEA Board of Governors, "re-establishing full and sustained suspension of all enrichment-related and reprocessing activities, including research and development, to be verified by the IAEA. Furthermore, the Presidential Statement requested in thirty days "a report from the Director General of the IAEA on the process of Iranian compliance with the steps required by the IAEA Board, to the IAEA Board of Governors and in parallel to the Security Council for its consideration."

With typical diplomatic alacrity, the United States proceeded to issue statements which questioned its commitment to a diplomatic solution. Secretary of State Condoleezza Rice, remarking on the debate unfolding in the Security Council, noted that "Perhaps one of the biggest challenges that we face is the policy of the Iranian regime, which is a policy of destabilization of the world's most volatile and vulnerable region. And it's not just Iran's nuclear program but also their support for terrorism around the world. They are, in effect, the central banker for terrorism around the world." Clearly the United States was casting a larger net on the issue of Iran than simply bringing a nuclear enrichment program to heel.

This reality was reinforced by Ambassador Bolton's remarks at the same time, in which he stated that "When you see the risk of a government led by a president like Ahmadinejad, a man who has denied the existence of the Holocaust, who has said Israel ought to be wiped off the map—imagining somebody like that with his finger on a nuclear button means that you can't take any option off the table if you believe, as President Bush does, that it's unacceptable for Iran to have nuclear weapons . . . As long as the hard-lined mullahs are in charge, we think they're determined to get them and we're determined to stop them." Reading between the lines, it was clear that both Rice and Bolton were espousing a policy of regime change.

These comments were not simply off-the-cuff remarks, but rather reflective of official U.S. policy as set forth in the new 2006 version of the National Security Strategy of the United States, released in March 2006. In addition to reinforcing the previous policy positions that endorsed unilateralism and preemptive military intervention, the new National Security Strategy singled out Iran as representing the greatest threat to the United States of America. The document introduced Iran as a nation that had "violated its Non-Proliferation Treaty safeguards obligations and refuses to provide objective guarantees that its nuclear program is solely for peaceful purposes."

The 2006 National Security Strategy went on to state that "the proliferation of nuclear weapons poses the greatest threat to our national security," and declared that the United States was "committed to keeping the world's most dangerous weapons out of the hands of the world's most dangerous people." The document declared that this could be accomplished only by "closing a loophole in the Non-Proliferation Treaty that permits regimes to produce fissile material that can be used to make nuclear weapons under cover of a civilian nuclear power program." This paragraph directly contradicted the language the United States had agreed to when referring Iran to the

Security Council in February 2006, in which it noted that the referral was operating in full respect to the provisions of the NPT, especially those provisions concerning a nation's right to pursue the peaceful use of nuclear energy.

But the most pointed comments came when the National Security Strategy took on the issue of Iran. "We may face no greater challenge from a single country than from Iran," the document read.

> For almost 20 years, the Iranian regime hid many of its key nuclear efforts from the international community. Yet the regime continues to claim that it does not seek to develop nuclear weapons. The Iranian regime's true intentions are clearly revealed by the regime's refusal to negotiate in good faith; its refusal to come into compliance with its international obligations by providing the IAEA access to nuclear sites and resolving troubling questions; and the aggressive statements of its President calling for Israel to "be wiped off the face of the earth." The United States has joined with our EU partners and Russia to pressure Iran to meet its international obligations and provide objective guarantees that its nuclear program is only for peaceful purposes. This diplomatic effort must succeed if confrontation is to be avoided.
>
> As important as are these nuclear issues, the United States has broader concerns regarding Iran. The Iranian regime sponsors terrorism; threatens Israel; seeks to thwart Middle East peace; disrupts democracy in Iraq; and denies the aspirations of its people for freedom. The nuclear issue and our other concerns can ultimately be resolved only if the Iranian regime makes the strategic decision to change these policies, open up its political system, and afford freedom to its people. This is the ultimate goal of U.S. policy. In the interim, we will continue to take all necessary measures to protect our national and economic security against the adverse effects of their bad conduct. The problems lie with the illicit behavior and dangerous ambition of the Iranian regime, not the legitimate aspirations and interests of the Iranian people. Our strategy is to block the threats posed by the regime while expanding our engagement and outreach to the people the regime is oppressing.

Unfazed by what virtually amounted to a declaration of war, the Iranian government responded by conducting a full-scale operation of a 164-ccentrifuge cascade, successfully enriching uranium up to 3.5 percent, sufficient for operating a nuclear energy reactor. The Iranians declared themselves to be in "full possession of the nuclear cycle," and that this step was "irreversible." There was some question as to whether the Iranians actually achieved the results they declared, but verification actions by the IAEA, in accordance with the standard safeguards agreement, confirmed that Iran had in fact produced low-level enriched uranium.

The Iranian goal in moving forward was to establish a precedent of possession, to show that since it already possessed enrichment technology, and had demonstrated its ability to enrich, there could be no talk of moving backwards. Iran declared that it was prepared to meet with the Europeans to discuss a diplomatic resolution to the crisis that recognized Iran's right to possess the full nuclear fuel cycle, a capability which was no longer theoretical.

On April 29, 2006, Mohammed El-Baradei reported to the Security Council, as requested in the Presidential Statement, that the IAEA continued to not be in a position to confirm that Iran's nuclear program was exclusively for peaceful use. The weakness of this statement was noteworthy in relation to the harsh comments put forward in the National Security Strategy of the United States. Furthermore, El-Baradei underscored the strategic benefit gained by the United States in helping create an environment in which Iran would stop its cooperation with the IAEA. As opposed to earlier reports in which El-Baradei and his subordinates were able to provide detailed technical reports on Iran's programs, and demonstrate progress forward regarding clearing up remaining issues of concern, in his April report El-Baradei noted that the drastic cut-back in presence by the IAEA in Iran meant that the IAEA knew very little about what was actually going on inside Iran. The United States exploited this ignorance by expanding its rhetoric about the threat posed by Iran, knowing full well that as long as IAEA inspectors were out of Iran, there was no way El-Baradei could contradict them.

Iran exploited El-Baradei's frustration by declaring the very next day that it was willing to allow the IAEA back into Iran, operating under the provisions of the Additional Protocol, if the Security Council referred the Iranian case back to the IAEA. The Iranian move was well timed, given that on May 3, 2006 the French and British governments tabled a draft Security Council resolution, acting under Chapter VII of the United Nations Charter, which declared that "Iran shall suspend all enrichment-related and reprocessing activities, including research and development, to be verified by the IAEA," and put Iran on notice concerning ". . . its intention to consider such further measures as may be necessary to ensure compliance with this resolution and decides that further examination will be required should such additional steps be necessary," and that "full verified compliance by Iran, confirmed by the IAEA Board, would avoid the need for such additional steps."

But the harsh rhetoric of the Bush administration, and the timing of the release of the new 2006 National Security Strategy, had undermined any hope the United States might have had in gaining support for a Chapter VII resolution from the Russians and Chinese. On May 8 the Iranian president, ostensibly on his own initiative but in reality under the prodding of Iran's Supreme Leader, Ayatollah Khamenei, sent a personal letter to President Bush that offered an opening for further dialogue (the letter in reality was little more than a rant against U.S. policies). The Bush administration immediately renounced the letter, only to falter in the face of growing international criticism for such an undiplomatic response. On May 9, the French and British withdrew their proposed Security Council resolution text, confronted by strong Russian and Chinese opposition to any threat of sanctions against Iran. In its place, the EU-3 proposed to put together a new incentives package for the Iranians, attempting to restart the process of building on the Paris Agreement, which had stalled in August 2005.

Stinging from the rebuke by the Russians and Chinese at the Security Council, the United States, on May 30, 2006, changed course diplomatically. "To underscore our commitment to a diplomatic solution and to enhance the prospects of success, as soon as Iran fully and verifiably suspends its enrichment and reprocessing activities, the United States will come to the table with our EU-3 colleagues and meet with Iran's representatives," U.S. Secretary of State Condoleezza Rice said.

Within a week, the EU-3, represented by Javier Solana, presented Iran with a package of incentives that would help Iran build light-water power plants through joint projects; support Iranian membership in the World Trade Organization (WTO); and a U.S. pledge to lift certain economic sanctions against Iran.

On the issue of uranium enrichment, the proposal requires Iran to suspend all enrichment-related activities; however, the requirement did not preclude the future possibility that Iran could eventually develop indigenous enrichment capabilities once all outstanding questions have been resolved and international confidence has been restored in the peaceful nature of Iran's nuclear program. This detail represented a major step back from the previous U.S. position, backed by Israel, of not one spinning centrifuge being permitted to operate in Iran. Iran's initial response was cautious, with the Iranian Foreign Ministry noting, "the proposals contain positive steps and also some ambiguities which should be removed."

President Bush seemed to warm up to the Iranian comment. "I think that is positive. I want to solve this issue with Iran diplomatically," he said.

However, behind the scenes in Tehran, the Iranian government was dissatisfied with the EU-3 package. It prepared a counterproposal, one that agreed to enter into talks with the EU-3 and the United States without any preconditions, especially ones that would require Iran to suspend enrichment activities. In exchange for no preconditions to talks, however, Iran was prepared to offer limits to its nuclear program, including drastically reducing the number of centrifuges it could operate—proposing that it would operate only three 164-centrifuge cascades, instead of the massive 50,000 centrifuge operation it had originally planned.

Not to be outdone by the Iranians, President Bush quickly responded by giving a national policy address while speaking to the graduating class of the Merchant Marine Academy, at Kings Point, New York, on June 19, 2006.

"Iran's leaders have a clear choice. We hope they will accept our offer and voluntarily suspend these activities so we can work out an agreement that will bring Iran real benefits," Bush said. He threatened Iran's leaders with progressively stronger political and economic sanctions from the Security Council, adding that if the offer is rejected, "it will result in action before the Security Council, further isolation from the world, and progressively stronger political and economic sanctions.

"The United States has offered to come to the table with our partners and meet with Iran's representatives as soon as the Iranian regime fully and verifiably suspends its uranium enrichment and reprocessing activities," Bush said. "I have a message for the Iranian regime: America and our partners are united. We have presented a reasonable offer. Iran's leaders should see our proposal for what it is: a historic opportunity to set their country on a better course."

Bush made it clear that Iran's nuclear program was not the only problem that existed between the two countries. The President described Iran as "one of the most difficult challenges facing the world today," not only based upon its nuclear activities, but also, echoing the National Security Strategy document, for its ongoing support of terrorism, poor human rights record, and constant threats against Israel.

In a not-so-veiled threat that more than hinted of regime change, Bush said his administration was providing more than $75 million in 2006 "to promote openness and freedom for the Iranian people." The Iranian people "want and deserve an opportunity to determine their own future, an economy that rewards their intelligence and talents, and a society that allows them to pursue their dreams," Bush said, adding, "We look forward to the day when our nations are friends, and when the people of Iran enjoy the full fruits of liberty, and play a leading role to establish peace in our world."

As the President's speech made crystal clear, the United States, as it had with Iraq years before, was simply unable to disassociate a policy of regime change with a policy of non-proliferation. The United States, as the 2006 National Security Strategy made quite clear, was committed to a policy of regime change in Iran, and was using Iran's nuclear program as a smokescreen to facilitate it. And as the "Downing Street Memo" so clearly demonstrated with Iraq, the Bush administration would not hesitate to "fix the facts" around this policy. This is the uncomfortable reality that underscores any development in the see-saw diplomacy that has marked developments concerning Iran's nuclear program since August 2002—that in the end, the only policy objective acceptable to the Bush administration regarding Iran is regime change.

Conclusion

ALMOST FOUR YEARS TO THE date that the Iran crisis got jump started with the Natanz-as-nuclear-weapons-plant briefing by the NCRI, the world stands on the brink of the abyss of yet another tragic, avoidable conflict in the Middle East, with the United States and Iran squaring off for a confrontation of global consequences. For the moment, the threat of conflict seems to have been quelled, with the historic U.S.-backed EU-3 incentives package, accompanied as it is with the promise of direct U.S.–Iranian discussions, having received a lukewarm response from the Iranian government. In an increasingly complex political environment, this cooling of tensions could be seen as a vehicle for reducing the pressures being exerted on a Republican-controlled White House by fellow Republicans in both the House of Representatives and the United States Senate who have come under fire from their respective constituents over the issue of failed foreign policy and perceived weaknesses in the national security of the United States derived from such a failure. Iraq weighs heavy on the minds of all Americans, and indeed people from around the world, and any American-backed policy initiative that appears to back away from extending the conflict in the Middle East into Iran, and possibly beyond, is a much welcomed development.

However, there is much to be concerned of when it comes to the newest U.S.-backed initiative. First and foremost, one must question the genesis of such a dramatic change of course in national strategy, and wonder at the depth of support such a sea change in policy has within the Bush administration. One only needs to concentrate on assessing the White House at this point in time, since Congressional engagement on the issue of Iran has been superficial to the point of being non-existent. Likewise, one must assess the policy position of the Iranian government in acceding to consider the U.S.-backed incentives plan. If in the end the U.S. government is willing to allow Iran a face-saving way to retain a small, closely monitored nuclear research program inclusive of enrichment technologies, while facilitating Iran's acquisition of nuclear energy capabilities in the form of light-water reactors, and the Iranian government is willing to back away from its publicly stated position concerning its inherent right to indigenously develop and field the complete fuel cycle associated with nuclear energy, then there may yet be a real opportunity for peace.

It is, in the end, not simply about American–Iranian posturing. Critical to this equation is the role played by the EU-3, backed up by Russia and China, in riding herd on both the United States and Iran throughout the process of negotiated settlement as it unfolds. There is an absolute requirement for the European Union–Russia–China front to hold firm not only to the letter, but also spirit, of the new agreement, and to present a solid front to both America and Iran throughout the process. However, this is problematic, as each of the consortiums of states involved in drafting the incentives package comes at the problem with a differing point of view, as well as varying levels of commitment to the overall process itself. If the incentives program were part and parcel of a comprehensive crisis resolution program seeking to reconcile the United States and Iran, there might be hope for a meaningful and solid role for the European Union–Russia–China consortium in reducing the threat on American–Iranian conflict.

However, the fact that the United States refuses to include in the incentives package any notion of security guarantees for Iran casts a shadow over the entire proceedings. Void of any security guarantee for Iran, the incentives package is in reality nothing more than a stalling tactic in support of a larger U.S. policy objective of regime change in Iran. In the end, it is this larger policy objective which will ultimately alienate the Iranians, and fatally divide the European

Union–Russia–China consortium. If the United States shows any hesitation in living up to its end of the deal regarding Iran's nuclear capability, and if Iran in turn balks, it is highly questionable if the solid front currently presented by the European Union–Russia–China would hold in terms of referring Iran to the Security Council for economic sanctions. This in turn would facilitate on the part of the United States a rush toward resolving the Iranian crisis through the unilateral application of military force. As such, the current euphoria over the U.S.-backed E.U. incentives package is sadly misplaced. Rather than pulling back from the abyss of conflict with Iran, America and the world are simply pausing before one last, mad rush forward.

One of the curious aspects of the current U.S. posture vis-à-vis Iran is its inherently contradictory positioning contrasted with established U.S.–Iran policy from 2002 until just prior to the fielding of the E.U.-incentives package. Some questions immediately come to mind. First of all, the United States has repeatedly stated that Iran has a secret nuclear weapons capability, one that operates outside the bounds of IAEA weapons inspections. If this is still the case, there is nothing about the European Union incentives package that fundamentally changes this "fact." How then will the Bush administration choose to deal with the covert Iranian nuclear program it claims to exist?

When one factors in the publicly stated position of Israel and the pro-Israeli Lobby operating in the United States, it appears as if the Bush administration has completely caved in on the issue of Iran. The Israelis have loudly proclaimed their position that any Iranian acquisition of nuclear enrichment capability represents a red line that cannot be tolerated in the interests of Israeli national security. Both Israel and the United States maintain that such a program exists inside Iran, operating outside of the scope of the declared enrichment activities monitored by the IAEA. In fact, John Bolton, echoing similar charges made by Israel, has gone so far as to assert that Iran has already enriched enough uranium to make several nuclear weapons, making any discussion concerning ongoing monitoring and verification efforts by the IAEA moot in the extreme.

Since it is only the IAEA-monitored enrichment activities which are verifiably subject to the freeze restrictions imposed by the E.U.-incentives program, in order for the United States and Israel to maintain any consistency and credibility there must be not only a continued call for expanded IAEA access to facilities in Iraq that are not currently under the monitoring of the IAEA inspectors, but also an active search for the highly enriched uranium Bolton and the Israelis claim already exists. Given the fact that the United States has refused to include any security guarantees to the Iranians, and that the policy of regime change in Tehran still dominates the senior-most hierarchy of the Bush administration, there is little likelihood that the Iranian government would accede to any wildly intrusive regime of inspections which opened up its national security secrets at a time when the United States continues to plot the demise of the Iranian theocracy.

Many of the facilities that would be targeted for such expanded inspections are considered by the Iranians to be extremely sensitive, as they relate to legitimate national security and defense programs, and as such would not be opened for such intrusive investigations. And any refusal by Iran to permit inspections of these facilities would be shown by the United States and Israel to be clear-cut proof that Iran is non-compliant, feeding the conspiracy theorists in the United States and Israel who have committed to the existence of an Iranian nuclear weapons program, regardless of what the facts are, and as such defining Iran as a threat worthy of military intervention. In short, the Bush administration will resurrect its old adage, overused in the build-up to war with Iraq, that the only way to disarm Iran is to lead a coalition of the willing into Iran to remove the regime of the Mullahs from power.

Void of a complete reversal in policy objectives on the part of the United States, including a rejection of regime change in Iran, and a willingness on the part of the Bush administration to muzzle Israel over the issue of Iran (something no American administration, Republican or Democrat, has ever shown a willingness to do in modern times), the path forward is sadly predictable.

Regime change in Iran is a topic everyone in Washington, D.C., knows about, but no one wants to discuss, at least openly. Typical of this approach is the speech given by Ambassador John Bolton to B'nai B'rith International, a Jewish humanitarian organization, in May 2006, in which he commented on the possibility of an incentives package to get Iran to cease and desist on its nuclear enrichment program. "This is a sign to the rulers in Tehran that if they give up their long-standing support for terrorism and they give up their pursuit of weapons of mass destruction, that their regime can stay in place and that they can have a different relationship with the United States and the rest of the world," Bolton said. While many marvelled at the benevolence of the U.S. position, what remained unsaid was the extreme hubris, and underlying reality, of what wasn't said: that if Iran did not "play ball," then the Iranian regime would not, in the minds of policy formulators in Washington, D.C., be allowed to stay in place. Once again, the world finds itself on the brink of another Middle East war in which the United States is using trumped-up charges centered around false threats of weapons of mass destruction as a smoke-screen to hide its true policy objectives of regime change.

Unless a new domestic imperative can be found within the United States that can influence such a sea change in the Iran policies of the Bush administration, the current lowering of tensions appears to be nothing more than a politically motivated maneuver on the part of the Bush administration to remove Iran from the politically charged lead-up to the November 2006 mid-term elections. The Bush administration seems to be gambling on its ability to breath life into the false hopes of the E.U. incentives package until after the November 2006 elections, at which time the United States will be able to orchestrate the demise of the incentives deal, and resume its way down the path of military confrontation with Iran, the goal being the removal of the Iranian theocracy from power.

It is essential, therefore, that Iran not be removed from the public debate here in the United States. War with Iran must be discussed, because the ultimate policy objective of the Bush administration regarding Iran is war. Such a public discussion and debate would be readily had if the Bush administration had not accepted the E.U. incentives program, because the American public would have no choice but to respond to the increasingly bellicose posturing of the Bush administration. Faced with the ongoing devolution of the situation in Iraq, the U.S. public most probably would have rebelled at the notion of yet another Middle Eastern war.

Thanks to the astute maneuvering of the Bush administration, it now appears as if Iran will no longer be on the front burner of American domestic political discourse in the weeks and months leading up to the critical November 2006 elections. Failure to so engage, however, only increases the likelihood of war with Iran. A failure to have a national debate, dialogue or discussion on the totality of issues that comprise U.S.–Iranian relations means that, in the minds of the American electorate, the only issue that defines U.S.–Iran relations is the nuclear issue, and that this issue is under control, at least for the time being.

For Americans who were introduced to the concept of fire as a result of the Great Chicago Fire, fire is a horrible and irrationally terrifying phenomenon, as opposed to being a process that is part of nature, and which can produce energy in a manner useful to all of humanity. The same can be said about the manner in which nuclear issues were introduced to the United States. Rather than a force which has the capability of doing great good, Americans view nuclear issues from the perspective of Hiroshima and Nagasaki, of children hiding under desks during Civil Defense drills, and as the potential bringer of global holocaust. As such, whenever any nuclear issue is raised, it is done from a negative context, void of balance.

This reality has been exploited to the maximum extent possible by the Bush administration when it comes to the issue of Iran and its nuclear programs. Iran, we are told, is a nation awash in a sea of oil and natural gas, and as such has no legitimate claim for a nuclear energy program. We are not made cognizant of the reality, and inherent complexity, of nuclear energy, so that we can better understand what it is Iran is trying to accomplish, and how to contextualize the nuclear technologies Iran seeks to pursue. For most Americans, use of the term "nuclear" does not engender visions of peaceful energy, but rather horrific destruction. It is this pre-inclination toward negativity that allows the Bush administration to get away with an extremely sophomoric approach toward assessing Iran's pursuit of the atom.

For these reasons, Americans have allowed themselves to be cowed by a Bush administration, together with a compliant Congress and media, which grossly misrepresents Iran's nuclear energy program as being something that it is not. We hear from the Bush administration that Iran is awash in a sea of oil, and that there is no justification for any nuclear energy program. But even a cursory look at the facts backs up the Iranian contention that it needs an alternative energy source for domestic consumption requirements if it is to remain economically viable in the decades to come. The Bush administration contends that Iran lacks the indigenous uranium ore to justify a home-grown centrifuge enrichment program, and that Iran would use up its entire uranium stockpile fueling its planned reactor capability in just one year. However, any sound calculation of Iran's uranium ore reserves holds that Iran can indigenously enrich enough fuel to power a dozen reactors for more than thirty years. And this number does not take into account the fact that Iran has claimed to have discovered even more uranium ore reserves.

The Bush administration has misrepresented the capabilities of the Iranian enrichment program, and irresponsibly inserted red-herrings into the equation, such as the maddening discussion centered on the "whole body counters" involved with the Lavizan–Shian research center. In short, the Bush administration, with the able help of the Israeli government and the pro-Israel "Lobby," has succeeded in exploiting the ignorance of the American people about nuclear energy technology and nuclear weapons so as to engender enough fear that the American public has more or less been pre-programmed to accept the notion of the need to militarily confront a nuclear armed Iran, even as they continue to pay the price, both in terms of money and blood, for a similar misadventure in Iraq.

But while the American public may be pre-programmed to accept the necessity of war with Iran, even if no such necessity exists, there has been no effort to prepare America, or even the world at large, for the awful reality of what a war with Iran would entail. On this, U.S. Secretary of State Condoleezza Rice is correct: Iran is not Iraq. While Iran has been subjected to a punishing unilateral economic embargo on the part of the United States, it still is able to trade with the rest of the world. As such, Iran remains very much a modern nation state with access to the complete spectrum of technologies that are available to the rest of the world. This includes military technology. Iran is a vastly larger country than Iraq, with a correspondingly larger population and military. The Iranian people are a proud people who cherish their culture, history and independence. Any notion that the Iranian people would somehow stand idly while the United States bombarded their nation or occupied their soil is tragically unfounded. Iran would resist any attack against its soil with all of the considerable means available.

Any aerial bombardment of Iran would result in the immediate attack by Iranian missiles on targets in Israel, followed by a major Hezbollah rocketing of northern Israel. If U.S. military forces were deployed from the soil of any nation within striking distance of Iran, those nations too could be expected to come under Iranian attack. Iran will fire missile barrages against American forces in Iraq, and then engage the entire coalition occupation force on the ground, either with Iranian paramilitary forces infiltrated into Iraq, or using Iraqi proxies in the form of the various pro-Iranian Shi'a militias that are in power in Iraq today. American freedom of movement, such as it is, will be eliminated almost overnight. Lines of communication with American logistics bases in Kuwait and Jordan will be cut, and the sole remaining line of communication through Kurdistan into Turkey, already tenuous, will become untenable. American forces will become almost exclusively dependent on aerial re-supply, which will expose American helicopters and aircraft to great risk from Iranian surface-to-air missiles. Americans will be forced to abandon some bases in favor of consolidation of resources, and eventually America will be forced to quit Iraq altogether or suffer extremely heavy casualties (Iranian intensification of the conflict in Iraq could have U.S. casualty figures approach weekly KIA/WIA rates similar to those suffered during the Vietnam War).

Iran will do its utmost to play the oil card, not only shutting off its exportation of oil and natural gas, but also threaten the oil production of Iraq, Kuwait, UAE, and Saudi Arabia, either through missile attack or direct action by pro-Iranian Shi'a activists or an Iranian military commando unit. U.S. naval forces operating in the Persian Gulf will be put at risk, and there is a real possibility that Iran would succeed in sinking or heavily damaging a number of U.S. capital warships, including any aircraft carriers that might be operating in the region. There is a better than even chance that Iran would succeed in shutting down the Strait of Hormuz, choking off the global oil supply.

The Iranian reaction will have global reach, with Iranian agents or their proxies conducting terror bombings, kidnappings and/or assassinations of American, Israeli, and allied forces, diplomats and civilians. Attacks will definitely occur in Europe, and may even spread to American soil.

Any American ground invasion of Iran would be doomed to fail. While there can be no doubt that American military might would succeed in gaining a significant foothold inside Iran, either by a coastal landing around Bandar Abbas on the Persian Gulf coast, or a ground assault emanating from Azerbaijan or Iraqi soil, the conflict would quickly bog down. America simply does not have the conventional combat power to fight a sustained ground combat action in Iran. The scenario most likely to be faced will be akin to that experienced by American forces in Korea in 1951 when China entered the war. At best we would see an epic attack in another direction, such as the 1st Marine Division pulled off at the Chosin Reservoir. At worst, we could see something along the lines of the total collapse of the VII Army Corps when surprised by the Chinese troops.

Faced with such a disaster, the United States would have no choice but to escalate the conflict along military lines, which means to engage Iran with nuclear weapons. At this juncture, the equation becomes unpredictable, the damage done incalculable, and the course of world history, including America's role as a viable global leader, would be seriously altered. The harm inflicted on the United States, directly and indirectly, as a result of any decision to employ nuclear weapons will be fatal. America's prestige and standing on the global stage has already suffered greatly from its ongoing misadventure in Iraq, and its incomprehensible strategy of world hegemony disguised as a global war on terror. A war with Iran will not only cause whatever good will the world held in reserve for America to rapidly dissipate, but also subject America to economic and physical harm.

Americans must keep in mind that today the global energy market operates on rather slim, and thus fragile, margins. Given the increased demand for oil, and a failure of the oil market to develop and exploit new sources of oil, the oil industry is operating at a mere 2 percent of excess capacity. This means that when one adds up all the oil consumed on a daily basis, the global oil industry produces that amount plus 2 percent. This figure is barely enough to handle even the slightest upswing in economic activity, and is already being stressed by the continuing demands brought on by the combination of America's endless thirst for oil, and the booming economies of China and India. Iran alone accounts for nearly 4 percent of the world's oil. Simply taking Iranian oil off the market means that the world will be operating at a negative 2 percent capacity, meaning there is not enough oil to meet the daily demands of the global economy. Factor in the fact that war with Iran will likely adversely impact oil production in Iraq, Kuwait, the UAE, and Saudi Arabia, there is a real danger that the world may well be facing up to a 20 percent negative production capacity. Given the demand for oil, and America's dependence upon foreign oil supplies, oil prices will do what any commodity in demand does when there are finite sources and infinite demand—explode.

The price of oil will skyrocket out of control as a result of any American invasion of Iran, and the destabilization inflicted on the world energy market will be made permanent if America employs nuclear weapons. Every American businessman who needs to factor in the cost of oil in the bottom line of the company being run must understand that they will face almost immediate financial ruin as a result of hyperinflation brought on by oil prices reaching in excess of $150–200 dollars per barrel over a sustained period of time. The American consumer will suffer, and nearly every aspect of the American economy will suffer a collapse along lines not experienced since the Great Depression.

The war with Iraq hurt America in ways most Americans could not see. The Bush administration and Congress, backed up by a resilient American economy, were able to soften the blow of the disaster that is the war in Iraq. However, in doing so, there is no longer a reserve of economic strength upon which America can fall back onto to shield the detrimental economic impact that a war with Iran will bring. America will literally hit economic rock bottom, with all that entails. One only needs hearken back in time to post–World War I Germany, where Germans suffering under hyperinflation had to use wheelbarrows to bring in enough cash to buy food. The American dollar will become worthless, and with it the entire American economy. The global economy will take a hit, for certain, but no country will suffer economically like the United States should the Bush administration pursue armed conflict with Iran.

There can be no doubt that a war with Iran is detrimental to the national security interests of the United States. Nothing good can come from such a conflict, only bad. One could put forward the argument that a U.S.-led invasion of Iran that checked Iran's nuclear ambitions and removed the regime of the Mullahs from power would be beneficial to Israel, and as such represent a policy worthy of implementation. This is dangerous thinking from two aspects. First is the absurd notion that such a policy would benefit Israel. As has been pointed out, any conflict between the United States and Iran will immediately spill over to include Israel. Four conflict fronts will rapidly manifest themselves, with the potential of more to follow. Iran will attack Israel directly with long-range missiles; Hezbollah will saturate northern Israel with short-range missiles and direct-action attacks by commando/terrorist units; Hamas, united with the PLO, will launch similar attacks from Gaza and the West Bank; and every Israeli diplomatic or economic interest abroad will be open to terrorist assault. The cost to Israel will be horrific and devastating, not only in terms of life lost, but also economic damage done. How anyone who proclaims to be pro-Israeli could ever support such a course of action is beyond me. I am pro-Israel, and as such would never endorse a policy course of action that would subject Israel to such pain and suffering. Iran's threats to Israel today are purely rhetorical. Iran poses no direct threat to Israeli security that warrants any form of preemptive military action, especially when it comes to Iran's nuclear program.

As a commissioned officer in the United States Marine Corps I spent a considerable amount of time and effort in January and February 1991 attempting to locate and interdict Iraqi missiles in western Iraq before they could be launched into Israel. I have toured the "bone yards" in Israel where the shards of Iraqi missiles rest, a reminder that even a nation as strong as Israel is not immune to attack. As a U.N. weapons inspector I worked closely with the Israeli government to eliminate Iraq's weapons of mass destruction, including the very same ballistic missiles that once rained down on Tel Aviv and Haifa. I have been to Israel, and understand the precarious security situation Israel finds itself in today. I have stood on the heights of the Judean Hills overlooking the Mediterranean Sea, and understand just how narrow and fragile the physical reality of Israel is. I have gone up the Golan Heights, and looked back on the Sea of Galilee, and fully comprehend why Israel believes it must hold a strategically dominating position vis-à-vis its neighbors. As someone who has placed my life on the line in defense of Israel, I have a vested interest in the continued existence of the State of Israel free of the tyranny of fear and oppression. I am a true friend of Israel, a status that goes far beyond simple hyperbole and rhetoric, and is instead backed up with sweat and deeds.

However, I am first and foremost an American, and a fervently patriotic one at that. As such, I subordinate my national interest to nothing other than my country. As close as the relationship that exists between the United States and Israel might be, it does not make us one with the other. There is the United States, and there is Israel. These are two completely distinct nations, and should never be treated as one and indivisible. Where American and Israeli interests coincide (and there are many places) I have no problem with our two nations working hand in glove for our mutual benefit, as two close allies and friends should. However, when our interests diverge, then I as an American insist on the right to disagree, and to express this disagreement as I see fit, up to and including public pronouncement of this disagreement and implementing courses of action that reflect this disagreement. Friends can disagree and still be friends. But friendship is strained when one party seeks to exert its will and influence using unfair and disingenuous tactics.

The conflict currently underway between the United States and Iran is, first and foremost, a conflict born in Israel. It is based upon an Israeli contention that Iran poses a threat to Israel, and defined by Israeli assertions that Iran possesses a nuclear weapons program. None of this has been shown to be true, and indeed much of the allegations made by Israel against Iran have been clearly demonstrated as being false. And yet the United States continues to trumpet the Israeli claims, and no individual more loudly so than the U.S. Ambassador to the United Nations, John Bolton. Bolton's pro-Israeli stance has elicited absurdly disturbing remarks by the Israelis themselves that bring into question the objectivity of Mr. Bolton when it comes to representing American, vice Israeli, interests.

On May 22, 2006, at a B'nai B'rith breakfast meeting in which John Bolton had already spoken, Israeli Ambassador to the United Nations Dan Gillerman declared Bolton to be the sixth Israeli diplomat assigned to the United Nations. Gillerman also noted that if the B'nai B'rith membership, historically unquestionably pro-Israeli, were counted, the Israeli Mission would in fact be one of the largest at the United Nations. While these comments were presumably made tongue in cheek, they do reflect a reality that cannot be ignored:

Israel's national interests are pursued by a network of individuals and organizations that far exceed its tiny diplomatic representation here in America. Israel counts on many, including Americans in public and private sectors, to act as an extension of Israel when promoting and implementing policies that involve Israeli interests.

Israel is not alone in this activity. Many nations maintain large and active lobbies in the United States in order to promote their individual interests or concerns. None, however, bring to the table the scope and clout of the Israeli Lobby. None operate in the brazen manner in which this Israeli Lobby has grown accustomed to operating, in which the lines which distinguish America and Israel are blurred to the extent that a serving American Ambassador can be openly referred to as an Israeli diplomatic resource. One of the largest and most influential members of this Israeli Lobby is the American–Israeli Public Affairs Committee, or AIPAC. Over the years, AIPAC has exerted its influence over the U.S. Congress and the Executive Branch of government to a degree unparalleled by any other single nation or group of nations. AIPAC operates as a de facto agent of the State of Israel, and yet does not need to register as such.

The duality of loyalty inherent in AIPAC, where Israeli interests continuously trump those of the United States, even among Americans, has been highlighted by the ongoing espionage scandal in which two senior AIPAC officials were indicted as part of an effort to have classified U.S. information pertaining to Iran transferred through unofficial channels to the Israeli government. One must question the true motivation of any so-called friend when, in a relationship as open and transparent as the one enjoyed between Israel and the United States, one party (Israel) sees fit to stoop to actions which violate American law, as well as the very spirit of friendship that is supposed to exist between the two nations.

It seems that, while the American supporters of Israel tout the common goals and interests that bind our two nations, in reality they operate a distinctly Israel-first policy. While I respect and defend Israel's right to place its own interests above and beyond any other nation, including the United States, I fervently reject, and am appalled by, any action undertaken by those who proclaim themselves to be American which subordinates American interests to those of Israel, especially when the stakes of such an issue put American lives on the line. I joined the U.S. Marine Corps, and took an oath to uphold and defend the Constitution of the United States against all enemies, foreign and domestic.

I have gone to war, and would do so again, to defend the ideals and values set forth in the U.S. Constitution. There are times when, in so defending the Constitution, I may be called upon to act in a manner which defends the territorial integrity or interests of another nation, should such interests be entwined with those of my country. This is why I fought in 1990–1991; to defend the letter of the law as set forth by the United Nations Charter, and approved by the Security Council of the United Nations and the Congress of the United States, in coming to the defense of Kuwait following Iraq's wanton invasion and occupation of that nation in August 1990, and to participate in combat operations in western Iraq designed to interdict Iraqi SCUD missiles from being fired against Israel. One could say that I fought in defense of Kuwait and Israel during that conflict, but let there be no doubt: I fought only for America.

I can justify American lives being put on the line to stop missiles being fired against Israel back in 1991. I can justify America coming to the aid of Israel militarily if Israel itself were subjected to illegal acts of aggression. If Iran were to attack Israel without provocation, I would argue long and hard for America to come to the aid of its friend and ally. But I cannot tolerate the idea of America being pushed into a war of aggression against Iran when Iran threatens neither Israel nor America. And this is what is happening today. Israel has, through a combination of ignorance, fear, and paranoia, elevated Iran to a threat status that it finds unacceptable. Israel has engaged in policies that have further inflamed this situation. Israel displays an arrogance and rigidity when it comes to developing any diplomatic solution to the Iranian issue. And Israel demands that the United States take the lead in holding Iran to account. Israel threatens military action against Iran, knowing only too well that in doing so Israel would be committing America to war as well. When it comes to Iran, Israel can no longer be said to be behaving as a friend of America. And it is high time we in America had the courage to recognize this, and take appropriate actions.

The Israel Lobby will scream bloody murder at any inkling that Israel is somehow betraying America, or that the Israeli Lobby puts Israeli interests ahead of the United States. This is its right. However, it then invokes the ugly specter of anti-Semitism, and drags out the memory of the Holocaust, and attempts to smear anyone who dares speak out in a manner critical of Israel or the Israeli Lobby as an anti-Semite and someone who has shamed the memory of the six million Jews who perished during the Holocaust. This is a sickening and deeply disturbing trend that must end. Israel may hold a special status here in the United States, but it is no greater or less than the status held by other close friends and allies, such as the United Kingdom, Canada, Japan, Germany, or any other.

Most Americans would reject outright any effort by one of our allies to limit fair debate, discussion, and dialogue here in the United States about the nature of American relations with any given state. And yet America as a whole remains mute to the interference by the Israeli Lobby into any meaningful discussion of American–Israeli relations. The end result is that Israel and the Israeli Lobby are herding America down the path toward war with Iran, and most Americans remain ignorant and/or indifferent to this fact. The proof is in the pudding; even as the world debates and discusses the June 2006 incentives package offered to Iran, Israel has already proclaimed its opposition to any such negotiated settlement, and AIPAC has initiated a full-fledged lobbying campaign targeted at the U.S. Congress to keep America on track toward conflict with Iran. No one in the world wants such a confrontation, only Israel. Let there be no doubt: if there is an American war with Iran, it is a war that was made in Israel and nowhere else.

If there is to be peace with Iran, the United States must find a way to bring to reign Israel's attempts, directly and indirectly, to unduly influence the formulation and implementation of U.S. foreign policy. Organizations such as AIPAC must either have the scope and scale of their operations severely curtailed, or be forced to register as an agent of a foreign power. It is fine to be sympathetic and supportive of the state of Israel. I know I am. But it is never acceptable as an American to subordinate the national interest of your homeland for the sake and benefit of another nation. In the past, such behavior has been likened to sedition and treason. And just because the action is undertaken on behalf of Israel does not make it any less so than if it had been done on behalf of any other nation. National loyalty is a one-way street, and in America, for Americans, that one-way sign points only toward the United States of America.

Reigning in the Israeli desire for armed conflict against Iran would provide the United States with a tremendous amount of room from which to begin negotiating a non-violent solution to the Iranian crisis. First of all, America buys time from which it can more sanely and sagely assess Iran's nuclear programs and ambitions. Second, it provides America with an opening to engage in sincere one-on-one negotiations with Iran void of the poisoning brought on by the Israeli call for conflict. Third, it removes Iran as a preconceived regional threat, and as such allows the United States to modify its posture vis-à-vis other regional issues, especially those involving energy policy in the Caspian Sea basin. In this day and age of energy shortages, the vast energy resources of the Caspian Sea basin hold the key to global economic stability and growth for the foreseeable future. A conflict with Iran would devastate the Caspian Sea basin, destabilize it politically, and retard its development for many years or even decades.

The United States, like the rest of the world, should be concerned about issues such as human rights and individual liberties in nations such as Iran. But we have no right to interfere in the affairs of a sovereign state to the point that we pursue a policy of regime change in respect to a legally empowered government. The best regime change policy the United States could engage in vis-à-vis Iran would be to stabilize relations, recognize Iran diplomatically, lift the unilateral American economic embargo, and initiate a program of intensive cultural and economic exchanges which would do more to moderate Iranian society than any program of containment and destabilization being considered by the Bush administration today. Iran is not a threat to America. In fact, the Iranian nuclear energy program should be viewed by the United States as desirable, given that its objectives are to increase the viability of Iran as a net exporter of energy during a time when the world's hydrocarbon energy resources are diminishing.

A sound American–Iranian relationship based upon mutual respect, non-aggression, and increased economic interaction will stabilize the Middle East and the world at large. Europe, Russia, China, and India with reap tremendous economic benefit. Israel will find its strategic position strengthened, not weakened, as Iran will seek to moderate its role and influence in the region along lines more beneficial to economic growth and prosperity. In doing so, new markets will be created for Israel to exploit. Energy supplies and prices will be stabilized. And, given America's role as a global leader and power, all of this will act to the benefit of America, which will likewise share in the economic boost that will result from such a policy course. When one compares and contrasts this boost with the economic disaster that any war with Iran would bring with it, the boost becomes a boom, with the economic differential being measured globally in the trillions of dollars.

But, most important of all, no American soldiers, sailors, airmen, and Marines will have to die on Iranian soil, or fall in combat in another theater because of any American aggression against Iran. No Iranian civilian needs to die due to the American bombardment of their homes, and no Israeli needs to cower in fear inside an air raid shelter as Iranian missiles rain down on their cities. People around the world will not have to do without as a result of the economic devastation that would fall out from an American–Iranian war. And the reputation of America, already badly scarred as a result of misadventures in years past, will be given a huge healing boost, enabling America to re-assert itself as a force of global peace and stability, as opposed to one of hegemony, death, and destruction.

It is not too late for America to change the course it has been charting for the past few years. But this course change will not happen on its own volition. It requires an engagement by the American citizenry on a scale that has not been witnessed in recent times. It requires a rejection of the Bush administration's policies, and of the Bush administration itself. It requires a Congress reinvigorated with new blood that can only come about through an engaged and informed electorate. It requires a fundamental re-examination of how the United States will choose to interact with the rest of the world in the years to come, whether we will still adhere to the hubris of having 300 million people dictate the terms of coexistence to a world of several billions, or operate with continued national impotence as another nation, Israel, dictates national security policy for all America. This requires a national debate, discussion, and dialogue on these very important issues, a dialogue that must take place sooner rather than later.

Iran is the one issue that can destroy America in the years ahead. As such, it must be elevated and injected into the national discourse as soon as possible, with as much urgency and passion as exists concerning Iraq. Americans from all political walks of life must empower themselves with knowledge and information so that they can overcome the fear born of ignorance and engage on this most critical of issues. Iran, Israel, weapons of mass destruction, and the role of America in an ever complicated world must become the fodder of political debate at every level of the electoral process in the United States. Failure to do so is not simply a failure of citizenship. It is a facilitation of disaster that will touch us all.

Postscript

THE DANGER OF WRITING A topical book is that events often outstrip the time-line-driven realities of publication. On the surface, this seems to have been the case with certain aspects of *Target Iran*. As of the end of July 2006, the theoretical "konseptsia" embraced by Israel that I warned about in Chapter One, linking as it does the issues of Hamas and Hezbollah with the nations of Syria and Iran, has become an ugly reality with the ongoing Israeli-Hezbollah and Israeli-Hamas conflicts. The hypothesis of an ugly northern front between Israel and Hezbollah has become reality, with hundreds of Hezbollah rockets pounding northern Israel, and Israel in turn launching devastating aerial and artillery bombardments of its own.

The political "Israeli trap" warned about in the original manuscript has likewise moved from the realm of theory into stark reality, with the United States Congress, in bilateral fashion, blindly supporting Israel on the issue of Hezbollah, with seemingly total disregard for the complexities of the actual situation. This Congressional action mirrored a similar rubber-stamp approval of the Israeli actions in Lebanon by the Bush administration, actions so void of any notion of pragmatism and balance as to make the United States appear in the eyes of many around the world, especially Muslims and Arabs (but increasingly others in Europe and Asia as well), indistinguishable from Israel, a tragic blend of proxy and facilitator that only diminishes the stature of the United States.

Throughout the unfolding conflict between Israel and Lebanon, one theme remained consistent in both Tel Aviv and Washington, D.C.—that the ultimate responsibility for the violence in southern Lebanon rested not so much with Hezbollah, but rather with Iran. As such, the conflict between Hezbollah and Israel has become a sort of war by proxy, pitting Iran against the United States. Given the hyperbole and irresponsible rhetoric that has been in vogue in the ranks of the Bush administration and much of the mainstream media here in the United States when it comes to the issue of Iran and its nuclear program, such a war by proxy is a very dangerous development.

America's founding father, President George Washington, strongly counseled against American involvement in "entangling alliances," and yet on the issue of Iran and its nuclear program, our collective entanglement with Israel threatens to take a minor regional problem (the Israeli-Hezbollah conflict) and turn it into a wider conflict that has far-reaching implications for the entire world (any US-Iran conflict). If one looks at the demographics and geopolitical realities of the Israeli-Hezbollah conflict, it is nothing more than a regional conflagration that has as much significance as the ongoing violence in Chechnya or the simmering unrest between the Republic of Georgia and the breakaway territory of Abkhazia.

The difference in these conflicts is Israel, which has used its unmatched ability to lobby and influence American politicians and policies so that its struggle with a legitimate Lebanese popular resistance movement—Hezbollah—has taken on global consequences that far outstrip any real impact of such a conflict. As such, a moderate border dispute has become, in the eyes of many, the first front in a major struggle that pits the United States (and Israel) against any and all in the Middle East who do not support either the concept of regional hegemony by Israel or global hegemony by the United States. The larger target in this mix is, of course, Iran, which has been singled out by both Israel and the United States as the ultimate "problem" that must be resolved if the Israeli-Hezbollah conflict is to be terminated in a manner beneficial to both Israel and the United States.

Amazingly enough, the Israeli-Hezbollah conflict has helped push the issue of Iran's nuclear program off the front burner of international concern. The world went from debating the allegations of

Iran's clandestine development of nuclear weapons to Hezbollah's (Iran-facilitated) launching of short-range artillery rockets into northern Israel. The disparity between the true global threat potential of these two issues highlights the reality that all of the hyperbole and rhetoric emanating from the United States (and Israel) regarding the imminence and severity of the Iranian threat, in the form of a nuclear weapons program, was little more than empty speculation designed to prop up the real policy objectives embraced by both Washington, D.C., and Tel Aviv concerning the isolation and ultimate removal of the Iranian theocratic regime in Tehran. With Israel now indirectly engaged in combat with Iran, at least in the minds of those who buy into the notion of war by proxy, the Bush administration has de-emphasized its "sky is falling" warnings of an Iranian nuclear weapon with a more events-driven rhetoric that seeks to label Iran as the world's leading state-sponsor of terrorism. The goal remains the same —to isolate and destabilize Iran.

But even in this deft maneuvering of politically motivated semantics, the Bush administration, and indeed the State of Israel, cannot escape the history of their collective effort to label Iran as a nuclear proliferation threat requiring urgent action. With Israel's stockpile of U.S.-provided "bunker busting" bombs, originally acquired to target Iran's nuclear infrastructure, now being expended in southern Lebanon and Beirut, the immediacy of any Israeli aerial attack against Iran has been considerably diminished (there seems to be little talk about how Israel ever expected to be able to accomplish anything more than triggering a wider Iranian-U.S. conflict in bombing distant targets in Iran, when its vaunted Air Force was having so much trouble targeting Hezbollah targets right along its border).

The danger of the Israeli "konsepstia" linking Hezbollah with Iran is not diluted by the growing reality of the impotence of the Israeli military in southern Lebanon, but rather exacerbated. Israel will never be able to defeat Hezbollah decisively. The main reason is that Hezbollah is not a nonstate terrorist movement, as portrayed by Israel and the United States, but rather a legitimate expression of the people of Lebanon, primarily Shi'a, who rose up in response to the Israeli invasion and occupation of Lebanon in 1982. Israel's ongoing actions against Hezbollah are not only militarily inconsequential but ineffective and counterproductive, as they simply feed the very dynamic that gave birth to Hezbollah and facilitated its growth. In many ways the inability of Israel and the United States to recognize this reality is mirrored by the similarly unrealistic analytical framework that has been constructed concerning Iran and its government. Both Israel and the United States labor under a model of action that seeks to isolate the Iranian government from the Iranian people, in total disregard for the historical and political imperatives that link the two (namely the dictatorial rule of the American-backed Shah of Iran). The ongoing actions of the United States and Israel serve not to weaken the bond between the Iranian people and the government of the mullahs but rather strengthen it.

The real danger of the Israeli-Hezbollah conflict is that in casting it as a larger conflict between the United States and Iran, Israel and its American proxies have not only made resolving the Israeli-Hezbollah conflict virtually impossible but likewise have made the possibility of a larger US-Iran conflict a very distinct reality. The logic model is simple: the more Israel tries to defeat Hezbollah militarily, the stronger Hezbollah becomes. As Hezbollah gains in strength, Iran will be blamed, making any reduction of Hezbollah linked to a similar reduction of Iran. By casting Hezbollah as a nonstate terrorist organization, Israel and the United States in turn are casting Iran as a state sponsor of terrorism. This model eliminates the need of the United States to deal factually with issues such as Iran's nuclear program.

The inability of the US Congress to act in a rational manner when it comes to matters pertaining to the security of Israel means that the stage has been set for a replay of the environment that existed in Washington, D.C., in the months prior to the invasion of Iraq in 2003, when the Bush administration was able to hype up a nonexistent Iraqi WMD threat by noting that it did not want a "smoking gun" to come in the form of a "mushroom cloud." As Israel flounders in Lebanon, and political pressures are brought to bear on Washington, D.C., to resolve this conflict by confronting Iran, the implausibility of an Iranian nuclear weapons program will once again be drowned out by the fear-inducing rhetoric of the Bush administration, which will once again hype up a nonexistent threat while leading America, and the world, down the path of yet another war of aggression in Iran.

The only hope in preventing this from happening is for the American people, and indeed people all around the world, to liberate themselves from their ignorance on the issue of U.S.-Iran relations, especially when it comes to any talk of an Iranian nuclear weapons program, as well as the role played by Israel in exaggerating any threat posed by Iran. This liberation can only come through the empowerment that accompanies the accumulation of knowledge and information. This is the true goal and objective of *Target Iran*: to help facilitate this intellectual "liberation" by providing an analytical examination of an issue that has been for some time clouded over with misinformation and irresponsible rhetorically laced speculation. If anything, the outbreak of conflict between Israel and Hezbollah in the summer of 2006 only reinforces the need for this book.

Afterword

SINCE THE PUBLICATION OF *Target Iran* in hardcover last year much has happened regarding the issue of Iran's nuclear program and America's policies toward Iran. As an author, I am very proud to be able to say that the research and analysis in the original edition of *Target Iran* has withstood the test of time. As someone concerned about the future of the world, however, and my country's role in shaping this future, I am deeply troubled. The Bush administration, it seems, is as committed in the summer of 2007 to a decisive confrontation with Iran as it was in the summer of 2006. This remains so despite the fact that the American people, in resounding fashion, rejected the pro-war policies of the Bush administration, at least as they were being carried out in Iraq, by electing in November 2006 a Democratic majority to both the House of Representatives and the Senate.

Elsewhere, in Europe particularly, there seems to be a collective unwillingness and inability to deal realistically with the threat of American imperialism as it manifests in Iraq and, increasingly, against Iran. Europe is trapped in the mistaken belief that it can dissuade and/or influence American policy by enabling a policy of "tough diplomacy," which somehow buys time for America to recognize the error of its ways. But "tough diplomacy," which over the years has transferred the Iranian nuclear case from the halls of Vienna, where the International Atomic Energy Agency (IAEA) held sway, to the halls of New York, where the American-dominated United Nations Security Council sits, has only succeeded in paving the way for the legal and diplomatic facilitation of an American war on Iran, a war that today seems more and more likely.

The ongoing diplomatic crisis over the proposed installment of an American anti-missile defense system in Europe, ostensibly as a shield against Iranian attacks—with a radar system deployed in the Czech Republic and missile interceptors deployed in Poland—not only serves as a how-to manual for the implementation of the classic "divide and conquer" tactics the Bush administration has used so effectively in mobilizing support for its Iran policies in Europe, but also shows how the United States can manipulate any given political situation in Europe simply by alluding to the existence of a threat (in this case, Iranian ballistic missiles) that has no foundation in reality. One only has to look at a map and project the maximum operating range of Iran's still-in-development Shahib-3 missile from its north-ernmost operating area in Iran (Tabriz) to realize that its 1,200-kilometer range potential falls more than 1,000 kilometers short of the radar sites supposedly being designed to detect its launch, and more than 2,000 kilometers short of the missile interceptors said to be designed to down these missiles. American logic in claiming Iran as the threat source for this missile defense shield is almost as absurd as Europe buying into this logic with a straight face. (Only the increasingly taciturn Russian president, Vladimir Putin, seems capable of calling a spade a spade on this issue.)

The escalation of words, and deeds, by the Bush administration regarding Iran continues to push the war of rhetoric into an actual shooting war. The president's decision to send a second aircraft car-rier battle group to the Persian Gulf, where it can be reinforced on short notice by a third and fourth carrier battle group from the Pacific Fleet and the Atlantic Fleet, combined with the decision to deploy U.S. Patriot antimissile batteries to the Middle East region, continues the process of moving military forces into place while the Bush administration aligns its foreign and domestic policy in a manner reflective of its long-term intent to remove the Iranian theoc-racy from power, using any excuse possible as justification. These moves are very much in keeping with the promises made by the Bush administration to the Israeli government that the political victory of the Democratic Party in November 2006 would not derail America's (i.e., the Bush administration's) plans vis-à-vis Iran and the Middle East region as a whole.

If Israel is the instigator, and America the implementer, then Europe must be recognized as the facilitator of war-as-regime-change with Iran. Europe, both in terms of the European Union as a collective (with Javier Solana representing it as its foreign minister) and the so-called E.U.-3 (France, Britain, and Germany) as a separate entity bridging the United Nations (where France and Britain have permanent seats on the Security Council) with the European Union (where these same three nations enjoy an overwhelming influence), has proved that in the end, on issues that matter, it is incapable of pulling together a truly independent foreign policy that can be formulated or implemented free of American influence and dominance. In the case of Iran, Europe continues to function as America's puppet.

America has long since perfected the tactic of "divide and conquer" regarding Europe, effectively using the expansion of NATO and the expansion of the European Union as points of leverage to push aside and isolate any European nation or group of nations that would dare rise up in opposition to a particular American policy initiative. The promise of NATO membership and American support in any application to join the European Union has been more than enough to sway the so-called "new democracies" of Eastern Europe into embracing their past totalitarian tendencies to fall lockstep in place behind the leadership of a powerful authoritarian figure, in this case an America possessing all-too-imperialistic trends.

As such, a weakened Europe has been bullied into casting a harsh glance at Iran's nuclear ambitions, all the while forbidden to question America's (and Israel's) motives in confronting what all facts point to as a peaceful energy program operating in complete compliance with Iran's obligations under the non-proliferation treaty. In doing so, Europe has fallen into a trap from which there is no escape. By buying into America's inflated concerns over Iran—derived as they are from a flawed Israeli "konseptsia," which skews intelligence and related analysis in a manner that embraces only those findings that support Iran as a nation pursuing nuclear weapons ambitions—Europe has enabled the United States to create a diplomatic and legalistic infrastructure that supports war.

Europe's first mistake was accepting America's insistence that Iran suspend its enrichment of uranium without first setting the terms and conditions for such. In choosing to pursue the so-called E.U.-3 track with Iran, all Europe did was legitimize America's contention that Iran was pursuing an undeclared nuclear weapons program. The Tehran Declaration of November 2003 purported to recognize Iran's rights under Article IV of the NPT. However, Europe quickly moved away from the concept of a temporary suspension of uranium enrichment by Iran until the IAEA could ascertain the true intent of the Iranian nuclear program in a verifiable manner. Instead it turned toward the American line of permanent suspension, which denied Iran its rights under Article IV while demanding that Iran submit to unprecedented levels of IAEA inspection activity, above and beyond even those required by the so-called Additional Protocol, which infringed to a significant degree upon the sovereignty and legitimate national security of Iran.

Europe never once significantly questioned the underlying motivations of America's policy direction with Iran. Jack Straw, the one-time British foreign secretary, let it slip that an American military attack on Iran was "inconceivable" and that any pre-emptive use of nuclear weapons by the United States against Iran would be "completely nuts." The quintessential European poodle, British Prime Minister Tony Blair, subsequently sacked Straw, allegedly after having received a telephone call from the White House complaining of the British diplomat's choice of words.

Thus chastised, and ever the compliant servant, Europe continued to point an accusatory finger at Iran every time the Islamic Republic balked at the unrealistic and unjustified demands made by the international community through the IAEA and the UN Security Council. Even Jack Straw complained that Iran had, at every turn, "overplayed its hand." But how does a nation overplay a hand that is undeniably founded in the letter and intent of international law? At every step of the way, Iran's right to, and need for, nuclear energy as an alternative to consuming ever-increasing amounts of its domestic supplies of oil have been documented. Iran's rights under Article IV to pursue the enrichment of uranium for peaceful uses are likewise crystal clear. However, its continued efforts to do so have been painted by Europe as being of "concern."

Without a shred of evidence beyond the rhetoric of Washington,

D.C., and the posturing of Tel Aviv, Europe has bought into the operating premise that Iran's nuclear ambitions are military in nature, and not civilian. Europe went along with the American demands that the Iranian case be transferred from the IAEA to the Security Council. Operating under a cloud of self-delusion that this was somehow just the political trick needed to convince the Iranians to back down, Europe all the while ignored the bellicose statements of U.S. Ambassador John Bolton and others concerning the "threat to international peace and security" posed by Iran's "nuclear weapons" ambitions.

In July 2006, as Israel was engaged in a bloody struggle along its northern border with the Lebanese Hezbollah party, the United States finally was able to get the Security Council of the United Nations to pass Resolution 1696 under Chapter VII, demanding that Iran suspend its enrichment of uranium. The majority of the Security Council viewed the resolution as a vehicle for pressuring Iran to negotiate a reasonable settlement to the ongoing dispute over its nuclear program. The resolution endorsed the proposals of China, France, Germany, Russia, Britain, and the United States, with the support of the European Union's high representative, for a "long-term comprehensive arrangement, which would allow for the development of relations with Iran based on mutual respect and the establishment of international confidence in the exclusively peaceful nature of Iran's nuclear program."

The British ambassador summed up the European stance concerning Iran and the need to pass a Security Council resolution. He said he was "deeply concerned over Iran's failure to cooperate fully with IAEA." After more than three years, the British ambassador stated, the agency was still "unable to conclude that there was no undeclared nuclear material or related activities in Iran, including activities with a possible nuclear military dimension that remained unanswered." At no time did the British ambassador state that Iran was pursuing a nuclear weapons program. The British decision was based on procedural objections, namely that Iran had not responded to earlier demands by the Security Council, and before that Europe, to suspend its nuclear enrichment program. For the British, and Europe as well, Resolution 1696 represented a logical escalation of diplomatic pressure on Iran.

The Russians and Chinese maintained positions similar to that of Britain (and France). The Russian ambassador went out of his way to note, "It followed from the resolution, any additional measures that could be required to implement the resolution ruled out the use of military force." The Chinese, for their part, said the resolution had "stressed in many paragraphs the importance of finding a negotiated solution through political and diplomatic efforts." Like the Russians, the Chinese noted their opinion on the "irreplaceable key role of IAEA in handling the issue" of Iran's nuclear program. This position echoed the longstanding Chinese belief that the Iranian case was best served in Vienna, not New York City.

Both the Chinese and Russians knew only too well the dangers of bringing an issue before the Security Council that was closely linked to a unilateral policy objective in Washington, D.C. However, all parties firmly believed that they could manage both Iranian intransigence and American bellicosity. No one for a second believed that the United States would dare embark on another Middle East adventure while so deeply embroiled in the ongoing debacle of Iraq.

If this was indeed the thinking, it showed a dangerous disregard (and complete ignorance) of the genuine foreign policy objectives of the Bush administration regarding Iran. John Bolton, the former U.S. ambassador to the United Nations, when speaking about Resolution 1696, noted Iran's ongoing defiance of the international community by its continued "pursuit of nuclear weapons." Not a single other nation involved in the Security Council action had even alluded to the existence of a nuclear weapons program ongoing in Iran, once again illustrating the disconnect between Washington, D.C., and the rest of the world. By passing this resolution, Bolton noted, the Security Council certified that Iran's "pursuit of nuclear weapons constituted a direct threat to international peace and security."

Resolution 1696, Bolton said, was an initial step toward holding Iran and its nuclear weapons program to account. However, Bolton underscored that if Iran chose not to comply with the will of the Security Council by continuing to develop weapons of mass destruction (again, a term no member used except the United States), then the Security Council needed to be prepared to adopt measures under Article 41 of the UN Charter. While the world sought incremental diplomacy, the United States pursued an incremental approach toward legitimizing war.

Security Council Resolution 1696 was adopted in July 2006 under Article 40 of Chapter VII of the UN Charter. This article holds that

"In order to prevent an aggravation of the situation, the Security Council may . . . call upon the parties concerned to comply with such provisional measures as it deems necessary or desirable. Such provisional measures shall be without prejudice to the rights, claims, or position of the parties concerned. The Security Council shall duly take account of failure to comply with such provisional measures." Article 40 represents a safe measure to undertake if one's intentions are purely diplomatic. The only problem is, once you have exhausted the provisions of Article 40—namely, when a nation such as Iran refuses to comply—there is, as Ambassador Bolton noted, only one direction to go: adoption of an Article 41 resolution.

Under Article 41 of Chapter VII, the Security Council may "decide what measures not involving the use of armed force are to be employed to give effect to its decisions, and it may call upon the Members of the United Nations to apply such measures. These may include complete or partial interruption of economic relations and of rail, sea, air, postal, telegraphic, radio, and other means of communication, and the severance of diplomatic relations." The problem with an Article 41 resolution is that, like a measure passed under Article 40, once confronted with noncompliance there is nowhere to go but upward in the cycle of escalation, invoking the specter of military action per Article 42 of Chapter VII. Article 42 states, "Should the Security Council consider that measures provided for in Article 41 would be inadequate or have proved to be inadequate, it may take such action by air, sea, or land forces as may be necessary to maintain or restore international peace and security. Such action may include demonstrations, blockade, and other operations by air, sea, or land forces of Members of the United Nations."

Those who support the use of "tough diplomacy" against Iran should never forget this: that in adopting the position of confronting Iran over its nuclear program, they are choosing the rule of might over the rule of right. Iran has the rule of law on its side. It has every right to pursue the nuclear programs it has. It is only because Israel and its American sponsor and protector have chosen to draw a red line over the issue of uranium enrichment that the world has taken the position it has vis-à-vis Iran.

Israel's stance is indefensible, and yet no one appears to be capable of publicly saying so out of fear of being called anti-Semitic. First and foremost, as a nation that has consistently refused to sign the NPT and instead has pursued its own covert program to acquire nuclear weapons, Israel has no moral authority to demand that the world hold to account a nation that is simply engaging in activity that it is permitted to do in accordance with its legal rights under the NPT. The Israeli desire to maintain a nuclear monopoly over the Muslim world is a misguided and dangerous policy that should not be endorsed or defended by Europe or the world.

Israel has determined that the maintenance of its nuclear monopoly not only dictate that it and the world seek to stop the proliferation of nuclear weapons in the Middle East (a defensible policy objective, especially if it were to include the elimination of Israel's own considerable stockpile of nuclear weapons) but also the acquisition of any technology that might have "dual-use" capabilities, which can be used in both the peaceful pursuit of energy as well as the development of nuclear weapons. The enrichment of uranium falls into this category. It is mind-boggling how Iran's pursuit of enrichment technology for peaceful energy in complete accordance with its rights under Article IV of the NPT has become a "threat to international peace and security" worthy of Security Council intervention.

Iran's reaction to the passage of Resolution 1696 was, if anything, predictable. Reiterating its right to enrich uranium under Article IV of the NPT, Iran rejected the Security Council resolution and, in keeping with its promise to hold the IAEA accountable for its decision to transfer the Iranian case to the Security Council, started cutting back its cooperation with the IAEA to levels representing only those that were required under the standard safeguards agreement. In stark contrast with the Security Council demands that Iran stop its enrichment program, the Iranians instead stepped up their work. P-1 centrifuges were tested at the Natanz Pilot Fuel Enrichment Plant, both in single-centrifuge, ten-centrifuge, and twenty-centrifuge arrays. While most tests were conducted under vacuum, meaning there was no insertion of nuclear material into the centrifuge, the twenty-centrifuge and 164-centrifuge cascades were tested with small quantities of UF6, totaling some six kilograms of material. The feeding of UF6 into the 164-centrifuge cascade was resumed on August 24, 2006, in direct defiance of the Security Council. Iran declared that the 164-centrifuge cascade had succeeded in enriching uranium to five percent U-235. The IAEA has not been able to independently verify the completeness of the Iranian work, although a limited analysis of environmental samples derived from this work seems to confirm the veracity of the Iranian claims.

In addition to the initial 164-centrifuge cascade already in operation at Natanz, the Iranians progressed toward the installation and operation of a second 164-centrifuge cascade. In August the IAEA installed additional monitoring cameras to keep tabs on this new cascade, and also proposed the implementation of a more stringent program of remote monitoring to compensate for the fact that the limited frequency unannounced access inspections normally associated with verification could not be readily accomplished at a remote site like Natanz. Iran refused to discuss these measures.

On July 26, 2006, on the eve of the Security Council's vote on Resolution 1696, the IAEA carried out a "design information verification" (DIV) visit at the Fuel Enrichment Plant (FEP) at Natanz, where construction was ongoing. This inspection went off without a problem. However, during the course of the inspectors' visit to Iran between August 11 and 16, Iran declined to allow the IAEA to carry out additional DIV inspections at Natanz, stating that the frequency of inspections was, in the opinion of the Iranians, "too high." The Iranians noted that in 2003 the IAEA had performed a total of three DIVs at Natanz, three more DIVs in 2004, fifteen DIVs in 2005, and twelve DIVs as of August 2006. The IAEA explained that the DIVs were an integral part of the agency's ability to carry out its mission, and Iran relented, allowing the IAEA to conduct the DIV at the FEP in late August 2006.

The IAEA continued to play political games in the name of verification. While the issues surrounding the existence of highly enriched uranium particle contamination had been worked out in detail between the IAEA and Iran, the IAEA, under pressure from the United States, kept the issue open by noting that it would require an understanding of the scope and chronology of Iran's centrifuge enrichment program, as well as full implementation of the Additional Protocol, before the IAEA could provide credible assurances regarding the absence of undeclared nuclear material and activities in Iran. In short, the IAEA continued to state that while it had not discovered anything of a prohibited nature ongoing in Iran regarding the NPT, it could not rule out the possibility that something, somewhere, somehow, might

actually exist in Iran until Iran agreed to allow the IAEA unprecedented access to sites and facilities above and beyond that required by
the NPT. In short, having found no evidence of wrongdoing, the IAEA
was finding Iran guilty until Iran could prove its innocence.

Ratcheting up the pressure, on October 16, 2006, the IAEA wrote
to Iran noting that it had failed to address the agency's longstanding
verification concerns with "the necessary transparency to remove
uncertainties associated with some of its nuclear activities." Iran
responded with a letter on November 1, 2006, stating that it "is prepared to remove ambiguities, if any, and give access and information
in accordance with its Safeguards Agreement." Iran was sticking to its
guns, doing only what was actually required by the NPT regarding its
nuclear programs, nothing more. In direct defiance of the Security
Council's demands that it cease enrichment operations at Natanz,
Iran not only continued to operate its initial 164-centrifuge cascade
but, in October 2006, initiated operations involving its second 164-
centrifuge cascade, inserting UF6 gas into this cascade on October
16. Between November 2006 and February 2007, a total of sixty-six
kilograms of UF6 was declared by Iran as having been enriched (environmental samples taken by IAEA inspectors showed a maximum
enrichment of 4.2 percent U-235, indicative of the level necessary to
operate a nuclear energy power plant and far less than the level
usable in any nuclear weapons program).

Iran's continued intransigence vexed many in Europe. In September French Foreign Minister Dominique de Villepin, in talks with
Italian Prime Minister Romano Prodi in Rome, stated, "We cannot
accept that Iran does not respect commitments it has made in the
past." De Villepin pressed Prodi for cooperation between France and
Italy over what he termed the "Iranian problem," something Prodi
agreed to do. Prodi seemed to have forgotten the entire sorry episode
of Europe's caving in to American pressure in the run-up to the 2003
U.S.-led invasion of Iraq, when Europe had played along all too will-
ingly with a "get tough" diplomatic line being pushed by America,
only to be caught out in the end when the United States went to war
as it had planned to do all along.

The same mistake was being made, this time regarding Iran. The
French-Italian hard line was being set on the eve of a visit by Javier
Solana, the European Union's foreign policy representative, to hold

face-to-face talks with Iran's chief nuclear negotiator, Ali Larijani. As expected, the E.U.-Iranian talks went nowhere, with Iran refusing to budge and Europe trapped in its hard-line position. The stage was being set for the final phase of the American plan to set the European Union and the Security Council down the path to war with Iran, from which there would be no turning back.

Perhaps the Europeans were being lulled into a false sense of security in light of the fact that President Bush and the pro-war party that had dominated America since the horrific events of September 11, 2001, were on the verge of suffering a disastrous setback at the polls. On November 4, 2006, the American people reversed the reins of power in the U.S. Congress, voting Democratic majorities in both the House of Representatives and the Senate. The Democratic Party had run on a strong anti-Iraq War platform, and many in the United States and around the world believed that the reticence displayed by the newly empowered Democrats in Congress toward military misadventure in Iraq would automatically translate into hesitancy to expand America's military engagements by extending the conflict in the Middle East to include Iran.

If this was the Europeans' point of view, then they must have been ignorant of the words and actions of the mainstream Democrats in America during July and August 2006, when Israel was locked in combat with the forces of the Lebanese Hezbollah. The Democrats were practically falling over themselves in a rush to microphones and television cameras, where they loudly defended Israel's actions while condemning the Hezbollah-Iranian "axis" as a threat to global security. The Democratic Party is as incapable of standing up to Israeli wrongdoing as its Republican counterparts. Furthermore, Democrats' "antiwar" posturing on Iraq isn't drawn from any deep-seated moral belief that war (especially an illegal pre-emptive war of aggression) is wrong but rather that the war in Iraq is one that America is losing; and since it is a Republican administration that is paying the political price for going to war, the Democrats are all too eager to jump on any band wagon that delivers some sort of political advantage.

Within weeks of their stunning electoral victory in November 2006, the Democrats who now control Congress made it clear that they view a nuclear Iran as a grave threat to American national security interests (Speaker of the House Nancy Pelosi), and they refused to rule out military action as a means of dealing with the Iranian nuclear "threat" (House Majority Leader Steny Hoyer). While supportive of a symbolic vote expressing dissatisfaction with President Bush's new "surge" plan for victory in Iraq, even though providing both the funding and the legal framework for such an expansion of military effort, the Democrats in Congress have done little in the face of the increasing reality that the new Bush administration policy for Iraq is little more than a smoke screen for a widening of the war effort to include Iran. Newly appointed Defense Secretary Robert Gates, during a mid-January 2007 visit to NATO, let it be known that the "surge" in U.S. military forces into the Middle East was really intended as a show of force against Iran. The rhetoric from Washington, D.C., has become increasingly bellicose, with everyone from the president on down speaking of the Iranian "threat" and the need to confront it "sooner rather than later." Adding final insult to injury, the newly elected "antiwar" Democrats stripped language from defense funding bills that would have required the president to seek the consent of Congress prior to launching any military attack against Iran. The primary reason cited for this egregious smear of Constitutional mandate: such language would be "harmful" to Israeli national security.

This, of course, was a direct result of the pressure brought to bear on American politicians by Israel. Within days of the stunning Democratic victory in the November 2006 elections, Israeli Prime Minister Ehud Olmert visited Washington, D.C., where he exacted promises from President Bush and his administration of resolute support over the issue of holding Iran to account. Europe is no stranger to this kind of strong-arm pressure; in October 2006 Italian Prime Minister Romano Prodi was caught on television being on the receiving end of a pre-press conference "coaching" by Ehud Olmert. The Israelis have mastered the art of turning Europe's historical shame into modern Israeli advantage, just as they have used their lobbying skills in the United States—via the American-Israeli Public Affairs Committee, or AIPAC, and other pro-Israeli lobbying groups—to push for pro-Israeli policies in the American body politic. The end result is that, in their collective inability to say no to Israel, Europe and the United States are effectively saying yes to war. The difference here is that while Europe continues to believe that war with Iran is unthinkable, their American counterparts are busy planning for just that eventuality.

As was the case with Iraq, the Bush administration has effectively deployed the "diplomatic" smoke screen to confuse Europe and the world (and many in America, as well) about its true intent regarding Iran. In December 2006, the United States finally got what it had been looking for: an Article 41 resolution against Iran that imposed economic sanctions (albeit limited in scope) on the Iranian nuclear and ballistic missile programs. This resolution, 1737, continued the process of targeting Iran's legally permitted activities under the NPT, declaring that:

> Iran shall without further delay suspend the following proliferation sensitive nuclear activities:
>
> (a) all enrichment-related and reprocessing activities, including research and development, to be verified by the IAEA; and
>
> (b) work on all heavy water-related projects, including the construction of a research reactor moderated by heavy water, also to be verified by the IAEA.

Resolution 1737 also put in place economic sanctions, declaring that "all States shall take the necessary measures to prevent the supply, sale or transfer directly or indirectly from their territories, or by their nationals or using their flag vessels or aircraft to, or for the use in or benefit of, Iran, and whether or not originating in their territories, of all items, materials, equipment, goods and technology which could contribute to Iran's enrichment-related, reprocessing or heavy water-related activities, or to the development of nuclear weapon delivery systems (i.e., ballistic missiles)."

Resolution 1737 gave Iran until the end of February 2007 to comply. As with the case of past Security Council actions, Iran showed no intention of caving in. A visit by IAEA inspectors to Iran in January 2007 revealed that the two 164-centrifuge cascades continued to operate, but only sporadically so. Single-machine tests were also conducted to evaluate the mechanical functioning of the centrifuges Iran planned to use for its larger ambitions concerning a 3,000-centrifuge cascade. But the inspectors found that Iran was nowhere near actualizing this goal. The underground facility at Natanz, ostensibly the projected home to as many as 50,000 centrifuges, remains empty. This facility has been the target of the verbal threat-mongering coming out of Tel Aviv and Washington, D.C., and would be the logical target of any military strike on Iran's nuclear program. It sat empty and unused.

The IAEA inspectors involved in the Natanz visits believed that the lack of progress shown by Iran underscored earlier assessments that the Iranians have significant technological hurdles to overcome before there can be any talk of an expanded enrichment program. Iran continues to have problems with the actual centrifuges, both in terms of single-machine operation and also linking them together in larger cascades. Likewise, any time the Iranians inserted the molybdenum-contaminated UF6 derived from Iran's indigenous uranium manufacturing program (as opposed to the pure stocks of UF6 Iran purchased from China in limited quantities in the early 1990s) into the centrifuges, the molybdenum clogged the extraction holes and pipes, causing the centrifuges literally to rip themselves apart.

The reality of Natanz was not being embraced by those promoting war with Iran. Rather than acknowledge that the Iranians were having extreme difficulty bringing their nuclear enrichment plans to fruition, the United States and Israel contended that Natanz was simply a front designed to mislead the world about Iran's true intentions. In the same way that the United States (and, to a lesser extent, Israel) used the findings of the UN weapons inspectors against Iraq (inspectors found no evidence of ongoing WMD activity, but the Bush administration argued that this only proved Iraq had hidden these programs from global scrutiny), the United States again twisted the facts concerning Iran's nuclear program in order to justify military confrontation. The fact that the IAEA found nothing in Iran that could constitute a threat only proved, in the minds of those who formulate policy in the Bush administration, that the IAEA was incapable of uncovering the true extent of the Iranian threat.

The deadline for Iranian compliance with Resolution 1737 came and went, and in March 2007 the United States pushed through a new resolution, 1747, again passed under Article 41 of Chapter VII, continuing its condemnation of Iranian intransigence and expanding economic sanctions to entities related to the Iranian Revolutionary Guard Command and Iranian ballistic missile activities. The expansion of the Iranian nuclear crisis to include non-nuclear matters such as the IRGC and missile programs reflected the overarching policy objectives of the Bush administration regarding Iran, objectives that have little to do with nuclear matters and everything to do with regime change. Recent developments that have the CIA admitting it is providing support to Pakistani-based terrorist groups responsible for political assassination inside Iran (including a bomb explosion in the Iranian city of Zahedan, which killed more than a dozen IRGC members), the U.S. military taking hostage five Iranian diplomats inside Iraq, and President Bush authorizing a covert finding that mandates the CIA-driven mission of regime change in Iran underscore the fact that while there still may be some months before overt war breaks out between the United States and Iran, for all intents and purposes the war has already begun.

Thus, while the world labors under the impression that the Iranian crisis can only be resolved through diplomacy, especially a direct dialogue between the United States and Iran, the United States is marching toward war. U.S. Secretary of State Condoleezza Rice has ruled out direct negotiations between Iran and the United States on the issue of Iran's nuclear program, and the Bush administration has further clouded the situation by blaming Iran for America's ongoing failures in Iraq. We now have a situation where Iran is being accused not only of developing nuclear weapons but also of waging a proxy war against America by supporting anti-American elements in Iraq. Strangely, the United States is not accusing the Iranians of supporting the Sunni insurgents but rather the Shiite militias that make up the backbone of the Shiite-dominated government in Iraq today, the same government the United States claims to support.

The convoluted strategy of the Bush administration in Iraq has created a situation in which the future of Iraq can only be assured through decisive U.S. engagement with Iran. Thanks to the incompetent fumbling of the Bush administration in forming the current Iraqi "democracy," the situation has emerged that has a very pro-Iranian government in place today in Baghdad. Rather than admit it has failed in Iraq, the Bush administration, by confronting Iran decisively and aggressively, seeks to kill two birds with one stone. If, by attacking Iran, it can achieve the demise of the Iranian theocracy, it will also break the grip on Baghdad politics that Tehran currently enjoys. This in turn will help facilitate the conditions for the return of normalcy and stability in Baghdad and all of Iraq.

This is little more than a continuation of the regional transformation policies derived from the National Security Strategy of the United States, as most recently promulgated in its March 2006 version. The belief that this document represents the discredited vision of a defeated policy is dangerously misplaced. The Bush administration has shown that it will not let American electoral politics interfere with its larger global ambitions. The president and his administration seem hellbent on engaging Iran militarily. What was once "wild speculation" has now entered the mainstream. The Arab press, reporting on alleged discussions between American diplomats and regional officials, now talks openly about the inevitability of an American attack on Iran sometime in 2007. ING, the international investment bank, began warning its investors about the potential negative impact of what it increasingly viewed as the likelihood of an American attack on Iran sometime in the first half of 2007. The fact that, as of June 2007, such an attack has not materialized in no way diminishes the reality, potential, and probability of such an attack taking place during the remaining tenure of George W. Bush's presidency.

There will be a war between the United States and Iran, unless some dramatic intervention occurs that changes the political dynamic in Washington, D.C. Unfortunately, the principal power capable of forestalling such a conflict, the U.S. Congress, remains asleep at the wheel or dangerously compliant toward such an attack. Israel, exerting heavy pressure on the United States, appears resigned to a war with Iran, and with it an expanded conflict with Hezbollah in Lebanon and Hamas on the West Bank. Europe continues to operate in a lethargic manner, either ignorant or mute to the dangers of a U.S.-Iran military confrontation. European complicity in setting the stage for this conflict will not escape the scrutiny of history, no matter how vigorously denied by its politicians today. Neither will Europe's subservient role vis-à-vis the United States be papered over. Europe will yet pay a heavy price for its inability and unwillingness to stand up to the United States in the face of American imperial policy.

But at the end of the day the ultimate condemnation for any conflict between the United States and Iran must be reserved for the American people. Suppressed by the narcotic of consumerism, whereby the addiction to oil-based energy makes them deaf, dumb, and blind to the realities of what is transpiring around them, Americans have forgone their responsibilities of citizenship to such an alarming degree that they have not only created a vacuum in the system of representative democracy that ostensibly reigns supreme in the United States through their collective nonparticipation in national elections, but also remain alarmingly indifferent to the variety of special interests that have emerged to fill this vacuum and thus direct the course of American policy at home and abroad. That the military-industrial complex, which President Eisenhower so sagely warned against, has emerged to dominate American economic and national security affairs is one thing; that we, the people, have ceded our responsibilities of citizenship to agents of a foreign power, which is the only interpretation possible when it comes to explaining the influence exerted on America's Iran policy by Israel and the pro-Israeli lobby headed by AIPAC, represents a completely different level of civic decline.

When, in the future, the history books are written about the events transpiring today, I venture to wage that the war in Iran, like the war in Iraq before it, will be seen as a symptom of the larger decline of the American nation brought about by the abject failure of its citizens to assume the mantle of responsibility mandated by the ideals and values set forth in the Constitution, which bound them together as a collective. While such an epitaph is undesirable, in this case, unless measures are taken otherwise, it will be most deserving.

Scott Ritter
Delmar, New York
June 10, 2007

Bibliographical Notes

WHAT IS FASCINATING ABOUT THE writing of this book is that while its content and analysis is decidedly different from much of what is available in the open press, the sources used in compiling this book are, for the most part, readily available to the general public. I have, of course, made considerable use of resources not so available, namely individuals who have first-hand access to information and activities pertinent to the subject addressed herein: Iran and its nuclear program. In writing this book, I have been very careful to protect the identities of those individuals who shared their experiences and expertise. For this reason, a detailed system of footnotes would be self-defeating, specifying as it would where a particular item or data point came from and, where such a footnote did not exist, highlighting the fact that a particular piece of information came from a human source. I chose not to use footnotes in an effort to protect those who agreed to assist in the compilation of information used in this book. I do not think this book suffers as a result.

Likewise, in writing this book, the sourcing of certain events becomes self-evident, as dates, names and places are specified. In the day and age of Google and other search engines, a simple key word check would allow any reader to ascertain the accuracy in which I quoted an individual or document, as well as the manner in which I placed it in context to the overall text.

There are some general sources available that the reader of this book may wish to access, as I did, in an effort to build a broader foundation of knowledge upon which to better assess this book. "The Manipulator," an article by Jane Mayer published in *The New Yorker* magazine on June 7, 2004, is a particularly good analysis of Ahmed Chalabi and his relationship with the US Government.

"MEK: A Terrorist US Ally?" an article by Daniel Pipes and Patrick Clawson, published in the *New York Post* on May 20, 2003, and "Exiles:

How Iran's Expatriates are Gaming the Nuclear Threat," by Connie Bruck in *The New Yorker,* March 6, 2006, provide contrasting points of view on the Iranian resistance group, the MEK. The National Council of Resistance of Iran also provides press releases and transcripts of briefings in its Web site, www.ncr-iran.org. The role of the MEK in US policy planning regarding Iran, as well as a great overall treatment of U.S.-Iran policy, is covered in Seymour Hersh's article "Plan B," in the June 28, 2004 issue of *The New Yorker.*

Israel is a complicated subject to write on, and much of what I write is based upon my first-hand experience. However, some useful sources which I used to fill out my research included "Israel's Intelligence Scandal," by Uri Avnery, published in *Counterpunch,* June 21, 2004, and "Cause for Concern," by Sara Leibovich-Dar, published in *Ha'aretz,* February 18, 2003. Former Israeli Defense Minister Moshe Aren's book, *Broken Covenant,* published by Simon and Schuster in February 1995, provides an interesting insight into U.S.-Israeli relations at the time of the first Gulf War in 1991.

The issue of nuclear enrichment and nuclear weaponization is complicated enough without having the matter burdened by misinformation and exaggerations. A basic understanding of some of the fundamental issues which are relevant to the discussion in *Target Iran* can be had by reading Vivian Grey's *Secret of the Mysterious Rays,* published by Basic Books in 1966, and *The Fly in the Cathedral: How a Group of Cambridge Scientists Won the Race to Split the Atom,* written by Brian Cathcart and published by Farrar, Straus and Giroux in 2005. Allan S. Krass, Peter Boskma, Boelie Elzen, and Wim A. Smit have written an outstanding primer for placing nuclear technology and processes into the context of proliferation in their text, *Uranium Enrichment and Nuclear Weapon Proliferation,* published by the Stockholm International Peace Research Institute in 1983.

While it sometimes seems that much of what transpires in the realm of weapons inspections is secret, the fact of the matter is that the International Atomic Energy Agency maintains an extraordinary level of transparency about the work it conducts. Iran in particular has been well documented by the IAEA. The IAEA Web site, www.iaea.org, contains a number of "In Focus" articles, including "IAEA and the NPT," "IAEA and DPRK," and "IAEA and Iran," which provide links to official reports and documents that detail the work of the inspectors as well as the details of IAEA meetings in which official reports are made concerning a particular problem. In the case of Iran, almost every aspect of the IAEA inspections is covered in great detail in the IAEA reports that are accessible on the IAEA Web site.

The journal of the Arms Control Association, *Arms Control Today*, contains numerous reports and articles on Iran which expand on some of the material contained in the official IAEA documents. All issues of *Arms Control Today* can be accessed on the Arms Control Association Web site at www.armscontrol.org/act. If one wants to dig even deeper into the minutia of nuclear proliferation as it applies to Iran, www.armscontrolwonk.com provides a vast amount of data covering, as it proclaims, "All the stuff about WMD, intel and the national security bureaucracy by Dr. Jeffrey Lewis and friends too wonky or obscure for publication." I found the site fascinating and informative.

As a public service organization, the European Commission, like the IAEA, maintains a remarkable degree of transparency. Official documents, statements, and press releases can be accessed on its Web site at www.ec.europa.eu/comm/external_relations.

Other useful sources which touch upon material covered in this book include "The Wrath of Khan," by William Langewiesche, published in *The Atlantic Monthly* in November 2005. No better source on the A.Q. Khan nuclear blackmarket activity exists in the public domain. "The World According to Bolton," by David Bosco, published in the *Bulletin of Atomic Scientists* in July-August 2005, represents a very balanced look at a very controversial figure, Ambassador John Bolton. I found it very useful. Likewise Al-Jazeera's "People Profile" on Iran's Ayatollah Khamenei, published on November 29, 2004, provided unique insights into a man and government the West knows very little about.

Regardless of the quality of the sources listed above (which does not represent a comprehensive bibliography used in the writing of this book by any means), I remain solely responsible for the text of this book, including all facts and assessments. I hope that my reputation for integrity and analysis will smooth over any ruffled feathers that might occur because of a lack of suitable footnoting and source quotation. In the end it will be up to the individual reader to pass final judgment.

Index

93+2 program, 42, 56, 60

A
"A Clean Break," xxii–xxiii
Ab-Ali, 58, 60
Abu Tahir, Buhary Seyed, 113
Additional Protocol, 42, 56, 61, 71, 86, 103, 105, 117, 129
Afeka, 6
Aghazadeh, Gholamreza, 51–52, 57, 87, 95, 121
Agreed Framework, 46–48, 52–53
Ahmadinejad, Mahmoud, 173, 182, 187, 190
Al Aqsa Intifada, 30
Al Furat, 54–55
American-Israeli Public Affairs Committee (AIPAC), xxii, 25, 28–29, 132, 209
Amitay, Morris, xxii
Annan, Kofi, 45, 136
Arafat, Yassir, 23, 30, 33
Arak, xxv, 49, 56, 60, 70, 128
Arens, Moshe, 7–9
atom splitting, 36
Atomic Energy Organization of Iran (AEOI), 51
"Atoms for Peace" speech, 39
Axis of Evil, xxi, 43, 45, 53
Ayalon, Moshe, 32
Azeri nationalist movement, 29
Azur, 6

B
Baker, James, 7, 9
Bam, 105–6
Barroso, Jose Manuel Durao, 152–53
Barzani, Mullah Mustafa, 20, 29
Baute, Jacques, 52, 55, 66
Becquerel, Henri, 35, 37
Ben-Eliezer, Benjamin, xxiv
Berlusconi, Silvo, 152
Bernier, Michel, 159
Bertholot, Rene, 73
Bin-Nun, Avi, 8
bismuth, 117
Blair, Tony, 50, 77, 79
Blix, Hans, 45–46, 49, 51, 57
Bolton, John, 135–44
    and Iran, 102, 129, 160, 190, 199–201
    and Israel, 132, 208
    and North Korea, 48
    United Nations, 142, 168, 172–73, 178–79, 188
bone yard, 207
Boucher, Richard, 56, 59
Brill, Kenneth, 70, 83, 89

Britain, 50, 97, 114–15, 153, 155, 163
    See also EU-3
Brownback, Sam, 151
Buenos Aires, 22
Bush, George W., 43, 144–45, 150, 167–68, 178–79
    and Europe, 162–64
    national policy address 2006, 194–95
    State of the Union Address (2002), xx–xxi, 53, 137–38
Bushehr, 25, 59, 164

C
Cambone, Stephen, 137
Camp Ashraf, xx
Camp David talks (2000), 30
Carter, Jimmy, 47
centrifuge, 38–39, 59, 62, 95, 99, 117, 119, 157, 174, 185, 192
    See also P-1 centrifuge; P-2 centrifuge
Chalabi, Ahmed, xiii, xviii, xxii
Chamberlain, Neville, 163
Chatellerault, 73
Cheney, Dick, 7, 9, 44, 46, 49–50
Chernomyrdin, Viktor, 24
China, 69, 86, 95, 130, 160–62, 188, 198–99
Chirac, Jacques, 79
CIA, 99–100, 110
Clean Lab, 67
Clinton administration, 28, 113
CNN-ISIS broadcast, 55–56
Cockcroft, John, 36
Committee for a Democratic Iran, xxi–xxiii
Cresson, Edith, 73

D
Defense Industries Organization (DIO), 121, 123
diffusion, 38, 39
"Doctrine for Joint Nuclear Operations", 179
"Downing Street Memo", 195
Dror, Ya'acov Ami, 14, 33
Dubai, 184

E
Eagleburger, Lawrence, 6–7
earthquake, 105–6
Einstein, Albert, 36
Eisenhower, Dwight D., 39
El-Baradei, Mohammed, 34, 44–60, 174, 178–80
    biography, 42–43
    and Iran, 70, 83, 93–94, 100–105, 116–17, 128, 157–60, 164–65

and Iraq, 65–66, 121, 133
Nobel Peace Prize, 181
report to IAEA, 88–89, 192
Eternal Light (Operation Forough-e Jaavedaan), xix
EU-3, 97–99, 101, 104, 122, 153, 155, 157, 166, 173, 175–77, 194, 198–99
See also European Union
euro, 74
European Commission, 74–76, 82
European Constitution, 153
European Parliament, 74–76
European Union, 73–79, 82, 84–85, 91, 130–31, 152–53
See also EU-3

F
Fakhraver, Amir Abbas, 82
fatwa, 170
Fuerth, Leon, 24
Fhimahto, al Amin Khalifa, 114
Fischer, Joshka, 159
fission, 37
France, 76, 97, 153, 163
See also EU-3
Frattini, Franco, 101
Fuel Enrichment Plant (FEP), 61

G
gamma spectrometry, 67
Gates, Robert, 7
Gchine, 185–86
Germany, 25, 74–76, 97, 111–12, 153–55, 163
See also EU-3
Gil, Yehuda, 19
Gilad, Amos, 2–4, 7, 13–14, 19, 22–24, 27–28, 30–32
Gillerman, Dan, 208
Goldschmidt, Pierre, 49, 57, 60, 63–65, 68–69, 94, 121, 165–67, 174, 186
Green Salt project, 183–84, 186
Guardian Council, 170
Gulf War, 13, 112, 154

H
Haass, Richard, 7
Haifa, 6
Halevy, Efraim, 32–33
Hamas, 207
Hamza, Khidir (Saddam's Bombmaker), 44–45
Harmon, Jane, 164
Hasmonean Tunnel, 16
Heinonen, Olli, 49, 57, 60, 63–65, 69, 121, 167, 184, 186
Helms, Jesse, 142
HEU (high enriched uranium), 37, 87, 89, 94–95, 120, 123, 128, 133, 157, 180
Hezbollah, 16, 19, 22, 27, 207

the Holocaust, 1–2, 33–34
human rights, 82
Hussein, Saddam, xiii, xx, xxiii, 7, 15–16, 29, 32, 44, 51, 112

I
Ice Castle, 4–5, 10
imminent threat concept, 140
Institute for Science and International Security (ISIS), 55
International Atomic Energy Agency (IAEA), xxiv, 14, 34, 39–72, 94–106
origins, 39–41
safeguards, 41–42
Iran
earthquake, 105–6
future U.S. policy, 197–215
and Israel, 19–20
and Palestinians, 31
and Russia, xxi, xxiv, 19, 23, 25, 130, 164
Iran-Contra scandal, 22
Iraq
Kuwait invasion, 5
U.S. invasion, 32–33, 79–81
weapons of mass destruction (WMD), xxii, 30
Iraq Nuclear Verification Office (INVO), 49
Isfahan, 59, 70
Israel, 1–34
and Germany, 111–12
and Iran, 19–20, 208
and Iraq, 12
and Lebanon, 16
and Turkey, 21
U.S. relations, 33, 207–14
Israeli Defense Force (IDF), 4, 10–11, 14
Ivanov, Igor, 86

J
Jabr Ibn Hayan Multipurpose Laboratory (JHL), 62–63
Jafarzadeh, Alireza, xix–xxvi 60, 91–93
Jannati, Ayatollah Ahmad, 99
Jenin, 30
Jericho missile force, 8
Joliot-Curie, Francis, 36
Joliot-Curie, Irene, 36

K
Kahota, 41
Kala (Kalaye) Electric Company, 58, 60, 63–64
Kalaye, 68–70, 87, 92, 94–95, 123, 128
Kamal, Hussein, 44, 111
Karine A, 30
Karroubi, Hehdi, 60
Kashan (Nantz), 49, 55–56, 58, 60, 62, 84–88, 94, 99, 117, 128
Katsav, Moshe, 1

Kay, David, 97
Kazakhstan, 25
Kelly, James, 52
Kerry, John, 147
Khadafi, Muhammar, 113
Khamenei, Ayatollah Ali, 159, 169–72, 178, 181–82, 193
Khan, A. Q., 41, 110–13, 116, 165–66, 184–85
Kharazzi, Kamal, 86, 91, 101, 121
Khatami, Mohammad, 57–60, 81, 93, 99, 101, 105, 121
Khomeini, Ayatollah, 91, 169
Kolahdouz, 91–92
konseptsia, 3, 7, 27–28, 31
Kurds, 19–21, 29
Kuwait, 5, 210

L
laptop intelligencs, 183–84
Lashkar-Ab'ad, 95–96
Lavizan-Shian, 124, 126–27, 166, 185, 203
Lavrov, Sergei, 107–9, 120
Le Mortadella (Romano Prodi), 75–76, 79–81, 84, 152
Leakage Committee, 28
Lebanon, 16, 22
Ledeen, Michael, xxii–xxiii
LEU (low enriched uranium), 37, 87, 89, 94–95, 120, 128, 133, 157, 180
Libby, I. "Scooter", 137
Libya, 110, 113–16
Likud Party, xxiii, 16
liquefied natural gas (LNG), 130

M
McCain, John, 164
Megrahi, Abdel Basset Ali, 114
MI-6, 110, 112, 114–15
The Middle East Quarterly, 28–29
Missile Technology Control Regime (MRCR), 18
missiles, 5–11, 18, 23, 112, 154, 183
The Model Protocol, 42
Mofaz, Shaul, 1, 103
Molybdenum, Iodine, Xenon Radioisotope Production facility (MIX), 63
Mossad, 19, 102
Mujahedin-e Khalq (MEK), xix–xx, 28, 125, 147
Mukhabarat, 28
Mullahsby, 151

N
Natanz (Kashan), 49, 55–56, 58, 60, 62, 84–88, 94, 99, 117, 128
National Council of Resistance in Iran (NCRI), xviii, 28, 48, 92–93, 125, 147
National Security Strategy (2002), 138–41
National Security Strategy (2006), 190–93, 195

National Threat Assessment (1996), 23
NATO, 76
neoconservative policy, 138
Netanyahu, Benjamin, xxiii, 16, 27, 30
No-Dong missiles, 18
North Korea, 18–19, 43, 46–48, 52–54, 57
Nuclear Nonproliferation Treaty (NPT), 34, 40, 83, 150, 186
Nuclear Posture Review, 53
Nuclear Suppliers Group (NSG), 41, 72
nuclear technology, 37–39
    energy, 36, 202–3
    fingerprints, 66
    fission, 36
    transformations, 36
    weapons, 36, 40, 203

O
Ocalan, Abdullah, 21
OFEK-3 satellite, 27
oil, 204–6
Operation Desert Fox, 29
Operation Forough-e Jaavedaan (Eternal Light), xix
Operation Grapes of Wrath, 16
Operations Division B, 49
O'Reilly, Bill, 144
Osirak nuclear reactor, 146
Oslo Accord, 17

P
P-1 centrifuge, 113–14, 165, 185, 189
P-2 centrifuge, 113–17, 119, 122–24, 128, 133, 157–58, 165, 185, 189
Pahlavi, Reza, xxiii, xxv
Pakistan, 41, 110, 125
Palestine, 31, 33
Palestinian Authority, 27
Palestinian Security Service (PSS), 17
Pan Am Flight 103, 113
Parchin, 143, 166, 184–85
Pardis, Seyed Reza, 105
Paris Agreement, 155–57, 159–60, 163, 175–77
Peres, Shimon, 16
Pilot Fuel Enrichment Plant (PFEP), 61
PLO, 30, 207
polonium, 117–19
Powell, Colin, 81, 102, 104, 145, 162–63
pre-emptive actions, 140
Prodi, Romano (Le Mortadella), 75–76, 79–81, 84, 152
Proliferation Security Initiative (PSI), 115
Putin, Vladimir, xxiv, 107–9

Q
Quartet, 31, 32
Quayle, Dan, 7

R
radioactivity, 35
Rafsanjani, Akbar Hashemi, 60–61, 159
Rajavi, Massoud, xx
"Rebuilding America's Defenses", 137
Reeker, Phillip, xiii–xvii
relativity theory, 36
Rice, Condoleeza, 49–50, 54–55, 162–64, 167, 189–90, 203
Rishon Letzion, 9
Roentgen, Wilhelm, 35
Rowhani, Hassan, 91–92, 97, 100, 121, 131, 159, 164, 170
Rumsfeld, Donald, 76, 84
Russia, 17, 107–9, 164, 174, 187–88, 198–99
    and Iran, xxi, xxiv, 19, 23, 25, 130, 164

S
Sabra, 4
Saddam's Bombmaker (Khidir Hamza), 44–45
Safeguards Analytical Laboratory, 66–67
Saguy, Uri, 15
Salehi, Ali, 83, 90, 105
Samsami, Soona, 60
Sanders, Jackie, 132
Santer, Jacques, 73–74
Schroeder, Gerhard, 179
Scowcroft, Brent, 7
screening techniques, 67
SCUD-B missiles, 18
SCUD-C missiles, 18
SCUD missiles, 5–11, 112, 154, 183
Second Preparatory Committee (PrepCom), 71, 82
Seibersdorf Lab, 66–67, 87
September 11, 2001, 43
Shagand, 60
Shah of Iran, 19, 25
Shahib-3 missile, 18, 23, 183
Shalom, Silvan, 134
Shamir, Prime Minister, 8, 10
Shamkhani, Ali, 91
Sharon, Ariel, xxiii, xxiv, 30–31, 134, 143, 167
Shatila, 4
Shomron, Dan, 8
Simens, 25
Sobhani, Rob, xxiii
Solana, Javier, 102, 153, 155, 159, 193
Soviet Union, 17
State of the Union Address (2002), xx–xxi, 53, 137–38
Straw, Jack, 86, 155, 159

T
Tahir, Abu, 113–14
Tehran Declaration, 97–98, 103–5, 153
Tehran Nuclear Research Center (TNRC), 62

Tehran Statement, 177
Tel Aviv, 6, 9
Tenet, George, xxiv, 50
Tikva, 9
Trade and Cooperation Agreement (TCA), 82
tri-conic warhead design, 183
Turkey, 21, 29

U
United Nations, 24–25, 142
United Nations Monitoring and Verification Commission (U.N.MOVIC), 45
uranium, 35, 37–38, 58–59
    enrichment of uranium, 37–39, 167, 173, 192, 194
    HEU (high enriched uranium), 37, 87, 89, 94–95, 120, 123, 128, 133, 157, 180
    hexafluoride, 25
    lasers, 96, 119
    LEU (low enriched uranium), 37, 87, 89, 94–95, 120, 128, 133, 157, 180
    uranium-235, 37–38
    uranium-238, 37–38
    yellowcake, 50, 52, 58, 66, 127
URENCO, 39
U.S. Department of Defense, 179

V
Vashem, Yad, 1–2
Velayati, Ali, 91

W
Walton, E.T.S., 36
War of the Cities, 18
Whole Body Counters (WBC), 126
Wolfowitz, Paul, 137
Woolsey, James, xxii
World Trade Organization (WTO), 194
Workshop 1001, 114

X
X-Ray fluorescence, 67

Y
yellowcake, 50, 52, 58, 66, 127
Yom Kippur War, 20
Yongbyon, 53
Yunessi, Ali, 91

Z
Za'ira, Eli, 3
The Zanger Committee, 41
Zionism, 141–42